I0554786

The Long Road to Cullaville

The Long Road to Cullaville

Stories From My Travels to Every Country in the World

BORIS KESTER

THE LONG ROAD TO CULLAVILLE
Stories from my travels to every country in the world
By Boris Kester

Cover photo: Boris Kester
Near the summit of Mount Wilhelm
(4509m), Papua New Guinea

www.boriskester.com

Original title: *De lange weg naar Cullaville*
© Translation: Boris Kester – 2021 First Edition
Editing: Emma Wilson

Second Edition
Copyright © 2023 by Boris Kester
Published by Munn Avenue Press
300 Main Street, Ste 21
Madison, NJ 07940
MunnAvenuePress.com

All rights reserved. No part of this book may be reproduced in whole or in part without written permission from the publisher, except by reviewers who may quote brief excerpts in connection with a review in a newspaper, magazine, or electronic publication; nor may any part of this book be reproduced, stored in a retrieval system, or transmitted in any form or by any means electronic, mechanical, photocopying, recording, or other, without written permission from the publisher.

ISBN: 978-1-960299-02-4

Printed in the United States of America

Dedication

An té a bhíonn siúlach, bíonn scéalach
He who travels has stories to tell (Irish saying)

In memory of my cousin Sander and my friends Walter, Mark
& Marilyn, who had the misfortune of being in the wrong
place, at the wrong time.

Special thanks to Corona. Without you, I would have never
found the peace and time to write this book.

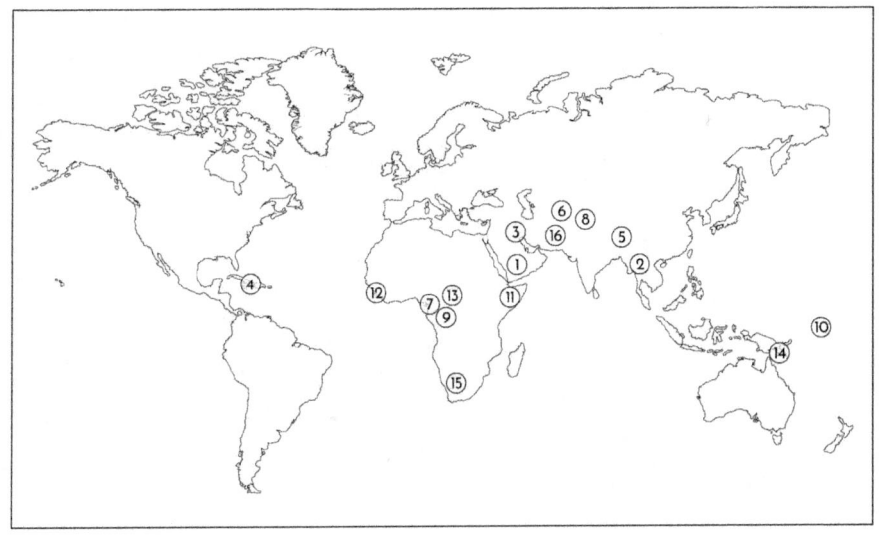

Table of Contents

Preface to the Second Edition

Step into the world of adventure, travel, and exploration with *The Long Road to Cullaville*. As the author, I can tell you that writing this book was a journey in itself. It was a labor of love, with countless hours of writing, rewriting, and polishing, but the moment I held the physical copy in my hands, I knew it was all worth it. And to see people lining up to buy the book and ask for autographed copies in my hometown of Leiden was a surreal experience.

Readers from all walks of life embraced my story, sharing how they were deeply moved by my tales of travel and self-discovery. Many readers told me the book made them laugh, cry, inspired them, and ignited a desire to step out of their comfort zones and explore the world. A few said they limited themselves to only one chapter a day, not wanting to end the book too soon. Some called it a travel thriller, filled with educational insights about our planet and its inhabitants.

I was humbled and grateful for the opportunity to share my writing with the world. Readers showed their appreciation by asking for autographed copies and many even asked for a second book. As I saw my book on bookshelves and libraries, I felt like my journey had come full circle. It was incredibly heartwarming to know my book was read the way I intended and that it touched my readers.

The response from the media was equally extraordinary. I was interviewed by newspapers, magazines, and radio, and was even given the opportunity to teach students at National

Geographic how to write travel books. The recognition and support are a huge inspiration for which I'm deeply grateful.

One of the most exciting suggestions came from a travel friend, who suggested the book should travel to every country in the world. From that moment on, I've asked readers to send me messages and photos of their book copies on location, and to date, it has traveled to 172 countries, with 21 more to go.

The process of publishing this first book also turned out to be an experiment that taught me a lot. I discovered some minor mistakes that needed correction. I found competent people to help me with all that is needed to publish a book and increase its visibility. I realized the book deserved a fresh start - and you are holding the result in your hands right now. I am even more excited about this second edition of my book than I was about the first.

And yes - I am writing that second book. Not only do I have many more travel tales to tell, my first book also turned around my life in unexpected ways. Bringing a copy to the protagonist of the first chapter turned out to be a bizarre adventure, which is a story that needs to be told. I started writing the second book only weeks after the first one came out. I have no title yet, but I know it will be about travel and love. I won't stop writing until I think it is at least as good as *The long road to Cullaville*. You can follow progress on BorisKester.com (sign up for the mailing list).

As I embark on this new chapter of my writing journey, I want to express my deepest gratitude to all the readers. You are my ultimate travel companions who have supported me and this book. Your unwavering support and open hearts have made this journey all the more rewarding. Thank you for allowing me to share my stories with you and for being a part of this fantastic adventure.

I invite you to sit beside me, and travel with me to places in the world you might have never heard of. Enjoy the read, enjoy the ride along *The long road to Cullaville*!

Leiden, March 2023

PREFACE

April 1965. The world consists of 124 countries and I'm just over five months old. My parents put me in a pram and take me on a journey. For the first time in my life, I cross an international border. We travel through Europe by train and take a boat to Crete. My parents discover the island on foot – with me in tow. On the way, the Greeks stuff me with treats, we sleep in a different place every night and I pose on the ancient stone throne of King Minos. My mum holds me while my dad takes my very first travel photo. Before I can even sit, walk, or talk, I learn the basics of travel. Transportation. Encounters. Discoveries. Adventure.

My childhood hero was Odysseus. His stories inspired me to dream about marvelous and dauntless travels to unknown places and about never giving up until you reach your goal. I wasn't even ten years old when I started keeping track of how many countries I had visited. Whenever we traveled to a new country, I would draw the flag in my diary with a multi-color pen and proudly add the country's number. Looking back in those notebooks, it's striking how happy I was when we visited a new place. New frontiers fascinated me intensely. Different people, different customs, different food, different money, a different language, and sometimes even a different script: every new country was a thrill. The rule at home was that you should have visited at least as many countries as your age. As a child, that wasn't difficult. On my tenth birthday, I had visited more than twenty countries in Europe and Asia.

Once I started traveling by myself, I made good use of Interrail. I traversed Europe to explore every corner. Travels to Africa followed. While it was fashionable to say that the world was getting smaller, mine just kept expanding. The famous paradox 'the more you know, the more you realize how little you know', is equally applicable to travel. The more I traveled, the more I became aware that there was so much more to discover. That realization made me restless and unsuitable for an office job. I resigned after four years. I then spent a year wandering through Europe and Africa to discover more new countries. After that, I also became restless inside university lecture halls and applied to be a flight attendant. This career enabled me to travel every week in between my lectures. After completing university, I decided to pursue a career in aviation because the irregular and unpredictable lifestyle suited my restlessness and wanderlust well.

Thus, my world expanded to include North and South America, the Far East and Oceania. Little by little, I conquered the planet. My yearning for the unknown made me explore countries that were new to me every year. The Internet enabled me to share my experiences and photos through my website: a continuation of the travel diaries I wrote as a child. In the meantime, I kept track of how many countries I had visited. To make things more complicated, new countries were born along the way out of a changing world order.

I had visited 117 countries when, due to a major earthquake in my personal life in 2008, I decided to travel differently. Instead of visiting one or two new countries every year, I decided to travel to all the countries in the world. I gave myself ten years to complete the remainder. The idea seemed absurd, but once it settled in my head, I realized that I had always had that goal – I just hadn't been aware of it. Hadn't I already started keeping track of how many countries I'd been to as a nine-year-old? It had just taken me more than thirty years to find out that it would be my quest to visit them all.

The half-century between my first and my last country was packed with travel, full to the brim with adventures, and chock full of encounters with a diverse range of people. In Mogadishu I ate gingerbread cookies with Somalis while my four body-guards kept a close eye on the area, their right hand on the trigger of their machine guns. Muslims got me drunk a stone's throw from the dizzying buildings of Samarkand, from where Timur Lenk once ruled an empire and where he is now buried. I sailed with betel nut traders on a boat down the pitch-black Sepik River in Papua New Guinea, under an infinite sky with so many shooting stars that my wishes were exhausted faster than I could think of new ones. On my way to the Central African Republic, I narrowly sped past a group of gorillas on the back of a motorbike. I came face to face with a brown bear in the wild Tian Shan mountains of Kyrgyzstan, got malaria three times, was trapped in a military base in Iran and crawled out of a car wreck with only minor injuries after a serious accident in South Africa.

June 2017. The world now comprises 193 countries. Just under Cullaville, I cross the last border of a country I have never been to before. I have visited all the countries in the world.

Soon thereafter, I realize that I have done something special. Even though I have many photos and stories of my travels published on my website traveladventures.org, I decide to do more justice to some of those adventures by writing a book. Once more, my restlessness plays tricks on me because I inevitably also continue to travel. After all, I know more than ever before that there are still so many places left to explore. It's thanks to the pandemic of 2020 and the associated lockdowns and travel restrictions that I'm finally forced to stay put and find the peace of mind and time to write this book.

For those who want to see images with the stories: go to BorisKester.com, or scan the QR code on the back of this book.

My gratitude I offer, first and foremost, to the tens, hundreds, thousands of people I met along the way. To them, I was a stranger, a curiosity, perhaps an intruder. Yet, they almost always lent a helping hand. Told me about their country. Showed me around. Protected me. Advised me. Offered me shelter, food and drinks. Even though they were often poor, they shared what little they had and allowed me, if only for a short while, into their lives.

Fortunately, I found many people willing to help me with the editing. Everyone who read along thus had a contribution to make to the realization of this book. I would especially like to mention the following friends. Marieke, who gave me precise feedback and made me realize the importance of formulating accurately. Sasha, who convinced me that long sentences do not make for great readability and who made me hunt for sentences of over 28 words. Gonneke, who was able to pinpoint sections which needed improvement and who gave me confidence in this book as a literary expert. Renata, who read along into the wee hours and proposed improvements at various stages of the manuscript. Maya, who posed questions regarding the content, which enabled me to improve the preface and introduction. Margreet, René, Francine, Steven and Suzan who all read one or more chapters and who pointed out potential problems and improvements. Several travelers whom I interviewed about the risks of traveling.

For this English version, I want to express my gratitude to native speakers who graciously read my first translated manuscript. Thank you, Carol, Maya, Mary, Sandra, Rose and Phil, Adam, and Jake, for the time you took to read and give me valuable feedback.

My sister Leila, brother-in-law Matthieu and niece Maite gave honest advice that made me look at the manuscript with different eyes. Finally, this book would by definition not have been written without my parents Caroline and Gerard, who passed on their travel gene, who taught me to look at the world with an open mind, never to give up, to throw myself into adventures and to trust in a happy ending. And that deserves my greatest gratitude.

Leiden, September 2021

INTRODUCTION

A ship in harbor is safe, but that is not what ships are built for.
—John A. Shedd, Salt from my Attic, 1928

You can never cross the ocean until you have the courage to lose sight of the shore.
—Christopher Columbus

'Isn't it dangerous to travel to all those weird countries?' That is the question I'm most frequently asked (after 'what is the most beautiful country in the world?'). Perhaps an obvious one to ask someone who has visited every country on earth. To me, it's all a matter of perception. My motivation to travel is fired by an unbridled curiosity for unknown places, for people with very different lives and for cultures that are remote from mine. I'm elated when I cross a border to a new country and can crave for all the new things I'm going to see and do. I can be intensely happy when I meet extraordinary people and when I encounter natural or man-made beauty that overwhelms me. When strangers invite me wholeheartedly into their lives. My heart starts to beat faster when I embark on something without having a clue how it will end. Where others might see danger, I see adventure.

After I decided to travel to all the countries in the world, I compiled a list of the 75 remaining. I used the only objective definition of 'country': the one used by the United Nations. At the time, it consisted of 192 countries; South Sudan was added a few years later. As soon as you divert from this list, you quickly get bogged down in a subjective, complicated, endless, and often politically charged discussion – which can be entertaining and exhausting at the same time.

Among the remaining countries were destinations that many would consider 'dangerous'. Somalia, Iraq, the Central African Republic and several others that, according to all current travel advice, had been colored deep red for years, and where you were advised not to go. 'Don't travel to Somalia. Are you there now? Leave the country as soon as possible [...] Serious crime occurs in this country; including armed robberies, kidnappings, murders, explosions, and sectarian violence.': I have read more compelling promotional holiday brochures. Nauru, Tuvalu and São Tomé & Príncipe: although not on the red list, I had never heard of them either. Where were those countries really, and how could I get there?

I quickly realized that I had set myself a goal of which I could not foresee the consequences. I wasn't even sure whether it was feasible. Excitement took possession of me. It was clear that I found myself at the beginning of the greatest adventure of my life. The more I thought about it, the more enthusiastic I got. It would certainly be exciting. But dangerous?

During one of my many Interrail wanderings, in my early twenties, I overheard a few young Americans exchange experiences about their travels across Europe. The sights not to be missed, the best food, the most beautiful cities. Barcelona, Venice and Athens were all high on their list. Then they talked about where you should avoid going. One of them mentioned Amsterdam. He had heard several stories of people who had been robbed. A girl supported him: she too had been told that it was unsafe. The others nodded in agreement. In no time, they labeled Amsterdam as the most dangerous city in Europe and decided to steer well clear of it.

I could hardly believe what I was hearing. They were

talking about my city! I lived in Amsterdam, cycled through it day and night without ever feeling threatened or unsafe. Yes, a junkie once stole my bike. But to call that dangerous? It made me realize for the first time how biased and unreliable the advice and warnings of others can be, how easy it is for people to frighten each other and how a bad reputation, once obtained, is very difficult to erase.

How often have I been warned during my ramblings about the people in the next village, the next region, the capital or (especially!) the neighboring country. They're all crooks, they're unreliable, it's dangerous: don't go there! Only to discover on the spot that the inhabitants received me like a prodigal son with the corresponding treatment. But when I left, they would warn against the residents of the next village. They *really* couldn't be trusted!

What is that about? Is there an ingrained sense of superiority in people? An aversion to everything different and odd? Fear of the unknown? The unknown is precisely what the traveler longs for, which drives him to go on and on to the next place he wants to discover. Granted, the unknown by definition also entails risk. But risk is not necessarily the same as danger.

By nature, humans are equipped to assess risks and make decisions when facing dire situations. Those decisions are by no means always rational. Our brains have set up a beautiful system in which fear, an expected reward and emotion work together to assess and act on risks. Confronted with acute danger, we have the well-known freeze, fight or flight reaction. That has helped humanity to survive for many centuries in all kinds of frightful situations.

In recent decades, we have done everything we can to eliminate as many risks as possible and make life as safe as we can. We have created labels, warnings, regulations and much more to achieve this which, in many cases, has certainly been useful.

For example, cars, airplanes and trains have now become so safe that we use them without even thinking about possible dangers, convinced that we will arrive safely.

Gradually, we have come to think that we can fully control life and that we can exclude all risks. We have forgotten that certain risks are inherent in life and that destiny still has the final say. Besides, taking risks doesn't always have to be negative. Look at it from the other side: if we never took risks, everyone would stay in their comfort zone. Many inventions and discoveries would never have been made. Columbus would never have crossed that ocean. We would never improve in our lives; we wouldn't dare to ask that girl or boy that we have set our eyes on for a date.

Travel and adventure go hand in hand. They don't exist without taking risks. Images and reports about terrorist attacks and insecurity flash around the world in a matter of milliseconds. They enlarge the risks, feed the fear and put the 'Dangerous' stamp on a country. Once obtained, it's very hard to get rid of. It's because of those images that people ask me if all that traveling isn't dangerous and if I have gone mad.

Reality on the ground is always different. Often very different. Especially because of the people I met on the way, I realized that the large majority of people around the world are kind to their visitors. This also applies to countries that are supposedly dangerous – or even more so there. Man is apparently keen to welcome the stranger and to protect him. That helped me a lot to have confidence and bring my travels to a happy conclusion. Was I scared? No. Fear is a bad counselor, especially for the traveler. This is certainly the case for the adventurer who wants to visit all the countries in the world.

In this book, I will take you along on travels where risk was unavoidable. In every chapter, situations arise where I had to make choices, often without overseeing the consequences.

Some stories are situated in countries that are generally labeled 'Dangerous'. Others describe adventures with people I met along the way and obstacles I had to deal with to achieve my goal, as well as moments where I was plain lucky – or not. The bottom line is that I rarely opted for the easy way. I leave it to the reader to judge the sanity of my decisions.

Allow me to take you to Somalia and Yemen, Cameroon and Kyrgyzstan, Nauru and Afghanistan – and other destinations that are probably very different from what you would expect beforehand. Just like those countries surprised me when I traveled there. And I always came back safely.

Chapter 1
Cupid Amidst Kalashnikovs

Yemen – 2004

Adventure begins where the familiar ends. A city you're visiting for the first time, a path you've never followed before, a mountain you've never climbed. Unknown scents, unusual sounds. Meeting people whose language you don't speak and whose traditions you don't know. Together with curiosity comes surprise and wonder about all that is odd. However strange the experience seems, the biggest mistake you can make as a traveler is to forget that *you* are the stranger. It's up to you to try and make sense of it all. It's crucial to leave your prejudices at home, together with stereotypes and clichés. Only then can you really start to appreciate your new environment for what it truly is.

When you arrive in a country you've never been to before, that amazement is all but guaranteed. Everything is new. You're besieged by impressions and you're often short of the senses to absorb it all. Gradually, the unfamiliar surroundings transform from curiosity to the stage of new experiences. You just don't know what meaning they will have in your life and what feeling they will evoke when, later on, you recollect the memories of your journey. The first moments, immediately after arriving in a new country, are often the most dazzling.

Everything is pure. You still have the innocent look of the child who is dying to experience something new and is open to anything.

Tonight, I have that innocent look. I zealously let my eyes wander over my new surroundings. Mighty towers rise all around me. White patterns are plastered above each floor. A red, green, blue, and yellow glow emanates from the *qamariah*, the refined stained-glass windows bricked up under the ornaments in the facades. The irregular decorations and windows make each building unique. The soft glow of street lamps makes the high walls glimmer dark yellow against the moonless night. The splendor of a thousand-and-one nights sweeps over me from all sides. It's well past twelve, I've just arrived in Sana'a and in half a day, I've been thrown back several centuries in time.

The advantage of arriving at night is that you prolong the exaltation of the first impressions until the next morning. As soon as the light falls through the dingy curtains a few hours later, I impatiently pull them open for my first glimpse of the city. Below me stretches a sea of beige-and-white tower houses that seem to have been scattered around randomly with between them dozens of stubby minarets pointing towards the sky. Sana'a is crying out to be explored and I rush down the stairs of my tower hotel to go outside and plunge into that sea.

For a few days, I immerse myself in one of the oldest continuously inhabited cities in the world. I can't get enough of wandering through the narrow streets and alleys and I'm enchanted by the buildings that make the entire inner city a World Heritage site. Not one of them is the same. Each house is painted in swirling lines of white, geometric patterns on the uneven walls. Here and there, men sit on wooden planks dangling from frayed ropes along the walls, touching up the plastered frames of the windows in dazzling white. Between the buildings, I find *miqshamah*. These palm-fringed patches of land where vegetables are grown are usually only visible from the roofs because they are well hidden between blocks of houses. They were once constructed here to keep the city supplied in times of siege. The fresh green contrasts with the terracotta walls that surround them. On the outskirts of the old city, I come to the pompous Bab-al-Yemen, the gateway to the historic center of Sana'a. Two Yemeni flags are draped over the archway, reaching all the way down to the street.

From the gate, the Souk al-Milh begins. The Salt Market. There are endless alleys full of market stalls and shops where robes, copperware, spices, traditional daggers, headscarves, mirrors, dates, toothbrushes made from *miswak*, grains, bowls, jars and, well, anything else you can think of is for sale. Here and there, a donkey or camel roams the streets. I wander through the market without anyone trying to sell me anything. At one point, I'm invited in for a glass of tea. The shopkeeper asks curious questions, just as I want to know everything about him. After all, he is the first Yemeni I've had a real conversation with. Just when I think he is going to try and sell me one of his copper coffee pots, he says: 'You probably want to see more of the city and don't have time to stay here any longer. Just know that you are welcome in our country. Welcome to Yemen.' With those last words, he puts his right hand on his heart.

While the Yemenis greet and warmly welcome me, I soon realize that there are hardly any women walking around on the streets. When I do see one, she is completely wrapped up in a dark *niqab* or *barlos*. In these wide, face-covering robes, only their eyes are visible through a narrow slit. I have to control my natural inclination to look into people's eyes and dare only cast furtive glances at the strips of facial skin between the dark fabric. Age-old traditions still have a firm grip on life in Yemen. Mecca lies a few hundred kilometers to the northwest. Yemen was one of the first areas where Islam gained a foothold and that influence is still tangible and visible. Legend says that Mohammed himself supervised the construction of the Great Mosque of Sana'a, a mere stone's throw from my hotel.

Here we come across the paradox of the traveler. On the one hand, I feel like I've won the lottery because everything indicates the country has stayed true to itself. It lives by traditions that go back many lifetimes. The whole inner city of Sana'a looks just like it must have done for centuries. People wear clothes that Yemenis have been wearing for a long time. Most of the items for sale in the market stalls were sold there hundreds of years ago. A foreigner here is a curiosity and a welcome visitor who is received with open arms, not a rich tourist on which locals jump from all sides to exploit. This is what I look for when I travel. This is exactly why I can fall in love with a country. Call it authenticity. A different world, almost without any similarities to my own, that I can marvel at and where I nevertheless feel at home.

At the same time, this uniqueness means that development in this country is stalled. The division of roles between men and women is persistent: Yemen continues to be a patriarchal society, just like others in the world. It will probably still look the way it does now for years to come, and women will play a secondary role for many more years. However, I do wish women a more equal role in society. When I told friends I was going to Yemen, their response was: 'Yemen? Are you out of your mind?' This is a country known for reports of calamities on the news, terrorism and kidnappings, not tourism and recreation. The isolation and absence of foreign influences allows the country to continue living on the same old footing. Which is precisely what I like so much about it.

Sana'a has made me hungry for more: I want to see the rest of the country. To do so, I need permits. Once I arrive at the relevant office, this turns out to be a formality. With the necessary documents in my pocket, I take a *bijou* the next day, the jumbled Yemeni version of Peugeot, the French car manufacturer. As soon as all the seats of this shared taxi are filled with passengers, it takes me west through a rough mountainous landscape. We're headed to the Red Sea, to Al Hudaydah, and then to Bait al Faqih. It's much warmer and more humid here than in high-altitude Sana'a. I go to the Friday Market, a sandy place on the outskirts of the city where you can buy everything and anything. Old TVs, electronics, plastic *Made-in-China* junk, but also gourds, spices and beans, fruit and vegetables, goats and cows. Here too, there are almost exclusively men around, dressed entirely in white and crowned with a red-and-white checkered headscarf or a white *taqiyah*, the Muslim headgear.

Then I continue to Zabid. Once the capital of the country, it has turned into a dusty village with dilapidated houses which were once white, most of which appear to have been abandoned. When I look closer, I see old, blue-painted and richly decorated wooden doors with heavy, handmade locks, framed by carved white walls. Ceilings with blue-yellow-red-gray motifs of flowers, leaves, stars, coffee pots and geometric patterns on beams in which you can still clearly recognize the original shapes of the tree from which they were cut. Small, white minarets with stubby tips lean against even smaller mosques.

Italian Director Pasolini lived here in the early 1970s and filmed his *Il Fiore Delle Mille e Una Notte*. The Flower of a Thousand and One Nights, also known simply as Arabian Nights: an erotic film about love and travel, and the essential role of fate, which so often links the two. In the strict Islamic society of Yemen, where sensuality remains hidden far behind those beautiful doors, it's hard to imagine that this film could have been made here. It's equally unlikely that the same fate would catch up with me a few weeks later in this same country.

From Zabid, I travel further south. The legendary hospitality of the Yemenis touches me more and more. As I get off the bus in Ibb, I want to pay, but the driver says that's not necessary. Someone else paid for me and he won't tell me who, so I can't even thank the donor. A little further on I ask for directions from a man who doesn't speak English, but who understands where I want to go because I say the name in Arabic. He hails a taxi, shouts my destination to the driver through the open window and pays him in advance, even though he doesn't come with me. When I arrive in Jibla, a bit further south, a passenger pulls aside my hand full of change just before I want to give it to the driver. He insists on paying for my ride, grabs my other hand and takes me to his home. We chat and drink tea, seated on cushions on the floor of the *mafraj*, the guest room. Friends join us, and then two women fill the entire carpet with bowls full of spicy chicken, meat, rice, vegetables, various sauces, several salads, and bread freshly baked in a clay oven. This would be the best meal of my entire trip.

After we've finished eating and my new friends have asked me all the questions you can ask a stranger with a limited knowledge of English, they take me outside. They tell me as best they can about the rich history of this town. Pride seeps into their words. When the local ruler Ali as-Sulayhi came to power towards the end of the eleventh century, he soon surrendered power to his young wife because he was paralyzed. She made Jibla the capital of Yemen and would rule the country for another seventy years as Queen Arwa. She also introduced a variety of ideas that are practiced to this day, such as terracing, a technique for growing crops on the country's steep, rocky mountain slopes. Arwa is one of the few women to have held power in Yemen. Moreover, she was supposedly both intelligent and very beautiful.

The question arises: what would she say about the position of women in modern-day Yemen? My friends sheepishly laugh at me when I ask. A woman in power is unthinkable in today's Yemen. They take me to the centuries-old mosque dedicated to the good-looking queen. One of the men has the key to the minaret, but it turns out to be blocked off due to renovation work. It's time for their afternoon prayers, so I have the opportunity to look around the historic building myself.

Then, it's time for the gentlemen to go in search of qat. For Yemenis, this is the highlight of the day. They chew on the leaves for most of the afternoon, constantly putting new ones in their mouths. After a while, their cheeks start to bulge, green slime comes out of their mouths and they talk more and more unintelligibly. Their mouths get fuller until they spit out the mucous liquid a few hours later. The green stains you see all over the streets are evidence of these daily rituals. My friends give me a few branches, but even after chewing on them for a while, they just taste like green leaves to me and I spit them out. It's unlikely I'll become a qat addict. While the gentlemen chew their first qat of the day, I wander through the narrow streets, past the stone houses and mosques of Jibla.

With my hand on my heart, I say goodbye to my friends and travel on to Aden, a port city on the south coast. A city with a completely different face and atmosphere. Much more modern, breathtakingly hot and humid. After the traditional Yemeni towns and villages, this is the first place in the country that looks vaguely familiar. It reminds me of modern cities on the Persian Gulf, but without the dazzling new glass towers. One day in this oven is enough. I move on quickly because there is much more to experience in this forgotten country.

First, a long bus ride to Mukallah, a long way east. Yemen has gained a reputation as a country where foreigners are often abducted. Since the government wants to promote tourism, it has recently decided to provide a soldier to foreigners on long rides. I'm assigned a youngster whose new uniform seems to have been tailor-made just a week before and with whom I can only communicate in sign language. The poor boy constantly follows me, sitting behind me in the bus with his gun on his lap. After a few hours, he is substituted at a military post by another young man. I have to abandon my attempts to talk to him because we don't speak a common language. At lunchtime, we stop and everyone gets out, my guard timidly following me with the Kalashnikov around his shoulder.

As in so many places in Yemen outside Sana'a, I'm soon surrounded by hundreds of men. From behind their backs, I can see the barrels of Kalashnikovs sticking into the air, while they carry a richly decorated *jambiya* on a belt around their belly. Without these traditional, curved daggers, a Yemeni man can hardly show himself on the street. While at first, I had to get used to this display of weapons, it soon became normal for me. I'm guessing that's because of the shy kindness of the Yemenis, which contrasts so strangely with the awe-inspiring weapons they carry. I increasingly get the feeling that the soldier is obediently following me around just for show. It seems to be a breeze to take him out and kidnap me.

Although I'm not scared of that. It seems that they treat you extremely well. Hostages are usually held in a village for weeks at a time, they get food in abundance, they get riding and shooting lessons, they are pampered in every way and they aren't hurt at all. The goal is to extract ransom money from the government that will help the community to finance a village school, a hospital or anything else of general use. You'd almost want to cooperate. The story goes that there are Europeans who come to Yemen specifically in the *hope* of being kidnapped. That is the extent of the legendary Yemeni hospitality.

It turns out that villages along the way are not in need of a new school building as I reach Mukallah at the end of the day. I thank my last guard for his good care by placing my right hand on my heart, which makes his eyes shine. I have to cancel my scuba diving plans for the simple reason that the only diving school in town has been closed for years. I manage to arrange for a car, with driver Mohammed and soldier-guide Ahmed.

The next day, we leave the Arabian Sea behind us and drive into the mainland. First, we ride through the canyon of Wadi Dawan with its pastel houses, crammed against the flanks of the rocky canyon. The lowest floors have no windows, making the

houses more defensible against attack. Yemen was once pros-
perous: the Romans called it Arabia Felix, Happy Arabia. But
the country has subsequently been the scene of tribal wars and
invasions for centuries, while its strategic location prompted
foreign powers to gain a foothold. It wasn't until 1990 that
North and South Yemen were united as one country, but
foreign interference continues to this day. Ahmed points to a
house in the distance and tells me that it belongs to the Bin
Laden family. It's impossible to tell what he thinks of him.

We drive on to Wadi Hadramaut and Shibam. I sit on the
edge of my seat when, in the distance, we see the outline of the
city rising from the wide valley. This is called both the Chicago
and the Manhattan of the desert. According to the Yemenis,
these are the oldest skyscrapers in the world. At the end of the
Middle Ages, the first eight-story clay creations were built,
giving Shibam a veritable skyline. As we get closer, I see that
the town is surrounded by palm trees and a city wall, which is
completely dwarfed by the white and beige giants towering
high above it. A little later, I wander through the narrow streets
where hardly any sunlight penetrates. Goats and donkeys roam
around. Occasionally, I have to jump away to avoid being hit by
garbage, carelessly thrown down from a high window. Every
building is unique, the irregular shapes show that they are
handmade. Because rain and wind gnaw away at these behemoths, the walls have to be renovated and plastered regularly.

Best of all, there is no souvenir stall to be seen, no pushy
carpet merchant, no tour buses or groups of people shuffling
behind a guide carrying a flag. I don't have to share this historic
World Heritage city with anyone. Apart from a few curious
children, who beg to be photographed, 'sura, sura!', the locals
let me walk through the alleys and take pictures without both-
ering me. When I walk around the outskirts of Shibam the next
morning, as the sun casts a warm glow over the mud skyline,

the children are nowhere to be seen and I have the city all to myself.

We drive further east and pass the enormous, white palace of Seiyun and the palaces of Tarim. To my surprise, I see that instead of stained glass, the windows of these buildings are decorated with elegant woodwork. The Hadramis roamed the Indian Ocean centuries ago and returned from Southeast Asia with inspiration to embellish their homes. We pass the huge, white-painted minaret of the Al-Mudhar Mosque, which at 53 meters is one of the tallest mud-brick structures in the world. Tarim is a center of Islamic learning, with one mosque for every day of the year, libraries and the largest number of descendants of the Prophet Mohammed. Here too, the proximity of Mecca is emphatically evident.

On the way, I notice black spots in the barren brown landscape with patches of green. It turns out they are women working the land. When I look closely, I see that they are wearing *madhallas*, pointed straw hats which make them very photogenic. I ask Ahmed if I can take a picture of them, but he warns me that they will pelt me with stones if I do. I only manage to take a few blurry pictures with my zoom. Further on, we stop at a place where the mud-bricks are made – the building blocks of the houses I see everywhere. Earth and water are mixed in a mold which is laid out to dry. The sun then bakes it into solid bricks. It's hard to imagine that things were ever different here.

We are on our way to Husn-al Urr, where a fortress once stood that defended the eastern entrance to Wadi Hadramaut. Neither Mohammed nor Ahmed know the place and I show them the way as far as I know it from descriptions I've found. When Mohammed asks a camel driver, it turns out we are close. We find a ruin: brown fragments of walls and an old well. There isn't much left of this defense post. Anyway, American drones don't care about fortresses, they fly high over them to hit their targets in their *War on Terror*. Fortresses don't matter anymore.

Back in Tarim, the time has come to say goodbye to Mohammed and Ahmed. I take the bus towards the west. After a long day through the desert with armed chaperones, I see the familiar buildings of the capital looming before me in the evening. I'm back at my familiar Old Sana'a Palace tower hotel.

After all the experiences of my journey through Yemen, the affection I began to feel for the country shortly after my arrival has grown into a blossoming love. Apart from the pristine beauty of the old cities and the captivating landscapes, it's mainly because I'm warmly welcomed everywhere I go. The people themselves have few possessions but insist on treating their visitor like a king. They share the little they have with me, while always respecting me and never harassing me. It is for these same reasons that the war, which would break out more than ten years after my visit, would deeply horrify me. These same simple and honest people end up paying the highest price.

During my last week in Yemen, I use Sana'a as a starting point for trips to places of interest in the surrounding area. In addition to the towns I can visit on my own by *bijou*, I want to go to Marib. This is the ancient capital of the kingdom of Saba and, according to some, the biblical city of Sheba. It's in a conflict-prone area: you have to arrange private transport and you need a special permit. A few years after my visit, it will be renamed 'the Capital of al-Qaeda in Yemen'. I'm back at the office of the Ministry of Tourism, which takes care of the permits. An official advises me to organize this trip together with others and sends me to a hotel where two foreigners are staying who are apparently also keen to go there.

Upon arriving at the place, I call their room and Misao, a Japanese woman, comes downstairs. She is the first foreigner and also the first woman I have talked to since I arrived in Yemen. Before deciding anything, she wants to talk to Carlos, her Colombian boyfriend. He's in town, so we walk in that direction to look for him. Misao's English is remarkably good, and for the first time in ten days I have a conversation that goes beyond the usual 'Where are you from', 'What's your name', 'How old are you' and 'How many children do you have' questions. It's great to talk about Yemen, about Japan and about traveling in general. It's nice to be able to talk to a woman again. We walk between the tower houses of Sana'a which are still as enchanting as when I saw them that first evening. A little later, we see four foreigners approaching in the distance. They immediately stand out among the other pedestrians. Even in the capital, foreigners are a rarity. Misao introduces me to Carlos and a German couple. Then my eyes turn to the woman standing next to them.

What couldn't have been more than a few seconds seems to last forever. Just like an innocent ray of sunlight ignites a bale of dry hay if you hold a magnifying glass over it, the intense look in her eyes sets everything in me alight. She looks at me half-mockingly. The sun creates a halo around her reddish hair. After weeks of surreptitiously glancing at narrow strips of female faces in search of eyes, I now take my time to absorb the details of her open face, on which the afternoon sun casts a warm light. The deep pink cheeks. The frown on her forehead. The light brown eyebrows. The straight nose. The white, regular teeth that frame a sparkling smile. But above all: those light green and luminous eyes that keep staring at me unabashedly.

The sounds of Sana'a no longer get through to me. The fairy-tale buildings have become blurry decorations in the background. My wife, who couldn't come with me to Yemen; Marib, Misao and the others; the impressions of my exciting journey: in one fell swoop, I've forgotten everyone and everything. This woman has instantly become the center of the world. My world.

When I traveled through Yemen, I had an eye for rough landscapes of rocky mountains and endless desert, for stone villages with centuries-old mosques. I talked and laughed with the colorful, warm, engaging Yemenis with the inevitable *jambiyas* around their waists. But a beautiful woman who looks at me defiantly, who holds out her hand to me and takes my breath away: I haven't seen that for the longest time. Here I am, about to touch her hand.

'Hey! I'm Nana, from Denmark.'

Our hands intertwine. We hold each other for much longer than necessary, looking into each other's eyes. I barely manage to say my name before my mouth becomes as dry as the desert I rode through the day before. Fortunately, someone suggests that we all go out to eat. I hastily take a sip of water.

Once we're in the restaurant, I manage to get a seat next to her. As soon as we're sitting at the table, we talk endlessly. It turns out that she has traveled around with the others for a few days and we exchange our experiences of Yemen. I listen to her voice and her light Danish accent, watch how she moves her hands, look at her face, watch how she smiles. I soon notice that she doesn't respect any conventions. She says the most unexpected things that catch me off guard and she has a wonderfully sarcastic sense of humor. She is elusive and free-spirited, tough and nonchalant, mysterious and seductive, and that makes her irresistible. I have to be careful not to be absorbed by her smiling eyes so as not to make a complete fool of myself.

She tells me she's in Sana'a for five weeks to study Arabic. That she's not seen much more than Sana'a itself and went to the limestone bridge of Shaharah the previous weekend, where she met the others. That she was touched by the warm welcome she received from the Yemenis, who apparently also take care of female foreigners. Then, in the middle of the conversation, she casually mentions her husband. My heart cringes. What was all that flirting about? That wink, that provocative smile, those radiant eyes and that hand I was allowed to hold for far too long? Or has my imagination run wild, driven by my simplistic male brain?

A little later, as we walk back to our traditional tower hotels, I wonder how I might be able to see Nana again. My heart skips a beat when Carlos suggests we have dinner together at six the next evening. We have arrived at the little square where I stopped that first evening to look at the stone towers around me. Even though I didn't know then what Yemen had in store for me, I sensed that it would be special. But I never expected that my heart would be racing like it is now. I frolic the rest of the way back to my hotel.

The next day, I continue to explore Yemen. I climb a rocky path to Kawkabam, a village dramatically perched on the edge of high cliffs, and then onwards to Thulla, which is famous for its stone houses. The unpolished beauty of the land continues to amaze me. I take pictures, read about what I see, and try to enjoy it. But it's not the same anymore. My head is gone. I only hear Nana's laughter and voice, see her eyes before me and count the hours before I can disappear into them again.

Back at the central square in Thulla, it takes more than two hours before all the seats in the bijou are taken and the driver finally turns his key. I look at my watch and calculate that there is still a small chance I'll make it. But there is traffic on the way, we have to refuel, passengers get off, others get on. By the time I reach my hotel, it's almost eight o'clock. My four new friends from the previous day have long since joined Nana in a restaurant I will never find.

If only I had left it at that! Now, seventeen years later, that's easily said. Our encounter has brought happiness, but also unfathomable deep sorrow. There were so many moments when things could have gone differently. So many coincidences, so many crossroads where I could have gone left and she could have gone right. How could I know that I was at a turning point in my life? I had to take fate into my own hands, I had to see those eyes again, see that smile and hear that voice again, feel that enormous tension again. I just had to know what it all meant. There was simply no other option – even though I'd been married for six years. It was terrible, but my desire to see Nana was simply too strong, or I was too weak to resist. The vagaries of Lady Luck, travel and love – the theme of Pasolini's film now has me in its grip, from which there is no escape. It dictates what to do. Fighting back seems futile.

I walk to the familiar square. Who knows, I might see her somewhere? A bright boy notices my eyes shifting back and forth and asks what I'm looking for. I shrug and tell him he can't help me. He doesn't give up and asks again. I casually mention Nana.

'Ah, but I know her! I know where she lives!'

'Where?'

'Around the corner. Come with me! I think she's home.'

My heart is suddenly pounding heavily in my chest. In the distance, I feel a glimmer of hope. Who knows, maybe she is already back from dinner? We walk to another traditional tower, into which the boy disappears while I wait outside. Of course, a single western woman who has been living here for a month stands out. No wonder this clever boy knows her. In no time, he is back, still panting after his sprint.

'No, she is not in her room.'

'What floor is this room on?'

'The fifth.'

'*Shukran!*'

A little later, I'm staring ahead of me in a neon-lit restaurant, steadily chewing on my chicken, not tasting anything. So now I know where she's staying, but what good is that? I can hardly wait in front of her hotel for her to come home. All sorts of other ideas pop into my mind but just as quickly seem ridiculous.

Then, suddenly, the pieces of the puzzle fall into place. All is not lost! I'll write a note to ask her out. It takes me an hour to come up with the words. After all, this is a note to a married woman I've only known for a few hours. So, it shouldn't be too heavy, but it should stand out, preferably with a big wink. But also, serious enough to make her say yes. I throw away one note after the other until I have a text that seems right to me. The exact words have long since been lost. It was about me proposing to meet again to find out once and for all which cheese was tastier: Danish or Dutch. Then, I take the time to write it down on paper. That also takes some time with my crippled handwriting.

Very early the next morning, I walk to Nana's guesthouse. When I arrive on the fifth floor, I see her door ajar. My breath falters – damn, she is awake! Luckily, she is not inside. Perhaps she has gone to the bathroom, which is one floor higher; floors are so small here that they don't fit together. She absolutely shouldn't see me now. I quickly put the note on the floor and rush down the high stone steps. I stand outside with a beating heart. I have pushed fate in the direction I wanted. There is no turning back now.

I'm going to Marib with Martin, a Dutchman with whom the tourist officer has hooked me up. Misao and Carlos have decided not to come. I experience the day as a half-dream. We drive through mountains, the wind creates a low-hanging mist of sand and we see columns of what was once the Temple of the Moon and the Temple of the Sun. These are remnants of a civilization that is thousands of years old. The Kingdom of Saba relied on the dam and the irrigation works which ensured that here, on the edge of the desert, an empire could flourish. When the dam collapsed, the Kingdom was doomed. We see the ruins of the old dam, as well as the new one, which is much more recent and has ensured that there are strips of green in the arid landscape. We see the ruins of a city; the Egyptians bombed it in a long-forgotten war in the 1960s.

Martin is happy to have met a fellow countryman. He is a guide in Syria and speaks fluent Arabic. I listen to his stories, do my best to seem interested and occasionally give him a friendly nod. But the back of my mind is busy. Will Nana be there tonight? Will I see her again? Or will she choose not to accept such an invitation? Was her flirting a fantasy born out of a long time without women around? If only I could press a fast forward button and know the answer. I scrupulously keep my little secret from Martin, listen obediently to the adventures of his group travel tours, while in my mind, like a nervous teenager, I endlessly consider my options: 'Yes', 'No', 'Yes', 'No'...

But first, we have lunch and, on the way back, we visit a qat plantation. Yemen is not rich in fertile land as it is, and the popularity of this green narcotic is replacing the cultivation of food, simply because it is more profitable – and, of course, because it is a substitute for alcohol. Men, including the many who are poor, spend a lot of money on the leaves; there is a lively trade in them. While we're here, the driver takes a few bunches to the city, where qat is more expensive.

He drops us off at my square in the city, where I talk a bit more with Martin. My heartbeat accelerates when I see Nana approaching. She has decided she wants to see me! Again, that sparkle in her eyes, that nonchalance in her posture, that smile. Again, it seems as if the world around me is dissolving and only she is left. She suggests that the three of us go for dinner. Oh no! That's not what I was longing for! Even though I haven't told him anything, Martin evidently senses what's going on. He wishes us a good evening and leaves.

A little later, we're sitting in a noisy restaurant. I manage to suppress my nerves and have a conversation. Now that I have her all to myself, I can look at her brazenly, listen to her and laugh with her. I thought about her for two days, imagining what it would be like to see her again. A whirlwind of feelings rushes through my body and I can't resist it, even if I want to. When I walk back to my tower hotel, after our goodbyes, I frolic across the street again. The guy at the reception desk is surprised by the huge grin on my face.

Back in my room, I acknowledge what is happening. After weeks of traveling through a country where men rule the streets, where women are dressed in all-covering robes, where every whiff of sensuality has been expertly squeezed out of public life and out of my mind on all sides, I've suddenly awakened. I instantly lost my heart to this elusive woman. Moreover, a married woman, who doesn't even live anywhere close to me and whom, in a few days, I may never see again.

The next day, I wake up with the same grin on my face as the one I wore when I entered my room the night before. It probably never left after I fell asleep. I float through the city, float through the countryside, float up the steps of the buildings of Yemen's symbol, Dar al Hajar – and at the end of the afternoon, I float up to the roof terrace of my tower hotel, because Nana is coming to see me.

When we finally sit on the roof, looking out over the old city and its ancient, brown and white buildings between the bare mountains, I realize how romantic Sana'a really is. I've been on this roof before and have known this view for weeks, and yet it looks completely different now. Nana has unwittingly added a dimension to this city, to this country, to this journey.

The sun is setting. From all sides, from hundreds of minarets, comes the sometimes plaintive, sometimes melancholic, but always overpowering chant of the *muezzin* to remind the faithful that it is time for the fourth prayer of the day. The vocal melee echoes against the mountains and comes back amplified, swirls around, before dissolving and disappearing into the falling night, towards the starry sky, towards Allah.

In the meantime, we continue to talk. In the back of my mind, all sorts of voices are chattering away. What's next? Meet again the next evening? Or make a more daring proposal and take a leap of faith? I just learned that I have a few extra days off, which allows me to stay in Yemen for a bit longer. With a big wink, Lady Luck pokes her head around the corner again: she clearly wants to give me more time with Nana. I'm determined to postpone my departure as long as possible. It gives me a chance to go to the Haraz mountains, which are too far from the city to visit in one day.

At the end of the evening, when she is about to return to her hotel, I gather all my courage. I feel like a pimply-faced adolescent who nervously picks at his sweater and would die a thousand deaths before daring to ask out the girl he's in love with. 'Would you like to come with me to the Haraz mountains this weekend?' The question seems to linger for an eternity in the dark Yemeni evening. For a moment, I feel like I've made a mistake. Then she says, beaming: 'Of course! I would love to go with you!' Inside I'm on fire now, with desire, excitement, joy. I flutter through Sana'a for a few more days while Nana studies Arabic.

In a desolate landscape of rugged mountains between which deep crevices have been cut, we stand among armed Yemenis in the back of a white pick-up truck. Nana is the only woman. We're on our way to stone towers that pierce the sky infinitely far above us. Slowly, pothole after pothole, bend after bend, the Toyota hauls us up the unpaved road towards Hajjara. Patches of mist swirl between the rocky peaks and it gets chilly. Despite all the beauty around me, my thoughts are elsewhere. I'm trying to imagine how this day will end.

After lunch, a few Yemenis give us shooting lessons. The simultaneously frail and tough Danish woman puts a Kalashnikov against her shoulder, aims, and fires. The shot echoes against the barren mountains around us. Then she fires again. The Yemenis look on in admiration and give her a thumbs-up. A woman who shoots: they've never seen that before. The shooting lesson is over immediately: they don't even offer me a try.

In the afternoon, we go for a walk and climb up to a lookout point. We're all alone on the top of the world and below, deep, deserted valleys stretch out between the pointed mountains where clouds now float between them. Silence. We no longer dare to look at each other. Don't dare to talk. Don't dare to make a sound. We don't even dare to swallow anymore. We walk back in silence.

Soon after we've had a simple dinner, the generator in the village switches off. Instantly, it's eerily quiet. The tension is unbearable and I propose going for a walk. Outside, the full moon casts a cold blue-white light over the jagged landscape, creating silhouettes of rectangular towers and sharp stone rock formations. We start talking again as soon as we leave the building. Cautiously at first, but we soon talk excitedly, if only to try and escape the insufferable nervousness.

Once we're back at our sober hotel, we can't escape our longing anymore. In a failed attempt at saying good night, Nana's mouth ends up on my shoulder. Trembling, I put my hand around her waist. For a moment, we hesitate. We both know that if we take the next step, there will be no going back. Then, our lips find each other inescapably. The first kiss is still tender, the next is outright desirous. With my other hand, I pull her slender body yearningly towards me, but that's not necessary anymore. Nana throws herself against me. We won't let go of each other now. The barrage that held back all the built-up tension and desire of the last few days breaks, just like the dam at Marib once did. A whirling tidal wave of churning emotions and bestial desire inexorably drags us along. Stronger and stronger. Further and further. Deeper and deeper.

Two days later, we have to let go of each other and say goodbye, without knowing if we will ever see each other again. Five days after that, I'm in Lisbon for work when I get a text from Nana. She has just landed at Kastrup but doesn't want to go home. She wants to be with me. We have to see each other, that much is clear. The next morning, I take the first flight to Copenhagen and go straight to the Little Mermaid. Nana doesn't want her friends to stumble upon us, and which Dane in his right mind would ever go to that little statue, the overrated *must-see* for every foreign visitor to the Danish capital? When we're finally entangled in an endless and voracious kiss, we hear the chatter of a thousand cameras. We look up to see a busload of Japanese tourists abandoning the statue and aiming their lenses at that melted-together couple on a bench.

The love of my life – yes, I was convinced of that. Within a week, Nana had split up with her husband and I had left my wife. Blazing love and desire and desperate grief for the lost loves we left behind lay close together in the months that followed. Love can be divine and devastating at the same time.

After two years of traveling back and forth, she came to live with me. We took all kinds of trips. When times were hard, when we clashed, all we had to do was to say 'Hajjara' to each other, like an enchanted password that opened all doors. It reminded us how and where it all began. How much we fell in love under the full moon in those rugged Yemeni mountains and how that attraction transcended everything else.

A summery August afternoon, a few years later. Just as love caught me off-guard in Sana'a, it was equally abruptly snatched away. The only time in my life I literally felt my heart break. The magic of 'Hajjara' had worn off and doors were hermetically sealed shut. I was desperate, but no matter what I tried, all my questions remained unanswered. For weeks I hardly slept or ate. I didn't know what to do with myself. Where the love of Yemen had made me flutter and frolic like a colorful butterfly in the bright sunlight, I now felt like living in a deep, dark cave. It was the beginning of a long process of mourning, of cutting ties, of a crushing grief that would haunt me for years.

My heart had to heal and to achieve that I decided to follow it. I needed a distraction. A life goal. Something that would keep me busy for a long time, that I could love unconditionally and that I could lose myself in without the risk of having my heart break again. Then it dawned on me. Travel! Of course! Travel like never before, travel to places I had never been before.

Travel: experiencing new adventures. Travel: a love that never betrays. The goal soon presented itself. I wanted to visit every country in the world. The first few trips certainly weren't easy because I missed Nana terribly. I screamed my lungs out against the rough, cold and dark emptiness of Iceland that somehow reminded me of the Haraz Mountains. In the months that followed, I discovered beautiful places and met extraordinary people. Tear after tear, journey after journey, adventure after adventure, I felt the pain melt away, even though it unexpectedly raised its hideous and ruthless head every now and then. Travel proved to be an excellent medicine.

Five months later, in a little church in San Andrés de Pisimbalá in Colombia, I cried tears of joy because for the first time I felt that I could be happy again. I never could have imagined falling madly in love that first night on that little square in the old town of Sana'a. Even less so that it would change my life forever and that I would end up traveling to every country in the world. Therefore, Signor Pasolini, I agree with you wholeheartedly. Travel, love and fate: they are intertwined. Inseparably.

Chapter 2
Here's Your Coke!

Myanmar – 2006

As I walk to the platform through the spacious railway station of Mandalay, holding the groceries I just bought in a plastic bag, a stream of people comes walking towards me. When I reach the top of the stairs, large baskets of food are moving up, with women underneath. Nobody is going down the stairs. This is strange because my train is leaving in a few minutes. I start to feel anxious and quicken my pace.

A little lower, I see others on the platform gathering their things and getting ready to make their way up. Another couple of steps down I see that the train has already started moving. That's my train. Is it leaving early? Is the conductor's watch ahead? Does any of this matter? The fact is, the long train is starting to move in fits and starts, to the sound of metal against metal. It's still more than thirty yards from me. Nana is on that train and she has all the luggage. I have some kyat with me, that's all. No passport, no money, no credit card, no clothes, no camera. Nothing.

I lunge down the rest of the stairs three steps at a time. I jump over a basket, slalom around people and luggage still on the platform, and accelerate to a full sprint as the train starts to pick up steam. The plastic bag with food and drink in my hand tries to keep up with me while it dangles along. The question now is how long it will take for the train to reach a speed that is impossible to run against. And where the end of the platform is.

Surprised Burmese people hang from the windows and look at me with excitement and a big smile on their faces. I'm an unexpected attraction at the beginning of their train journey. With a desperate leap, I barely manage to cling to the metal bar at the end of the train and I squeeze myself into the swaying wagon. The very last wagon. The end of the platform flashes away behind me.

After the excitement of the sprint, I feel calm. I only have to walk forward now. Nana has a stomachache. I bought her biscuits, soft drink and aspirin. She asked for it when I left her on the train after we settled down in our seats. I thought I still had plenty of time to buy those groceries. The pale blue plastic bag is now moist on all sides from the condensation of the ice-cold can of soda, which Nana hopes will make her feel better. However, I soon find out that I can't get out of this wagon. This is an attachment to the train and there is no way to access the other carriages.

The employee working on this wagon grins at me. He understands my situation but can't help me. It must be a comical sight: a foreigner with sweat gushing from all sides and a plastic bag in his hand, looking around desperately. For him, too, I'm a free attraction. Still, he can't explain to me what the function of this wagon is, or indeed of himself. It doesn't help that he doesn't speak a word of English. How can I make him understand that my girlfriend is in the front of the train, that she's sick, and needs me and the contents of the plastic bag?

We've embarked on a long ride that will take us through the night to Naba in the north of the country, where we'll take the slow train to Katha. Using gestures and by pointing at my watch, this employee of the Burmese railways manages to make me understand that the train won't stop for the next few hours.

I realize that Nana will also be seriously worried about me by now. I hope she hangs out of the window to see if she can catch a glimpse of me, so I stick my head out as far as I can when the train is going round a bend. I can see the entire train ahead of me and, at the very front, a locomotive pulling all these wagons through the Burmese landscape. I hope to give her a sign of life and reassure her by waving vehemently towards the front of the train. To my disappointment, I only see locals hanging out of the window and they wave back enthusiastically. Not a trace of Nana.

She must now assume that I'm not on the train at all. Our phones are useless in Myanmar: no coverage. How did we manage these situations in the pre-mobile phone era? What will she do when the train pulls in at the next station? Will she get out, taking all our luggage? Will she catch a taxi back to Mandalay and hope to find me there? I suppose she wouldn't stay on the train. I need to be with her before we get to the first station.

In the meantime, I keep trying to explain to the guy in this small carriage that I need to go further up the train. He understands me, but can only answer me with that sweet, almost apologetic Burmese smile. I'm trapped in this wagon, obediently following the rest of the carriages.

After a while, when the train slows down and heads up the gentle slope of a bridge over the Irrawaddy River, the fellow in my wagon gestures that by jumping out and running ahead, I should be able to get into the penultimate carriage. I look at him in disbelief. Even though the train slows down, his plan means that I will have to run faster than the train and then jump into the next wagon. And all that going uphill. If I make it, I'll be with Nana a few minutes later. But if it fails, I'll be on a railway bridge far out of town, with no road nearby, without money, luggage or travel documents. I'll only have the plastic bag with Coke as a consolation prize. My Burmese friend probably won't pull the emergency brake if I lag behind. But at the same time, I realize that the alternative, lingering in this wagon for hours, isn't attractive either.

There it is again, that choice which keeps on coming back. What should I do? Should I stick with the predictable and safe option, or go for the adventure and the uncertainty? In all respects, the rational choice of waiting patiently until we get to a station is far better than a risky jump between the Burmese sleepers. At the same time, I have a bag with food and drink that Nana needs to get well, which I have to deliver as soon as possible. Plus, I'm impatient. To my surprise, I tighten my grip on the plastic bag, look for a spot with fewer stones next to the sleepers, and jump.

The landing goes splendidly, and I try to carry the speed of the train into my sprint. I manage to overtake its speed. Slowly but surely, I work my way past the front of the last wagon. I can see the bar and the metal steps of the penultimate carriage in front of me. Now, it's important to catch up before we reach the highest point of the bridge and the train builds up more speed. Centimeter by centimeter, I succeed in doing so. When I'm under the bar of the stairs, I jump. I grab the metal with my right hand, while the abrupt movements make the plastic bag in my left-hand swing dangerously. All the while, I pray the plastic doesn't break – then everything would have been in vain.

The next moment, my right foot is on the bottom step. I put my second foot on the plank and now I have a firm grip on the train's handle. After the tension of the last minute, a sense of pride is taking hold of me. I made it! When I turn around, I look towards the broad smile of my Burmese friend with a look that radiates: 'I told you so!'

Now I'm in a normal passenger wagon. I walk through the carriages one by one, stepping over people on the ground, over baskets of merchandise, walking past locals also on their way north. I greet them all. I am euphoric: it's only a matter of time before I can hand Nana her order. I still have to go through about twenty packed carriages because our seats are in front of the train.

When I arrive in the front carriage, I'm met with cheers. Passengers applaud as I walk forward. I see a group of Burmese people and when I get closer they diverge. Nana is sitting in their midst. She turns around and I look into a tearful face. When she sees me, her moist eyes widen. She was convinced that I was still in Mandalay, or perhaps already in a taxi, on my way to the first station to intercept her (assuming the taxi would reach that station before the train, as well as the driver accepting a passenger without money).

It is time to open the plastic bag. It is time for Nana to drink the Coke she asked for, a desperate remedy to calm her stomach. When I bought the can it was ice-cold, but by now it's lukewarm. Still, I proudly say, 'There you go. Here's your Coke!'

Chapter 3
Tricky Training

Iran – 2001

While four strong hands hold me in a tight grip, I swiftly look back. I see a soldier closing the huge metal gate through which I was just dragged. It's impossible to escape. The hands pull me further and push me onto a bench. Once I sit down, I see about twenty soldiers in solid, pale green uniforms towering over me. They stare at me, poke each other in the stomach, point their fingers at me and smirk. Behind their heads I see the barrels of their guns sticking into the cloudless sky. Here I am in my tight, shiny, Lycra running clothes. The soldiers are talking to me, but they are speaking Farsi and I don't speak their language. A cursory glance at my sports watch tells me it's 7:44 am. I have no idea how I'll ever get out through that gate again, let alone catch my flight home that night.

A few days earlier, I had arrived in Iran for the first time in my life. Together with my colleagues, I had hired a van to drive south to Isfahan. It was the first time for most of the others as well. We all had that curiosity that comes with visiting a new country, so we spent most of the ride looking outside at this historic, controversial, and mostly unknown country. One of the great things about traveling: arriving in places of which you already have an image in your head, to then discover that the reality is different. Often completely different.

We stopped in Qom, a sacred city for Shi'ites. We saw hordes of believers clad in black, wandering around the shrine of Fatima Masumeh. One of Iran's holiest sites. Even though my female colleagues had been provided with black *chadors* upon arrival at the airport, they were given a more concealing dress at the entrance. This made it even harder to distinguish them from the other women around here as they were all wearing the same monochromatic garb.

From immense banners high above us, Khomeini and other gray-bearded ayatollahs stared sternly at the black ants crawling across the huge square. The Ayatollah, who had deposed the Shah in 1979 and started the Iranian Revolution, had died more than a decade before. He was depicted wearing a faded red robe with a gray shirt underneath, a black turban and a deep frown on his face. In the left corner of the enormous poster was an elegantly calligraphed slogan.

We saw a golden dome with walls tiled in blue and green and round minarets with intricate geometric decorations, honeycomb vaults in gold, green and blue, alcoves with count-less mirrors that multiplied all that beauty a thousandfold, spouting fountains that spread their soothing murmur across the marble floor. The builders of this sanctuary did everything in their power to inspire the devout pilgrim and overwhelm the innocent visitor. It's both impressive and suffocating, fasci-nating and frightening; especially because of the gaze of the omnipresent Ayatollah, piercing our backs wherever we go.

Driving away from the sanctuary and the all-encompassing, all-determining religious compulsion felt like liberation. After driving south for a few more hours, we arrived in Isfahan at the end of the afternoon, the second-largest city in the country.

I was preparing for my fourth marathon, which was to take place a few weeks later in Rotterdam. Determined to finally finish under two hours fifty, after three previous failed attempts, my colleague and friend Ernst and I went for a run right before nightfall. Despite the heat, we trained in long-sleeved running clothes so as not to cause too much offense in a country where you hardly see any runners on the street anyhow. We haphazardly ran up a nearby mountain and, when we turned around, were rewarded with a view of Iran's former Safavid capital. In its legendary heyday, this was one of the largest cities in the world. According to an Iranian proverb, Isfahan is half the world and I immediately believed that when I saw it lying at my feet.

The next day, we marveled at refined mosques and madrasas, palaces and squares where the colors blue and green predominated. We saw brightly colored yellow-red-brown-green-purple pyramids of spice in the huge covered bazaar, lit by beams of gray daylight streaming down through holes in the ceiling. We smoked hookah under an arch in the Khaju Bridge over the almost waterless Zayande River. The unconditional hospitality and friendliness of the people surprised us and was contradictory to what you hear about Iran in the West.

Isfahan felt like the opposite of Qom. There were no life-size portraits of sober, strict, religious leaders who kept an eye on everyone and who had a paralyzing effect on passers-by with their piercing eyes. Instead, we found young Iranian women who approached us and, when they were sufficiently close, moved their *chador* to the side. This instantly transformed them from walking dark covers into beautifully made-up, seductive women with coal-black eyes, dark hair and bright red lips. With a soft voice and in almost perfect English, they politely asked us where we were from and what our names were.

We visited a cemetery for the victims of the war against Iraq, which lasted most of the 1980s, took millions of lives on both sides and had no winner. Endless pictures of soldiers who died in vain before their lives had even begun to flourish. We saw a small photo exhibition of the battlefield, showing the most heinous atrocities depicted in black and white. The contrast with the colorful splendor and friendliness that surrounded us couldn't be bigger.

The evening before our departure, we had agreed to have breakfast at eight o'clock and to leave an hour later for the long drive back to Tehran. That way, we would be back in time for our flight to Amsterdam. I had become restless after a day without training and decided to go for another run in the morning. I set the alarm for quarter past six.

I sneaked out of the hotel and closed the door behind me as gently as I could. I ran up the same mountain where Ernst and I went for a run a few days before. It was a beautiful day. The blue, bone-dry air stood out against the barren mountains which still lay in shadow; the sun had also just woken up and had yet to hoist itself over the ridge.

Once I reached the top, I paused in the radiant light to consider my options. My watch said it was 7:08. The logical thing to do was to turn back, just as we had done on our first run: a guarantee to be back in time for breakfast. But it's boring to take the same way back. Before me, I saw a valley with lumps of beige-brown rocks without any vegetation. In the distance, I saw a black ribbon contrasting against the light brown. An asphalt road. On the west side of the ridge, I noticed another road leading back to the city. It should be possible to get to that main road around the mountain via the road at the end of the valley. I estimated the distance to be less than ten kilometers. I should be able to make it for the eight o'clock breakfast.

How many times had I been in a similar situation? In my heart, I already knew I was going to do it, but I just had to ignore the calculating, logical arguments of my mind to start the new adventure. Once more, I couldn't resist the strong lure of the thrill that lay ahead of me. I left the certainty behind, plunged into the valley and jumped between boulders as there was no longer a trail. The sun was burning my back and my sweat evaporated into the dry air almost instantly. In all directions, there wasn't a single person to be seen: the barren and empty Iranian landscape stretched out in front of me. Brown land-scape, blue sky: there were no more colors around. Has anyone ever run through this valley? Here I was, thousands of miles away from Rotterdam, training on a track no one had ever trodden before, to finally run that damned time I had set my eyes on. My heart was pumping adrenaline through my body and I felt a strong urge to scream out of sheer happiness.

Once I arrived at the asphalt road, I turned right. Euphoria was still seething through my body, especially when I looked back at the mountain I had just come running down from. There is nothing more beautiful than plotting your running routes as you go, especially in a country like Iran. It was weird that I didn't see any cars on this road. Perhaps it was still too early? Apart from the regular tapping of my shoes on the asphalt and my deep breathing, I heard nothing at all.

Suddenly, a shrill whistle cut through the silence of the blue morning sky. I ran on and the same piercing sound broke the morning silence again. How could that be, wasn't I alone? I stopped and looked left. My eyes got a chance to focus and I saw shadows in the light brown landscape around me. To my surprise, I noticed a well-camouflaged tower with barbed wire. When I looked more closely, I observed that the barbed wire belonged to a fence leading to another tower. On top of it, I noticed a man dressed in a green and brown uniform. He was wearing a gun on his back and had a whistle in his mouth.

A soldier.

He gestured for me to come to him. I anxiously walked towards him. As I got closer, I pointed my arm in the direction I was running and shouted, 'Isfahan?' I guessed he was less than twenty years old. He clearly didn't know what to do. This wasn't a well-used running track and it was likely I was the first foreigner he had ever seen here. Certainly, the first in running clothes. On the next tower, there was another soldier and they began to yell and gesticulate nervously at each other. I took a few steps forward and got ready to run on.

Just as I was about to set off for the last stretch towards the hotel, I heard a heavy vehicle pulling up behind the fence. A cloud of dust arose as it came to a halt. Once it had settled, I saw a truck with soldiers through the barbed wire. They were carrying guns over their shoulders. As soon as they stopped, some of them unlocked their guns and aimed their weapons at me. An intense fear shot through my body and killed the bliss I had been feeling only minutes earlier. Running away was no longer an option. I slowly raised my hands in the air.

In a flash, the images I saw at the photo exhibition the day before came back to my mind. What have those soldiers on that truck experienced, what have they seen in their military life, what have they been up to in the war against their neighbor? How high was their threshold for pulling the trigger?

Apparently, they were pleased with my raised hands; the truck started to move. With the vehicle driving away from me, I started running again. Just after half-past seven. I pressed the button on my watch again. My heart was pounding in my chest, this time not because of the effort of the run. After this delay, I could still have breakfast in half an hour. And arriving a few minutes late wasn't a disaster either.

A few hundred yards further on along barbed wire and watchtowers, I saw a group of soldiers walking up the road. Their truck was parked on the other side of the fence. The armed soldiers ran towards me. I immediately realized that my fate was now in their hands, that there was no escape, and I stopped running. Excited voices, curious looks: before I knew it, I was surrounded by men whose language I didn't speak. I tried again with 'Isfahan?'. I tried to show that I had nothing on me.

But the guy with the most stripes on his shoulder pointed to the large gate behind us, the only entrance in the barbed wire-protected area. Everything inside me was screaming not to go in there. I begged and gestured for them to let me go, hoping that these men would have the same kindness as the Isfahani. Or at least the spirit of the merchants in the bazaars here, where everything was up for negotiation. If only those beautiful Iranian ladies with their big black eyes were here. But in the meantime, two soldiers grabbed me and dragged me unrelentingly towards the gate.

So here I am, at an Iranian military base. Surrounded by Iranian soldiers I can't talk to. Iranian hospitality ended at the gate. Here, other laws apply. Stricter laws. The West has been at odds with this country since the 1979 Revolution. How will they see me? A runner from a faraway country who accidentally passed their base: no matter how logical the explanation may seem to me, these soldiers have no reason to buy it. They may as well see me as a spy disguised as a runner who has been sent on a reconnaissance mission. Running isn't a big sport here.

Rule number one for any traveler is to avoid military areas and that certainly applies to Iran. Stories come to my mind of innocent plane spotters being rounded up near military airports and sent to prison – and that was with allies in Europe. I'm carefully searched: at least they know that I have nothing with me and nothing to hide – as if you could hide anything in these tight running shorts.

In the meantime, one of the soldiers comes over and sits close to me. He starts picking at my watch. He is still a boy, with just a faint hint of what will one day be a mustache on his upper lip. He seems mesmerized, pushes buttons and looks at the display to see what the result is. I let him go and start saying goodbye to my faithful running buddy. I can't imagine it will still be on my wrist if I ever get out of here and I don't even care now. I would gladly give this watch to him if he could open the gate in return so I could finish my training session.

The soldiers are still talking in excited voices. One of them has a walkie talkie, maybe he could contact the police in Isfahan so I can leave soon? But then they ask, 'You, America?' For a short while, I wonder: should I say that I'm French or Spanish? Those countries are less openly supporting Israel, the archenemy of Iran. But if they find out I'm not telling the truth, I will have an even bigger problem. 'No, Holland', I answer, trying to give them my most innocent smile. Hopefully, they think of tulips, windmills and football players. But I'm met with angry looks: 'Holland: Israel.' The soldier who spoke gestures with his hands, making it clear that he thinks the countries are close friends. This is exactly what I was afraid of.

Then, a car comes over a hill on the military grounds. It stops a few meters from my bench. The men around me signal for me to get in. Now the gate is opening and they are taking me to the hotel, I think. It is 8:07 am and I will still be able to take a shower and have a quick breakfast before we drive back in less than an hour.

Only goes to show how naive I am. The car turns around and drives the other way. Away from the gate, further into the military base, until we reach a one-story building. Are these the headquarters? I ask the driver and the man who is accompanying me, but they don't understand. The latter orders me to get out and ushers me inside.

The room is small. Through a square window, the sun shines on a metal bed in a corner, over which a worn, grubby bedspread is sloppily draped. There is also a table and a chair. A plain-clothed man approaches me with an almost apologetic smile on his face. He shakes my hand, introduces himself as Reza and turns out to speak perfect English because he studied medicine in the United States. A ray of hope. Now I can finally talk to someone whose language I speak, so I can explain that I'm innocent. Now I can ask if they could call my guesthouse. He will understand that I mean no harm, accidentally ran past the military base, and help me get me out of here. He knows that those weird Westerners often go for a run and that there is nothing suspicious about it. Maybe he regularly went for a run himself when he lived in the US.

Unfortunately, it turns out there is no external phone line. He is not in a position to make decisions. But the hospitality of the country runs in his genes. So, it can be found here after all, even behind that heavy fence. He gives me a cup of tea. Before he leaves, he switches on a tiny black and white TV next to the bed. I mainly see static on the screen. But I don't want to watch TV anyway.

It's now 9:14. I can forget about the shower and breakfast and I should already have been on the bus with my colleagues. Now that I feel a little more secure, my thoughts focus on them. They must have finished breakfast, packed their luggage, and wondered where I was. They must be seriously concerned by now. They will undoubtedly try to find me – but where? No matter how hard they try, they will never find me here, in the middle of a tightly guarded Iranian army base. I try to imagine how I would react if I were in their position: a colleague who disappears without a trace. In Iran.

With a shock, I realize that, after having searched in vain, the moment will come when they decide to leave. They'll have no choice. Tehran is more than four hundred kilometers to the north. The return flight to Amsterdam can't be canceled due to Purser Kester's training. I don't want to think about what will happen when they are back in the Netherlands and I am still stuck at this military base. They won't find me here, but who will? Why couldn't I just turn around on top of that mountain and run down to the guest house? Why did I have to choose adventure over certainty?

When Reza comes back, I have had three cups of tea and my mouth is still bone dry. He tries to strike up conversation to reassure me, but I can't keep my mind straight. My thoughts are with my colleagues. What are they doing right now? Where are they? When will they decide to go back to Tehran and leave me behind? I try my best to be nice to the guy. He's my only hope here, my ally, the only one I can talk to, the only one who can convey what I want to say. He's also the only one who practices Iranian hospitality here. I try to explain to him how important it is for him to call my guesthouse. I feel that he understands and I believe him when he says there is absolutely nothing he can do before he disappears again. I'm alone once more and my thoughts are moving in all directions. The small TV continues to broadcast static and white noise.

It seems to take forever for him to reappear (oh, how time passes slowly). I can tell from his face that he has good news. No, calling is still impossible, but he asks me to follow him. I jump off the bed and follow my Iranian friend. He commands me to get into the car that brought me here. I thank Reza for his tea. As a matter of fact, I want to thank him for how he has received me here, how he made me feel human, but I just don't know how to put that into words so quickly.

Back at the gate, I'm told to sit on the bench again between the soldiers I can't talk to. There he is again: the guy who took a fancy to my running watch. He immediately sits down next to me and looks mesmerized at the leaping of the seconds. According to my watch, it's already past ten o'clock. But why isn't the gate opening, why aren't they driving me back to town?

Only when a black car approaches on the empty road does one of the soldiers walk to the exit and fiddle with the lock. The gate, which I thought would never open for me again, swings to the side. One of the men gestures for me to walk to the car and get in. I take the back seat: two men in dark clothes are seated in front.

Even though I'm wearing long-sleeved running clothes, I feel underdressed. When we get out of the gate, I have to make an effort to hold in a deep sigh of relief. Slowly, I feel the tension of being stuck on the army base flow out of my body. But a different stress is now becoming more urgent by the second. Will my colleagues still be there? 10:27, according to my watch. It can't be more than a ten-minute drive. We should have been a long way towards Tehran by now. Keep going, man!

But after a few minutes, the driver parks the car on the shoulder and turns off the engine. The men turn around. Now I can see them better. Their faces are serious, I see a frown between their black eyebrows and pitch-black hair. They explain in good English that they are from the Iranian secret service. 'Where are you from? Where is your passport? Why don't you have that with you? Your visa? You don't have a visa? What were you doing here at this base? What are you doing in Iran? What is your profession? How long are you here for? Are you traveling alone?' I can tell from their faces that they aren't satisfied with some of my answers.

When I explain what I do for work, they don't understand me. When I tell them that I don't have a visa, their eyebrows are raised. When I say I will only be in Iran for three days, they look at each other in bewilderment. When I add that my colleagues have probably already left, who knows, possibly taking my passport and luggage, they don't know what to do about it. In the meantime, the clock is ticking and I feel like screaming at them to take me back to the hotel.

With every minute that passes, it's less likely that my

colleagues will still be waiting. I feel an urge to drag the driver out of his seat, get behind the wheel and race full speed to the hotel. But I know I shouldn't get impatient. With supreme effort, I manage to stay calm and patiently answer all their questions without a word of dispute, all the while with a smile on my face that I'm sure looked forced. The only thing I'm thinking is: Hurry up!

Eventually, the driver starts the engine again. We drive along the road that I would have liked to run along, hours earlier. It turns out that my idea was correct. After we pass a barrier, the road comes out onto a larger road with traffic, where we turn right and soon enter the outskirts of Isfahan. My mouth is still dry when we turn into our hotel driveway. My heart skips a beat when I see our minivan. The doors are open and my colleagues are standing next to the vehicle. They were about to leave.

I get my luggage from the guesthouse and give my passport to the officers. They check everything and interrogate some of my colleagues. The manager of the hotel explains to them in Farsi why we don't have a visa, that we're only here for three days because we work for an airline and that everything is fine. It's past eleven when we start the long journey to Tehran and I hear the stories of the search.

They had split into groups. One group scoured the hill where Ernst and I had been running. That was a good thought. Some of the others drove across town to the local running track. They drove slowly so that they could search among the people on the street for their missing colleague. The manager made phone calls to hospitals and the police, until they no longer knew where to look and realized they had to get back to the capital to be on time for our flight. I try to explain how immensely grateful I am that I just met them before they left for Tehran.

Back at our hotel in the capital, I have a shower and change my clothes before I meet my colleagues for the flight. It's only when I'm home the next morning and tell everyone what happened that the goosebumps come, my knees feel feeble and tears fill my eyes. Only now do I have the time and distance to realize what I have experienced, how lucky I have been, especially considering how it could all have turned out very differently there, on that army base in Iran.

A few weeks later, the starting gun sounds on the Coolsingel in Rotterdam and the crowd of runners sets in motion towards the Erasmus Bridge. When I look around me, I know one thing for sure: none of the other runners has trained in the mountains near Isfahan. Beyond any doubt, I know that no one has had tea at an Iranian military base at the end of their training session.

I manage to keep my pace steady, not to lose much in the second half and to arrive at the time I have been dreaming of for years: 2:49.27 (I will further improve that time in the following years). Clocked by my trusty old sports watch that did not end up around the wrist of a young Iranian soldier.

Chapter 4
El Comandante Offended

Cuba – 2002

Two weeks after leaving Havana, we walk through the streets of Santiago de Cuba. So far, the country has disappointed us, mainly because the Cubans try to cash in on our presence at every possible moment and in every possible way. There is nothing wrong with people who try to make money from those visiting their country, especially in places where poverty reigns, but here it sometimes takes on absurd proportions.

One of the particularly low points was when a hooker in a bar reached into my trousers from the right, while my wife Daniela was standing to my left. Or the time we took a walk through the green landscape in the middle of the island, were invited into people's homes and were offered a coconut. When we wanted to leave after a fifteen-minute chat, the lady of the house demanded ten dollars for the coconuts. Cuban hospitality doesn't come free. And there were many more instances where the Cuban obsession with extracting foreign currency haunted us.

In Santiago, it strikes again. We pay an entrance fee at a restaurant so that we can attend the live music show while we eat. We even get a receipt for it. We look forward to attending an evening of Cuban music and are happy to pay for it. It's still early, so we have a drink first. When we ask for the menu, the waitress casually tells us that we have to pay extra if we want to eat, because there will be live music. I show her the receipt, but she talks her way out of it by saying that it's only valid for entry to the establishment. While the handwritten receipt clearly states that we paid to stay the whole evening. With music.

The next afternoon, we're walking through a suburb of the city when suddenly two boys on a bicycle attack Daniela from behind. They yank her globe necklace (received a few weeks earlier for her PhD) and take off.

I immediately give chase. I'm in training for a marathon and I want to see if they can escape me. Two guys on a bicycle surely can't go that fast. Especially not on this uphill road. My flip-flops clapper on the hot asphalt while I get closer and closer. The boy on the back of the bike anxiously watches me. He hadn't expected this. He clasps the golden chain in his hands and urges his buddy to cycle faster.

Just when I'm starting to wonder what I'm going to do when I overtake them (do I grab the boy sitting on the back or try to pull the guy up front off the handlebars; and more importantly, how do I get the necklace back?), the road flattens. Their bicycle starts picking up speed and with it, they fade from sight.

As I walk back to Daniela, defeated, I look towards the side of the road. Like everywhere in Cuba, people sit outside, they are talking, cleaning vegetables, or staring ahead, seemingly lost in thought. I ask around if anyone knows the boys, but they look the other way, as if nothing had happened and as if they haven't seen anything. A little later, we're at the police station, where the policemen do their utmost to ignore us.

When we finally get to talk to them, they still refuse to

help. Theft? No, they can't do anything about that. Theft doesn't exist in the communist state of Cuba. No, they don't want to go to the spot where Daniela was robbed. No, they don't want to question potential witnesses. No, they don't want to make a report. It's crystal clear that this robbery should be kept off the books so that Cuba can continue to live up to its image of a perfect state with only honest people.

The next day, we want to go to Castillo del Moro, a seventeenth-century defensive fortress about ten kilometers south of the city, at the entrance of the bay of Santiago. We hail a taxi, negotiate with the driver and agree at fifteen dollars. To and fro, including waiting time, obviously payable in hard US currency. The guy is quiet during our ride, we don't get to know him despite our attempts to start a conversation. At the fortress, we climb the walls that once guarded the entrance to the bay. At first, we think we have the fortress to ourselves, but after a while, we meet two Italians who have walked here all the way from the city. They ask if they can join us in our taxi. I ask the driver, who says it's not a problem. It turns out they are staying around the corner from our accommodation in Santiago and after they get out, we ask to be dropped off at a nearby square.

One of the habits I learned in dealing with taxi drivers (as long as you don't have luggage in the trunk), is get out first, then pay. I put my arm through the window and give the agreed amount to the driver. A few seconds later, while we're already walking away, we hear a roar coming from the car: the man gestures for us to come back. I ask him what the problem is.

In response, he lifts a small carpet that hangs down from

the dashboard. Under it, we see a meter, tucked away. It reads twenty-five dollars. I tell him that we agreed on fifteen, but the man claims that bringing the Italians along nullified our agreement. Except that we didn't drive for any longer than planned, it took the Italians barely ten seconds to get out and he gave his permission in advance and didn't say a word about a meter secretly running under his carpet. Or even worse, perhaps the meter isn't working at all and is actually stuck at $25? I try to say as kindly as I can that we have already paid the agreed amount, that we will leave it at that, turn around and pull Daniela with me. We walk into the square, palm trees above our heads, white benches and bushes all around and people lying in the grass enjoying the sun.

We're less than fifty meters away, when I suddenly feel a heavy hand on my shoulder. When I turn around, I stare into the face of a policeman. Next to him, his colleague and our driver. A few Cubans are watching from a distance, clearly feeling as if something is going to happen.

'You still have to pay this taxi driver.'

'I think you are mistaken. I have already paid the agreed amount.'

'You should have paid twenty-five dollars and you only gave fifteen, so ten dollars are still owed.'

'We agreed that the ride would cost fifteen dollars including the wait, and I paid exactly that. The driver is mistaken.'

Tempers are starting to rise. It's clear that the driver doesn't want to let his booty go. A small crowd begins to form around us. Momentarily, all the annoyances of the last few weeks are coming back. The devious ways Cubans constantly try to extort money from us. The aversion when Daniela was robbed, the unwillingness from the police to do anything about the theft or even to write a report about it. And now this taxi driver is 'forgetting' that an agreement has been made and the police are eagerly cooperating with him while they are unwilling to catch thieves. All the pent-up frustration is coming to the surface. And eventually, it explodes.

'Cuba is a country with eleven million thieves,' I yell at the police officers, the taxi man and the group of people around us.

Suddenly the racket stops. The officers look at me in shock. One of them reaches for the handcuffs hanging from the belt around his waist.

'Are you coming along voluntarily, or do I have to put on the handcuffs?'

'Why would you handcuff me? Where would we go?'

I'm still fuming, I think the situation is ridiculous and I want to move on, away from these agents, away from the driver. But we're trapped among dozens of people who are all staring at me.

'You just insulted El Comandante and that is a punishable offense. You will go to jail. You must come to our office. Will you join us, or should I use handcuffs?'

Finally, the penny drops. On impulse, I had just insulted all Cubans. El Jefe Máximo, Fidel Castro is obviously one of them, as a real man of the people. Oops. Sometimes it isn't convenient to speak the language of the country you're traveling through. I think it would be better to keep quiet now and just follow the officers. It's no longer a stupid argument about money. Now, it's about insulting a head of state in a country where you could go to jail for less serious offenses.

The police station turns out to be nearby. The officers immediately confiscate my passport and escort us to a dimly lit room. Daniela is nervous, says we should call the embassy, but then we realize it's Sunday. Despair radiates from her face and she begins to cry softly. Yesterday, she lost her necklace and now I'm on my way to a prison in Cuba. Between tears, she promises to bring me an orange every so often once I'm behind bars. That's a comforting thought.

After a while, we don't know what to say to each other anymore and we just hold each other tight. We wonder what's going to happen. I use the time to calm down and think carefully about the situation I'm in. I realize this is a delicate matter and wonder if the embassy would be able to help me, if they were open. In the Netherlands, you can be locked up for lesemajesty, but in Castro's Cuba, it's an even bigger offense. If one thing has become clear in these last weeks, it's that Fidel Castro is high on a pedestal, untouchable, uncontroversial (at least formally), adored, and the Father of the Country.

The more I think about it, the gloomier it seems. A simple argument with a greedy taxi driver threatens to escalate into a lawsuit for insulting the head of state and that can't be a good thing in Cuba. I wonder how I can still talk myself out of this if I'm even given the chance to do so. And what I'm going to do if I can't. Oh, that bastard with his sneaky meter!

When the officers come back after a while, they look stern. The driver is no longer with them and I don't see my passport either. They repeat their charges and, to my surprise, give me a chance to speak. I eagerly seize the opportunity.

'Obviously, my intention was never to insult anyone, especially not El Comandante. I made that statement out of pure frustration with the experiences we unfortunately had during our journey through your exceptional country. Yesterday, my girlfriend was the victim of a robbery involving violence. The taxi driver was also not straightforward and tried to rip us off. The incident with the cab driver was the straw that broke the camel's back. I hope you can understand our frustrations over the past few weeks and the taxi driver's dishonesty. I am sincerely sorry for insulting all Cubans. That was never my intention.'

Sometimes it is useful if you speak the language of the country you're traveling through. The officers look at each other. One of them nods and the other takes my passport out of his pocket. They show sympathy now, confirm that the driver acted unlawfully and that we're free to go. We thank the men very much. When the door closes behind us, we fall into each other's arms and we have to fight our tears. I'm glad that I'm not dependent on Daniela's oranges anymore and we celebrate that evening with a delicious dinner. Without music.

While we initially considered returning home immediately to flee from all the negative impressions, we decide that we don't want to end this journey on a bad note. That evening, we take the bus back to Havana and travel from there to María la Gorda, on the west side of the island. There, we let everything sink in and we're finally able to relax. The sharp edges of the unpleasant experiences we have had here are wearing off and we're starting to see the beautiful sides of the unusual island and its inhabitants. That Cuba is unique is beyond dispute. If only because of El Comandante.

Chapter 5
Hotel California

China – 2007

After leaving Xining, I was heading south and traveled through the desolate landscapes of Qinghai for eight days in a car with a driver. A region for which you didn't need a special permit and which was usually forgotten by travelers, travel guides and Chinese tourists. It housed snowy mountains and endless lakes with thick crusts of ice in which the impending, short summer already had struck deep cracks. There were abandoned monasteries and pilgrims making their way toward Lhasa while praying, on a journey that would take years to complete. Wild and colossal Tibetan mastiffs which I could only keep at bay by throwing stones. Every time I went for a walk, I had a few in my hand.

In a valley covered with a delicate layer of fresh snow, we came across a small monastery decorated with colorful flags, where a sky burial had taken place the day before. Dogs were munching on the remaining bones and small birds were pecking on bits of human flesh. Vultures had already eaten most of the corpse. After death, a lama reads from the Tibetan Book of the Dead for a few days. This facilitates the departure of the soul from the body of the deceased. Then, the remains are cut into pieces by *ragyabas* and fed to the birds. There I was, in the desolate Tibetan landscape, reflecting on death and transitoriness. Where I'm from, where corpses disappear into caskets or ovens, this is inconceivable. But what is our body once life has abandoned it?

I had been surprised by the motorbikes, washing machines, and other devices that stood around the nomad tents. Each tent had one or more solar panels to keep the machinery running. The occupants invited me into their fabric homes. There was always a TV inside. On a wooden cupboard, there was invariably an altar decorated with yak butter candles. Hidden behind some paraphernalia, a portrait of the Dalai Lama. These are prohibited in China, but without a police officer for miles around, no one would ever notice.

Furthermore, I had lost weight because I could barely eat the food and concluded that the Tibetan food was the most repulsive I had ever tasted. Yak meat that had hung in the air for months to dry so that it was rock hard, was better than everything else, but only slightly so. The yak butter tea tasted exactly like the scent of the yak butter candles I smelled in temples everywhere, so I constantly had the idea I was drinking candles. Vegetables were virtually impossible to find, if only because nomads don't cultivate them. I forced myself to eat, if only to prevent altitude sickness.

After this immersion in Tibetan life, I set out from Xining on a destination that has captured my imagination since I read Tintin as a child. Tibet. The 'real' Tibet, the huge country annexed by China in 1950. I have a permit for my one-man tour group, I don't need a guide and can travel freely throughout the region.

A year earlier, one of those impressive Chinese infrastructure projects had been completed: the railway to

Lhasa. It's unmistakably designed to connect the city and the region to the rest of China as it facilitates the mass migration of Han Chinese. It's also the highest railway in the world and was built across the rugged Tibetan landscapes in record time. Due to the altitude, the train has oxygen bottles in every compartment. Tanggula, at 5068 meters the highest station in the world, is higher than Mont Blanc. Besides the spectacular landscapes, what somehow sticks with me the most about the train journey are the golden deer on the dining car tables. I arrive at a grand, futuristic station in Lhasa in the evening. The next day, I'm longing for a surprise when I open the curtains of a modest room in a hostel: my first glimpse of the capital of Tibet.

Even though the sun has just risen, I can see it immediately. I'm late. Way too late. The city has already been converted into the umpteenth Chinese conglomerate with many uniform high-rise buildings and gray block boxes that you can also find in Shanghai, Xi'an, Xiamen or any other Chinese city.

On my first walk through the city, I discover that there is still a pocket of Tibet to be found. A memory of the original inhabitants and their culture, which is preserved as if it were an open-air museum. The Potala Palace, featured prominently on one hundred yuan bills, towers over the city just as it has for centuries. The Jokhang Temple still stands, as a huge magnet for all pilgrims who often walk for years to get here from distant regions. That is all the more improbable when you see how they move. They stretch their hands over their heads, bend their knees, throw themselves forward and end up lying on the ground, after which they get up and take a step forward, their hands again extend over their head, thus starting the next cycle. They wear thick gloves and knee pads because on their pilgrimage they go straight through endless landscapes with stones and bushes, through mountains and streams. I think back to the pilgrims I saw in Qinghai who won't arrive here for another year or two. The devoted travelers conclude their pilgrimage with one hundred and eight laps around the Jokhang – the sacred number for Buddhists.

So yes, there is still a bit of Tibet left in Lhasa. But only under the watchful eye of the Chinese rulers. Soldiers stand in a large circle around the shrine, keeping their weapons in their hands to supervise this never-ending stream of pilgrims. The Chinese rebuilt this part of the city when it owned Lhasa for twenty years, to keep everything under control. They did that for the Potala Palace too. A huge square has been laid out here, cutting the umbilical cord between the Potala Palace and the Jokhang Temple for good.

Because it's so sparsely populated, Tibet is difficult to explore by public transport. To visit Draksum-Tso, a mountain lake east of the capital, I decide to book a two-day tour with a Chinese-run travel agency. According to the advertisements, the purpose of the trip is to visit the lake. I don't like tours at all and much less so when a group is involved, but sometimes you can't escape it. It will prove to be one of the biggest mistakes of my life as a traveler.

When I open the door of the van the next morning, it turns out to be full of Chinese tourists. The driver and guide, too, are Chinese. It confirms the impression I already had in Lhasa: the Chinese own all businesses and push the Tibetans into the margins. I immediately get a bad feeling. A little later, we pick up another foreigner and since we already have a bond – if only because we are not from Asia and do not speak Chinese – we inevitably talk to each other. He turns out to be Dutch.

Meanwhile, the driver steers our minivan through the Tibetan landscape at high speed. At what seem completely random moments, the Chinese tourists stick their hands through the window to shoot a photo of the landscape rushing by, with their Japanese compact cameras. Those will surely be beautiful pictures, to prove to their friends at home that they have been to Tibet, even though most of them will be blurry.

After a few hours, we stop at a building with dark gray walls and a large yellow sign with red Chinese characters. The guide doesn't explain anything, I have no idea what this is, but the Chinese happily run inside. I follow suit and see herbs and leaves in baskets, posters with images of the human body, jars and boxes, everything with explanatory texts in Chinese. In the next room is a counter with a cash register. Now I finally understand: you can buy traditional, natural medicines here. I'm already outside when the Chinese are still filling their bags with purchased medicines and the cashier looks satisfied when they finally leave. We continue our race again, stopping at another shop, and I get more and more impatient. The lady at the travel agency hadn't told me this. Perhaps it was naive to think that a trip to the Draksum-Tso lake would go directly to the Draksum-Tso lake.

When we finally arrive at the lake and the driver parks our van in an area full of other minivans, our guide says we have forty minutes. His words sink into my stomach like a stone. A two-day expedition, with less than three-quarters of an hour at the destination advertised as the purpose of the trip? My rebelliousness against this whole tour is now starting to boil over and I decide to stay here for at least an hour. They won't leave without me anyway.

At the lake, I see the islet of Tashi, which can be reached by a floating bridge. I cross over and take my time to enjoy the giant mountains with their tops of snow, reflected in the lake's completely still water. It's so calm that it seems as if there is no water in the lake at all. The only evidence that it's actually there, is that the mountains are upside down.

I look around the small Tibetan Buddhist Tsozong temple on Tashi, with its brightly colored paintings on the wood, where red is the dominant color. Perilous-looking gods in dark blue, a horse in a lake, a female half-human, half-animal with an offering of fruit in a bowl rising from the waves. A huge prayer wheel with mantras carved in metal. If you set this heavy wheel in motion, the mantras will be sent into the universe. Six centuries old.

Then a group of Chinese tourists enters the silence of this shrine, laughing and stamping their feet. One of them is smoking a cigarette. They take photos, give the old wheel a huge swing so it obediently starts to move, sending an endless array of mantras into the universe, and ring the bell several times. A monk comes and tries to silence them – in vain. Moments like these make me wonder what the future of Tibet will be like. The train spews out hundreds of Han Chinese a day at Lhasa station and the province is set up as a vast open-air museum, viewing Tibetan culture as a funny, exotic curiosity rather than an ancient culture to be treated with respect.

Once back on the mainland, the forty minutes have long since passed. I walk along the shores of the lake, run into a small herd of yaks and watch Tashi from a distance. I fully enjoy the whole panorama of this tiny island in the grand landscape before returning to the van.

The others are of course already there because I should have been back half an hour earlier. I cheerfully greet them and take the only seat that is still left. The guide looks angry, slams the door and the driver hits the accelerator full throttle. We dash through the Tibetan countryside again at breakneck speed. Off to a new shop. I feel miserable and wonder how I will survive the next day. It will undoubtedly have more stops at more shops.

Then, I decide that I must take matters into my own hands and abandon the group. That evening, I read in my travel guide that a bus leaves for Lhasa from the village where we're staying and I decide to let my group go and return by bus. When I present my plan to the Dutchman with whom I share the room, he looks at me in shock due to the level of disobedience. But after a few minutes of reflection, he asks if he can come with me.

The next morning, our guide knocks on the door a few minutes after we were supposed to be in the minivan. I don't open, tell him through the door that they can leave and that we won't be coming with them. The Chinese man starts to scream and bangs on the door. I make sure it's properly locked. The guide calls the agency in Lhasa, probably to ask what he should do with us now. After he hangs up, he barks that I still have to pay for half of the tour (I paid half in advance), but I advise him that I won't do so, as I only did half the trip. The door endures some more abuse and then the fading echoes of footsteps in the hallway tell me he is leaving after all. His Chinese customers must be wondering what's going on and where those foreign guests ended up.

Freed from the scourge of the Chinese tour and enjoying the regained freedom, we hurry to the bus station and are soon on a bus full of Tibetans and a few Chinese people on our way back to Lhasa. On the way, the bus stops for a bathroom break. While I do what you're expected to do on such an occasion, a

Tibetan indiscreetly looks directly at my vital parts. Excitedly, he climbs back into the bus and as I walk the aisle behind him to find my seat, I hear him say something to the other passengers in a loud voice as he points to my crotch. All passengers laugh. I just laugh along with them. I will never know what he said.

Using Lhasa as a base, I visit several monasteries. Some by bicycle, the others by local bus. One monastery has an even more beautiful location than the previous one. In one of them, I witness a debating session with young monks. In another one, I see a hall full of young monks wearing yellow hats. Despite a few decades of Chinese rule, it seems as if everything here follows traditions just like it has for centuries. Nevertheless, the number of monks has been greatly reduced. Within the walls of Drepung, once the largest monastery in the world, ten thousand monks lived during its heyday – there are only several hundred left now. One year later, protests would take place in the run-up to the Beijing Olympics, killing dozens. In the aftermath, the Chinese shut down Drepung for five years. Just as they do with Ganden and Sera, the other large monasteries in the vicinity of Lhasa. Tibetan exiles have rebuilt these monasteries in Karnataka, in southwestern India, where they can operate without interference from the Chinese security forces.

From Lhasa, I want to go to Kathmandu and after the disaster of the Draksum-Tso tour, I'm determined to organize this myself. It turns out to be easy to find a few travel companions. I head west with a Dutch couple and an Australian woman. Fortunately, our driver Tsering is Tibetan, which feels better than driving around with a Han-Chinese.

We're traveling along a road built by the Chinese after their annexation in the 1950s, which they have christened the Friendship Highway. It offers an irresistible mix of ancient shrines and much older landscapes. The more we leave Lhasa behind us, the less the monasteries appear to suffer from the harsh hand of the Chinese. Nature is still as stark and magnificent as it must have been long before the Chinese invasion. Yamdrok-Tso, a lake shaped like a scorpion, lies among the bare brown mountains like a blue jewel casually thrown down by a giant. We walk around the fort of Gyantse and the monasteries of Pelkor Chöde, Tashilhunpo and Sakya. We see how the monks here are trying to cling to ancient traditions under difficult circumstances in their slowly crumbling empire of Tibetan Buddhism.

We have already made some headway west when we wake up one morning under an immaculate blue sky. I immediately feel the tension of the child in me on the day of my birthday and I already know what present I'm going to receive. We're on our way to Everest Base Camp, which I have been looking forward to for weeks. No: years. I have devoured many books about it and today I'm going to see it for the first time. Now, we only have to drive there.

We get a flat tire just before a checkpoint and we see that Tsering has dealt with this kind of situation before. Before we know it, we're on the road again, driving up bend after bend on a dirt road to Pang La, a mountain pass of 5120 meters (although some say it's even higher). Even though I have been at 3600 meters or higher for a while now, when I walk up a hill for an even better view, I feel that the air here is thin.

But I only really lose my breath when I reach the viewpoint and look south. Goosebumps run over my arms when I see the morning sunshine on the row of our planet's greatest giants, all dressed in immaculate white. The Makalu, Lhotse, Cho Oyu and, of course, Qomolangma, also known as Mount Everest. Four of the six highest mountains in the world, neatly in a row, all well over eight thousand meters, with several smaller peaks in between. From the pale brown mountain where we stand and where I see dozens of hairpin bends below us, these monsters seem to float like icebergs in the tranquil air. I don't hear any sound, as if we're already halfway towards outer space here. My eyes keep going from left to right and back again, over this high part of the Himalayas, this high slice of the world. The mountains seem to smile at me. A peaceful scene. Nonetheless, I'm looking at one of the most extreme and hostile places on Earth.

We drive down the stony road over numerous hairpin bends, lose sight of the giants and pass little villages with small groups of Tibetans in a wide, gray valley. Besides, we see no people and certainly no traffic. I'm trying to calculate what time we will arrive at Everest Base Camp and how much time I will have left to hike. I'm determined to go as far as I can.

Then, Tsering hits the brakes and I immediately notice in his face that something is very wrong. Our front tire is punctured – and we no longer have a spare. We look at Tsering, expecting him to fix this. But he walks to a hillock, sits with his back to the road and lights a cigarette. Our phones don't work here: only Tsering has one with the right sim card. But when we ask him to use his phone, he says he has run out of credit. He turns his back and continues to smoke. Now, this is the disadvantage of having a Buddhist driver: he resigns himself to fate and does nothing at all to solve the problem.

We diligently discuss the alternatives. We can't stay where we are. Although we're now lower than Pang La, the temperature here drops to well below freezing at night and we don't have the proper clothing or blankets for that. Waiting for someone to come by, after not having seen another vehicle for hours, doesn't make much sense either. After all, this is a dead-end road to Base Camp. So, we decide that the women will stay near the car and that the men will walk back to the last village. I estimate that it should be about five kilometers, less than an hour on foot. We should be able to be back before dark, hopefully with help.

Just as we get going, a truck miraculously appears from the direction of Base Camp. It stops. The Chinese driver gets out and when we point to the back of his lorry, then to ourselves and in the direction of the next village, a grin appears on his face. He takes a stick from his booth, writes $ 100 in the gravel and laughs, exposing a row of crumbling gray-black teeth. We turn around and start walking again. He taps our shoulders, smiles to apologize for his exorbitant suggestion for a two-mile drive, gestures towards the loading platform and we jump on the truck. Upon arrival in the village, we give him some yuan and soon come across two vans. It turns out we are extremely lucky today.

Japanese. That's a bull's eye: they immediately understand that they have to help us and for the umpteenth time I'm not disappointed in Japanese helpfulness. Within ten minutes, we're back at the car. Tsering is smoking yet another cigarette, still with his back towards the road. The ladies are jumping and waving their arms to keep warm. It's cooling down fast now.

The front wheel is quickly changed, our driver is told where to leave their wheel and while the Japanese drive towards Base Camp, we head north again, across Pang La, to Tingri. We get there just before it's completely dark. Fate has still been good to us and Tsering was proven right for waiting for things to sort out by themselves.

While our punctures are being repaired, Tsering charges his phone and as soon as possible, he calls the agent in Lhasa where I arranged the car. He talks excitedly into the phone, then hands it to me. The agent says that tomorrow we will have to drive directly to the border with Nepal. I make it clear that Base Camp was part of our six-day ride, that our driver took unnecessary risks by proceeding without a spare tire and that we're not willing to skip Base Camp. A heated discussion ensues. Tsering is on the phone, then it's my turn and then we talk to Tsering again as a group. The organizer insists that we continue to Nepal, but he is hundreds of miles from here in Lhasa and all he can do is shout into the phone. At the end of the song, Tsering quits his job on the spot and promises to take us to Base Camp.

So, the next morning, we drive up the sixty hairpin bends again, we get another stunning view of the highest mountains of our planet and we drive through the Dzakar valley, until we pass the point where we had to turn around yesterday. Everest comes back into view on the last straight stretch. We're now driving towards it, slowly zooming in on the pyramid-shaped giant.

There are two Base Camps: one for tourists and one for climbers. Base Camp for tourists consists of a row of tents made of yak hair. We leave our belongings in Hotel California, one of the accommodations that the Tibetan owner has named after the Eagles evergreen. The others flop down on their beds, tired after all the driving for the past few days. But I can't wait to hike to the real Base Camp, which is three miles closer to the mountain monster, and I'm out of the tent in ten minutes.

A few miles further south, I have an overview of the base camp for climbers. It's the right season: different colored tents with various groups of climbers are set up in clusters at the foot of the highest mountain on earth. I see a permanent building in the middle and assume it's the Chinese checkpoint. I have read that there is a steep fine for walking past Base Camp without a permit and I'm looking for a way to do just that without paying the fine. Giving it a wide berth seems the most obvious solution.

There are quite a few climbers around in the exclusive community, so I don't stand out. After speeding through the camp, I see two climbers coming down a path, assuming that it's the official trail to Camp 1 – and eventually, to the top of Everest. After a steep climb, I continue, heading south towards the wall, towards the highest peak in the world. Everest has me in a tight grip and pulls me up like a magnet. The office is already far behind me and excitement spurts through my body as I walk on, all alone, across the gray plain. Even though I'm above 5200 meters, I still have to crane my neck to look up at Everest, which it seems I can almost touch, but which nevertheless is still so far away. It's maybe five kilometers across, as the crow flies. I want to get as high as I can, but at the same time, I still have to go back to Hotel California tonight.

After a while, when I stop to take a picture, I hear a sound followed by a splash. Diagonally behind me, I see a small pond with rippling water in which a gray mass comes to the surface. Wait a second. I'm walking here on the trail that eventually leads to the top of Everest. Right? I peer around me and take a closer look underneath the rubble. It turns out I'm walking on ice.

Then the truth shoots through my head like a bolt of lightning. I'm walking in the middle of Rongbuk Glacier, which comes down from the north side of Everest. I hear more ominous sounds and I realize I have to get out of here as soon as I can, but also that I have to do it as carefully as possible. It's high time to focus on where I'm walking, instead of looking at the top of that giant a few thousand meters above me all the time.

Step by step, I try to walk perpendicular to the ice mass to the east side. I want to have solid ground under my feet. I slither over ice and walk past semi-frozen lakes with light blue ice in them, holding on to rocks here and there that I hope are stuck. There is no direct route, I'm walking where perhaps no one has ever been on regular hiking shoes and my knees seem to get more and more elastic. Finally, I jump from the last bit of ice onto the dark gray stones on the side of the moraine. I almost fall to the rocky ground to kiss it, but now I start to shake. For a moment, I give in to my emotions, but then I admonish myself: I have to go on, I want to continue. Up, up, higher up!

I try to climb a steep slope with loose stones, but that is harder than it looks. I slide down, come higher, slide again: it's a battle between gravity, rolling stones and willpower. I'm jubilant when I see a climber above me and when I'm with him I'm on the actual trail. Finally. It looks very easy now, compared to all the trouble I took to get here. The climber tells me we're at around a 5800-meter altitude. I calculate that I can no longer go up and hurry down, towards Base Camp and Hotel California. Half running, half jumping, half stumbling. I'm in a hurry, the sun has long since disappeared behind the enormous peaks, the light is slowly fading in the valley. I fall hard, my camera gets a big dent but still seems to work, and I keep walking. I can't help but glance over my shoulder at Mount Everest every so often, as if it were a woman I secretly lust after but don't dare to look in the eye because she's so beautiful.

I'm now too tired to worry about the Chinese checkpoint. The terrain is a lot more forgiving from Base Camp onwards. I walk as fast as I can on the gravel road, take a shortcut and see just enough to distinguish Hotel California from the other 'hotels' when I arrive at the tourist base camp. That night, I sleep under a thick pile of blankets in the unheated tent.

The next morning, I'm outside when it's still dark. It's fourteen degrees below zero and the water bottles next to my bed are solid ice. I sit on a rock in the semi-frozen river and watch as the sun casts its first rays on the pyramid of Everest, how the gray-pink mountain turns orange through all kinds of subtle shades and then slowly gets whiter. It seems so peaceful from here, this white mountain in the blue sky. A feathery cloud blows over the summit: Everest pierces the bottom of the jet stream that rages at that height. I try to imagine how climbers are busy up there, how they try to sleep in their flapping tents at that altitude, how they look out over the world, how they might attempt the summit today, how they all pray to their guardian angels to make it to the top and return safely from that extreme place that can be so cruel to its rare visitors.

We drive through rugged valleys via a shortcut back to the Friendship Highway, drive again on a high mountain pass in the green-blue-red-yellow-white prayer flags, descend through a spectacular gorge where storms have thrown chunks of mountain on the road. Tsering leaves us at the border. For the first time in over a month, I am below a three-thousand-meter altitude. The next morning, we cross the Friendship Bridge. We reset our watches by two hours and fifteen minutes (China has one enormous time zone, even though it's thousands of kilometers wide, and Nepal once decided to be five and three-quarter hours ahead of UTC). Then, we drive in humid temperatures to the pandemonium of Kathmandu.

Chapter 6
Muslim Vodka

Turkmenistan/Uzbekistan – 2010

After crossing the Caspian Sea by cargo boat from Baku to Turkmenbashi, my new travel companion Anneke and I had crossed Turkmenistan with the government-mandated guide. Beforehand, I was afraid that it would be a repeat of the deadly serious regulations in North Korea many years earlier. There, two guides controlled each other while providing a constant stream of propaganda. We were picked up in the morning from our room and taken back there in the evening. Even a short walk without their supervision was strictly forbidden.

However, those fears turned out to be completely unwarranted. Our guide Jenet happened to be a free-thinking woman who incessantly talked about her private life (peppered with rash details), who steered well clear from state propaganda and who didn't bother about conservative regulations. Instead of wearing one of the colorful traditional dresses which almost all Turkmen women wore, she donned half-length hot pants and a tight t-shirt. In Nokhur, a village in the southern Kopet-Dag Mountains that the country shares with Iran, she briskly approached a group of men to ask where we could buy beer, which elicited quite some frowns in this conservative Muslim village. We had a lot of fun with her during our ten days in the Turkmen dictatorship, which was in some ways more surreal than North Korea's.

Leader Niyazov, who died in 2006, placed his book *Ruhnama* (the Book of the Soul) on a pedestal higher than the Quran. It was compulsory to study and to have a working knowledge of this two-piece classic. For example, when taking your driving test, you could expect questions about its content to show that you were an honorable Turkmen. The same was true for university students doing an exam. Niyazov had made his subjects believe that whoever read the scripture three times was guaranteed to go to heaven. To underline the importance of the book, he immortalized it in a unique monument on Independence Square in the capital Ashgabat. A gigantic version of the *Ruhnama*, which opened every night at eight o'clock, while a spoken excerpt played for the bystanders. One year before his death, he blasted the first part of the book into space, so it orbits our planet to this very day. Take that, Kim!

Niyazov also filled the country with golden statues of himself. The most peculiar one we could see from our room in Ashgabat. It stood high on a huge tripod, turning every day with open arms towards the sun and was flooded in bright purple, green and gold light during the night. Moreover, he renamed the months of the year. January became Turkmenbashi, his self-chosen name, meaning Leader of the Turkmen (indeed, also the name of the port city on the Caspian Sea where we had arrived); April: Gurbansoltan, after his mother, and September: *Ruhnama*, after his book. A few years after his death and not long after our visit, his successor Berdimuhamedov decided to go back to the old system and the statues were removed. Although she didn't say so, we both felt that Jenet didn't like the extreme veneration of the leader who died, in part, due to exorbitant alcohol consumption. She regularly seemed embarrassed by the dead dictator's extravagant excesses.

What became clear during our trip through Turkmenistan was that Islam was experienced differently than in most Muslim countries. The will of the dictator was considerably more important than the much older set of religious rules. This became especially evident at the Turkmenbashy Ruhy mosque, where the minarets carried slogans from the *Ruhnama* and an inscription above the entrance stated that the *Ruhnama* was a holy book. This was the largest mosque in Central Asia, constructed of white marble with a remarkable amount of gold, thus following the style of the capital. Naturally, Niyazov himself was buried there, along with his family.

After a visit to the destroyed Silk Road city of Merv, we spent an unforgettable night at the bizarre Darvaza gas crater. It had been burning for more than forty years in the middle of the Karakum desert after an accident lit it up. The next day, we crossed the border into Uzbekistan. We traveled through the holy cities of Khiva and Bukhara. Uzbekistan has done much to restore its historic cities to their former glory and their efforts have produced beautiful madrasas and mosques with ornate domes, walls and minarets.

The last in this list of celebrated centers is Samarkand: the legendary city I had been dreaming of visiting for many years. After his visit to the city, Alexander the Great supposedly said: 'All I have heard about the beauty of Samarkand is true, except that it is much more beautiful than I had expected'. I was badly disappointed when we drove into town and saw only bleak 1950s Soviet blocks, instead of the magnificent buildings I had imagined. We decided to stay in a pleasant hotel with a private garden, near the medieval monuments of Samarkand, which we'd planned to explore the next day.

It's still dark when we leave the hotel. We want to see as much as possible in the relative coolness of the early morning. It ends up being a long day, during which we immerse ourselves in the restored splendor in and around Samarkand. At the end of the day, I have to admit that it surpasses the fantasies I had for such a long time. Alexander was right. Richly decorated madrasas in which blue and green predominate, marble tombs, gold-plated mosques, dazzling mosaics whose beauty takes your breath away. Samarkand is one of the oldest inhabited cities of Central Asia and experienced its heyday as one of the main sites of the Silk Road. Moreover, it's one of the most important centers for Islam studies. Samarkand was also the capital of the Timur-Lenk Empire and was conquered by both Alexander the Great as well as Genghis Khan.

We watch the sunset over the Registan's curious tiger-adorned Sher Dor madrasa, whose colors seem to get warmer by the minute, until they slowly fade away, leaving only the black silhouettes of the elegant buildings standing out against a dark blue sky.

The heat made us drink all day long, but we had nothing to eat. Except for one ice cream. It's time to look for a copious dinner. Walking back to the city, we pass large grounds. We see a crowd of people and fragments of exciting oriental music swirl towards us through the twilight, carried by the evening heat. We automatically walk towards the fence surrounding the area and see festively dressed people sitting behind tables. There is a stage, there are dancers, there is joy: something is being celebrated here.

Then, an older man emerges from the other side of the fence and invites us in. Even though our stomachs rattle, we can't resist. We want to see what is going on here. The man leads us across the grounds to the tables. On the way, he explains in poor English that a double wedding party is in progress. He points to an elongated table, covered with white cloth and decorated with yellow roses. Behind it, we see two young, shy couples flanked by their families.

Several dozens of round tables have been set up. Women and men sit separately. We're seated at a white plastic-covered table with middle-aged men. They seem to find it extremely interesting to have exotic guests and do everything to make us feel welcome. This mainly means that the small glasses in front of us are filled with vodka and that we're expected to make a toast and knock the glass back in one go.

There are bottles of Coke and Fanta on the table, but we're clearly not supposed to dilute our spirits. We cast a hopeful glance at the dishes on the table and see that they are virtually empty. The guests just finished dinner. We're too late. There is still a bowl with some fruit in it. I quickly grab a piece of watermelon, but that doesn't help much. My stomach continues to growl.

A man in a black and white suit comes to our table. It turns out to be the father of one of the brides. He insists on proposing a toast to the foreign guests and before we know it, our glasses are full again, we raise our shots, and knock them back all at once.

I'm starting to worry. We haven't eaten, rarely drink alcohol and now we are drinking at a brisk pace and on an empty stomach, swigging vodka like there's no tomorrow. Anneke doesn't share my concerns and loves the party. She visibly awakens as a result of the uplifting music.

In the meantime, the two dancers whirl between the tables on the grounds. When they get closer, I can see how beautifully dressed they are. Green robes that almost reach the ground, adorned with glittering floral motifs. One of them has a white feather on her head, the other a green one. Both have braids that almost reach their knees. With graceful movements, they turn in circles around the tables, where the guests sit and watch and clap to the beat of the music. The women receive thousand-Som notes from all sides. They are making a lot of money.

When they arrive at our table, Anneke can no longer hold back. She gets up and begins to follow the dancers. In her long, white dress she blends in well with the other two and she sways along as if she were the third dancer. The only thing missing is a feather on her head. She is completely absorbed in the irresistible music. The vodka makes her hips move even more smoothly and without inhibition. The men at our table admire her enthusiasm and soon one of them gets up to put money in the top of her dress. That sets a good example for the other tables. Anneke sways on and receives more and more money, until she needs to catch her breath and returns to our table. She flops down in her chair with a beaming smile.

Now our table is the center of all attention. The father of the other bride sees his chance and also wants to propose a toast: our glasses are quickly filled and again we gulp the vodka down in one go. No way we can cheat by secretly adding Coke or emptying the contents of the glass onto the ground. The men at the table closely observe every move we make. Nor can we refuse to toast to the father of one of the brides, who sees it as a great opportunity that he can add luster to his daughter's marriage with these strangers.

Then comes the moment I had already dreaded: the men at our table pull me out of my chair and push me towards the dancer with the green feather on her head. I feel dizzy when I stand, grab a chicken leg that I suddenly spot in a bowl on the next table and move cautiously towards the dancer. The main thing now is not to fall. At the same time, I need to pretend that I can dance while trying to bite off pieces of the cold chicken leg as inconspicuously as possible, in an attempt to neutralize the effect of the alcohol.

I move around the dancer, spin around in circles and let her spin around while I devour another piece of chicken. When I can no longer chew any more meat off it, I casually drop the chicken bone. Thousand Som notes from the guests now flow my way: they put them under the Turkmen *takyah* that I have been walking around with for more than a week. In turn, I give a few of them to my dance partner in a gesture of solidarity.

I'm happy to feel a sense of safety when I sit down at our table again. It's time for a new toast right away. So, we down a few more glasses of vodka, because yes, the fathers of the grooms would of course also like to toast to their newly married sons. In the meantime, I have to do my best to stay upright in a chair without armrests. The uplifting music seems to be getting louder and more shrill, the tables and people around me seem to vibrate and turn and when I look at Anneke, it looks like she isn't doing much better.

Just as I wonder how we can escape the overload of vodka without offending anyone, one of the Uzbeks comes towards me and lifts me from my chair. I give him an exaggerated hug, a kiss on the cheek and I shout that from today onwards we shall remain friends for life. By holding onto him tightly, I just about manage to stay upright. Another man helps Anneke out of her chair and she also relies heavily on her buddy. If my new friend lets go of me now, I will fall over. I'm afraid they will make us dance together. One thing is for sure. We would collapse straight away if we had to move autonomously.

However, our wedding friends take us to the exit and hail a taxi. When my friend lets go of me, I only just manage to grab the side of the car. As soon as I see the illuminated TAXI sign on the roof, a deep-rooted suspicion arises and alarm bells ring. Wait a minute: taxi. Does the driver know where we're going? What will the short trip cost? Who says we can trust him? But our friends are gesturing that it's okay, he knows where to go. We have already paid. Did we tell them where we were staying? Apparently so. The only brain cell in my head that was still working, is now also capitulating.

When we arrive at our hotel, we support each other through the courtyard. With our last ounce of consciousness, we manage to find our room and when we close the door behind us, we surrender to a night of deep sleep.

As soon as I wake up, I know something is off. My left leg is on the floor, I'm half lying on the bed. Alone. When I get up, I feel a blazing pain in my head. I see that Anneke is lying with her head on my leg, the rest of her body on the floor. After I wriggle out from under her and arrive in the bathroom, I'm in shock. On the floor, both in and beside the toilet, over the rug, against the walls: I see traces of vomit everywhere. A trail leads to the bedroom and ends at our bed. Fragments of memories emerge, but what happened after our return to the hotel remains shrouded in darkness. Judging from concrete evidence, I can imagine the rest. Perhaps it's better to leave it that way.

When Anneke is also awake, we do our utmost to clean up the mess. We scrub the floor with the rug (which had to be washed anyway) and rinse it several times under the tap. We scoop leftovers into the toilet and flush, time after time. We open a window to dispel the worst of the stench. But however hard we try, it turns out to be impossible to completely cover up the havoc of the night. When we speak to the owner of the guesthouse, we apologize and give her a few thousand Soms as a tip for the cleaning lady.

We have breakfast nearby. Even though we ended up not eating at all the night before, we have to force ourselves to eat something, but it's not easy. Our hunger has given way to headaches. Back in the guesthouse, the owner immediately approaches us. She has now taken a look at our room and starts to question us. What exactly did we do the night before? Why did we not just say *nyet* to the vodka? She makes it clear that a larger tip is in order and when we enter the room we can only agree with her. With a sigh, we fork over a few thousand Som. Anneke now has only half of her dance earnings left. We leave the window open to let the room air further and walk under the scorching sun to the famous mausoleums of Shah-i Zinda.

In front of the entrance, we see a group of elderly men praying, in tightly ironed shirts, black trousers, prayer cap and all. The mausoleums are a place of pilgrimage for Muslims, especially as one of the tombs is believed to belong to a cousin of Muhammad, who introduced Islam to these parts of the world back in the seventh century. I can't help but think back to the night before. For the first time in my life, I got drunk. Led by a group of Muslims. Despite the city's lavish Islamic history, seventy years of the Soviet Union have ensured that the vodka still flows freely here. Jenet would be proud of us.

CHAPTER 7
SPANISH ANGELS

Gabon/Equatorial Guinea – 2013

Now that I'm walking behind her, I can take a closer look at the woman. Her legs seem even longer than they really are because of the black miniskirt she is wearing and the stilettos pushing her heels upward. Her body is undeniably graceful. Caramel-colored and slim built. Long, black hair that almost touches her bottom. The exotic attraction of a woman of mixed descent. I follow her across the car park of the CKDO, Libreville's biggest shopping mall. Her hips make a continuous circular movement. Sometimes she stops and turns her head towards me; her black eyes urge me to follow and she makes a small gesture with her fingers whenever she thinks I'm hesitating.

She directs me to a black car with tinted windows. She unlocks the doors, chases a white poodle from her seat and gets behind the wheel. I take the passenger seat. After we close the doors, she turns to me and bends over, making her breasts fall halfway out of her black blouse. Despite the air conditioning blowing icy coolness through her car at full blast, I feel myself getting increasingly hot.

'Passport, passport photos and money,' she says matter-of-factly. In the meantime, her right arm reaches for the back seat. The little dog, whose name turns out to be Luna, has sat down on the visa application form that is already waiting for me. Reluctantly, I count the pile of money one final time. I had to withdraw it from several ATMs because the amount was too large for one transaction. But before I hand it over, I ask her again to confirm what we had agreed on earlier.

She takes out a sparkling, gold-colored iPhone from her bag and makes a phone call.

Meanwhile, I realize that I could buy that same phone with the pile of money lying between us. After a short conversation, she hangs up and assures me that I'm free to go wherever I want as long as I stay in the country for no longer than thirty days. To underline her trustworthiness, she not only gives me a receipt on which the amount of money and the services rendered are written in clumsy handwriting, but also her luxurious card. MME ARSENIA FRANCISCA MOLINA MANANGA – SÉCRETAIRE PARTICULIÈRE DE S.E. M. L'AMBASSADEUR. In case of problems: call! In fact, several telephone numbers are listed under her name.

When I open the door, the heat immediately forces sweat out of my pores, forming wet stains on my shirt. She has made me sweat, it has cost me a lot of money, but this quarter of an hour hasn't brought me what outsiders might have suspected when they saw me get into this dark car with this scantily clad woman.

A few days later, Arsenia calls me and asks me to come to a bar in town, where she turns up again in clothes that barely cover her. I get my passport back. Another empty page filled, this time with the coveted visa for Equatorial Guinea. I have taken the first big step towards entering one of the most difficult-to-visit countries in Africa and indeed, the world.

Traveling often starts with the question: do I need a visa for my destination? If so, how and where can I get one? What documents do I have to provide, apart from my passport – and for how long do they have to be valid? How many passport photographs should I bring? Where is the embassy and when is it open? How long does the application take? Conditions often differ between embassies, so it pays to do some research between the different embassies of the same country. Usually, you can find the answers on the Internet, but the lesser known the country is, the scarcer and often older and more unreliable the information. Besides, different conditions may apply depending on the requesting nationality. Overnight, countries can decide to complicate the visa application process, make them more expensive, stop issuing visas or, if you're lucky, offer visas on the Internet, issue them on arrival or stop requiring them altogether. On top of that, there are plenty of rogue websites offering visa services that you can pay for, but that will never get you one. In short, it's often a puzzle and sometimes a nightmare.

In the case of Equatorial Guinea, I soon found out that getting a visa was going to be a challenge. The more I looked into it, the more difficult it seemed to be. To begin with, the small country has very few embassies other than those of its neighbors, Cameroon and Gabon.

I came across a story about a couple who had traveled to Berlin, where one of its few embassies in Europe is located. They waited five days for the embassy to process their application and then flew to the capital Malabo with the fresh visa in their passports. Upon arrival, the authorities calmly announced that no foreigners would be admitted that day. They stamped the expensive visa void and sent the couple back to Europe on the same plane.

I read Heinz's story. A German who, like me, wanted to enter the country from Gabon, through the border town of Cogo. He crossed the border just after New Year's and when examining the fresh stamp in his passport in the evening, noticed that the official hadn't changed the year on his stamp. The next day, he went back to the office to have this mistake corrected. The same official who hadn't bothered to update his stamp accused Heinz of having exceeded his thirty-day visa: the infamous *visa overstay*. He was deported without mercy straight away.

Besides, I mainly came across stories of embassies that simply didn't grant the visa. Clearly, it was going to be a tough job. Even if I managed to get a visa in my passport, there would be no guarantee that I would actually be allowed into the country. Only those with an American or Spanish passport (due to oil trade and former colonial ties, respectively), or a citizen of one of the neighboring countries, are exempt from a visa. For all the others, there is a complicated route with hurdles, none of which you know how high they will be, or how many there are between yourself and the finish line.

A few weeks before my rendezvous with Ms. Arsenia, I try the consulate in Douala in neighboring Cameroon. It turns out to be closed. What catches the eye is the shiny bronze plaque on the consulate's façade. This gives it a luxurious look that contrasts with the ramshackle neighborhood where the building is located. I notice that there is no mention of working hours and the people living in the dusty street can't tell me when the consulate will open its doors.

When a taxi driver drops me off in Libreville a few weeks

later, at the address I found both on the Internet and in a travel guide, it turns out that the embassy has moved. I ask around and eventually find someone who can give me the new address. It turns out to be an extravagant, new building. Although there is still scaffolding on one side, this is evidently a rich country's calling card. It's much more prominent than the consulate in Douala with its shiny plaque.

I walk through the gate unhindered and enter a huge courtyard garden where I see a white tent with a table and chairs underneath. There are application forms and even pens next to them. I fill in a form and feel a glimmer of hope as I walk toward the building. Perhaps the embassy has changed its policy now that they have moved into this brand-new building?

But of course, it's naive to think that I would just walk in, submit my application and be able to collect my visa a few days later. Just as I set my foot on the last step of the marble staircase, a doorkeeper dressed in an orange shirt resolutely sends me back. I'm not allowed to enter the building in my three-quarter-length trousers.

I walk up to the Senegalese *gardien*, the guard of the property. A shy man in a shabby house next to the gaudy entrance gate. Obviously, he has done this before and lends me a pair of shiny, silver-gray trousers – six sizes too big for me. In any case, the trousers are now long enough and the orange man has no reason to stop me.

A little later, I'm sitting in the waiting room with my passport, passport photos, fabricated confirmation of a hotel reservation (not a single hotel had responded to my emails asking for the confirmation required for the visa, so I had no choice but photoshop it myself) and a completed application form. The interior, too, is an embodiment of grotesqueness. A massive, gleaming, wooden railing and bars frame the marble staircase. Dark wooden doors fit perfectly into equally dark door frames and stand out sharply against the white marble floor which radiates coolness.

After waiting for a while, the man in the orange shirt beckons me to follow him. I roll up my trousers for fear of tripping over them. The custodian leads me to one of the rooms in this spacious embassy, lets me in, points to a chair and closes the door behind me.

Across from me sits an elderly man behind a huge desk, strewn with piles of documents. He is reading a French newspaper, spread out in front of him. There is still ample spare room on the desk. The man says nothing and doesn't look at me, so my eyes wander through the enormous room. The walls are covered with bookcases. The flag of Equatorial Guinea stands pontifically in the middle of the room. There are six stars on the white band, a cotton tree and underneath the words UNIDAD, PAZ, JUSTICIA. Unity, peace, justice. That is reassuring. A large portrait of Obiang, framed in gold, hangs on the wall behind the reading bureaucrat. Since ousting his uncle in 1979 (and having him executed soon after), he is the second longest-serving president in the world. That is less reassuring.

The man reads his newspaper imperturbably. He doesn't look up, not even when he turns the page. Even when he reads the top of the newspaper and is almost forced to see me, he continues to stare stoically at the text. Or is he pretending? I sit still, leaving the initiative to the person from whom I need a favor. I look again at the interior, at the desk, the luxurious chairs, the trays of paperclips and other stationery on the huge table, the bookcases, the decorated ceiling. My eyes keep moving to the gold-framed portrait of Obiang. I try to gauge his personality. I try to imagine what effect almost thirty-five years of autocratic rule had on him.

The man reads on, turns a few more pages and ignores me, even when I allow myself a modest and inappropriate cough. I feel myself getting smaller and smaller, which is probably also exacerbated by my much too large gray trousers. I understand that this is a game and it seems best to play along. That means: don't make a sound, sit still and wait.

Then, suddenly, he folds his newspaper. He aims his gaze straight at my face and speaks to me in French. He acts friendly as if he hadn't just ignored me for more than ten minutes. He looks at my application form, flicks through my passport, asks questions about the stamps and visas he sees in it and makes a new pile of my documents on his exquisite desk.

Just when I think the application has been approved and will be processed, I'm about to get up and he nonchalantly asks where my invitation letter is. I don't have one. I try to give it a light-hearted twist. I have never been to Equatorial Guinea, right now I don't have any friends there and so an invitation is not yet feasible for me. I hope to make those friends through my visit – but I will need a visa to do so. The classic chicken-and-egg problem. The official is now resolute: no visa without an invitation. He unfolds his newspaper again. I have ceased to exist for him. There is only one thing left to do for me. I take my stack of documents and leave the room.

I hand the gray oversized trousers to the *gardien*. I make several phone calls to hotels in Bata, the largest city in continental Equatorial Guinea, only to find out that not a single hotel is willing to help me. They won't send an invitation because that would make them assume responsibility for me during my stay. I have a meeting with the consul of the Netherlands, who confirms that a visa for the country is extremely hard to get. He, too, doesn't know how I can get an invitation; at least, he can't help me with it. The same is true of a regional UN official whom I approached via Lars, a Danish friend in East Timor. Even for them, as UN representatives, it's difficult to get into the country. I knew beforehand, of course, that it would be hard, but now it seems almost impossible to cross the border.

That evening, I draft a statement in Spanish, to explain the reasons for my intended visit. I will use this certificate as a substitute for an invitation, as a kind of application letter. The next morning, I print it out and return to the embassy in the only long trousers I have with me. The *gardien* gives me a friendly slap on the shoulder and a smile when he sees my trousers: they fit better than his silvery ones.

The doorman is still wearing the same orange shirt and immediately makes it clear with a scowl that I should leave if I have come without an invitation. He has obviously been briefed by the old bureaucrat I don't even get to see. Orange man advises me to forget about Equatorial Guinea and think of a new destination, then he turns around and closes the heavy, wooden door in front of me. I'm beginning to realize that I have no choice but to follow his advice.

While I'm still talking to the *gardien,* a bald man enters. He is wearing a white *boubou,* the imposing, wide garment which makes West African men look so impressive. With his gold-rimmed glasses, he exudes a curious mixture of authority and friendliness. He asks me what I'm doing here. After hearing my story, he orders me to wait and disappears into the monumental building.

A few minutes later, he appears on the marble staircase: he gestures for me to come in and keeps the door ajar for me. I pass Orange man, who grimaces at me. The man with the gold-rimmed glasses clearly has some leverage here. He sends me into another richly decorated room, where a slim, elegantly dressed lady sits behind yet another impressive desk. She has light-colored skin: daughter of Spanish and Equatorial Guinean parents. I put my stack of documents on her desk, next to a sign that says: Madame Arsenia Francisca Molina Mananga – Sécretaire de l'Ambassadeur. A smile plays on her lips when she sees me and she asks me to sit down. Just as we start our conversation, we hear a knock at the door.

The newspaper-reading official of the previous day storms into the room. Has he been warned by Orange man? He has lost yesterday's composure and starts talking excitedly in Spanish to the woman. It doesn't occur to him that I can perfectly under-stand what he is saying. With broad gestures, he makes it clear to the lady that they are dealing with an 'extremely delicate case' – and he swings his arm in my direction. The woman, with whom I just spoke in Spanish, asks me to wait outside. Through an open window above the door, I hear a heated discussion between the two. He is aggressively trying to convince her to send me away without a visa, as he had done the day before. After a few minutes, he walks out of the room. His face looks like a thundercloud. I can't resist wishing him a good day – in Spanish. He doesn't look back and storms off to his room.

Arsenia beckons me inside again. She pretends nothing has happened, looks at all my documents, reads the letter I wrote, hears my explanation of my wish to visit her country and my aim to visit all the countries in the world. Before she can start harassing me about the missing invitation, I explain that I tried very hard to get it, that it didn't work out and that I decided to write the declaration instead. She nods understandingly. There is a moment of silence, then she says in passing that an invitation isn't necessary for a tourist visa.

Wow, after all the fuss the day before, suddenly it's possible to get a visa without an invitation? Did I just have the wrong person in front of me the day before? I can't believe my luck. 'Oh yes, the price is 400,000 CFA.' Again: Wow! A fat viper is crawling out of the grass now. That's about six hundred euros. My throat suddenly feels uncomfortably dry. The first thought that comes up: will the man with the golden glasses get a share of this? In the back of my mind, I quickly calculate my alternative: stay in Berlin for a few days, hoping to get a visa there, then buy a ticket to Malabo – altogether this will be much more expensive. And they can still send me back to Europe at the airport in Malabo without any reason. Moreover: who says the embassy in Berlin will give me a visa without an invitation?

I would like to know a few things. Can I use the visa to cross the border in Cogo, that is, overland from Libreville? Can I travel freely in Equatorial Guinea? Can I take photos there? She assures me that it's OK and says she is going to give me a visa that will allow me to visit her country without any further obstacles. She says they may ask for money at the border but urges me not to pay anything. I stand with my back against the wall, reluctantly choosing to accept the fee. To my surprise, she gives me back my passport and other documents and asks me to come to Supermarché CKDO at 1 pm the next day.

A few days later, I'm riding a shared taxi to Cocobeach, the last Gabonese village before the border with Equatorial Guinea. When we leave, the taxi is jam-packed, but most of the passengers get out along the way. To their chagrin, the policemen at the checkpoints we meet can't find anything in my passport or inoculation booklet to make me pay. When we drive into the coastal town, there is only one other passenger in the car next to me.

The streets of Cocobeach are almost empty – strange for an African border village. Usually, commotion arises because there is always something to be earned from people and goods crossing a border, but there is none to be seen here. Even the market is dead. I walk towards the border post: nobody there either. Again, I realize that this is not a normal African border. It dawns on me that Equatorial Guinea is unlike all other African countries.

After a while, a cheerful lady wearing a baseball cap arrives, who not only stamps my passport but also organizes a boat to take me to the other side of the border river Río Muni: to Cogo. To be sure that I can enter the country, she calls her colleagues on the other side – according to her, foreigners are sometimes sent back. Yes, she knows Heinz's story: five months earlier, he was the last foreigner to cross the border. She tells me that he hung around in Cocobeach for two days to recover from the shock of the treatment he received from the authorities in Cogo. When she hears what I paid for my visa, her jaw drops. She even makes a copy of my receipt as proof. Most people here earn less in a year than what I paid for a stamp in my passport.

A woman with a child arrives at the immigration building. The boatman is also there and asks for twice what my friend from immigration says is normal. After four hours of waiting and negotiating, he decides to go for it. In the meantime, the officer who has to draw up the official documentation for this boat trip – we are, after all, crossing a border – has fallen asleep with his head on his desk. We wake him up and after he prepares the papers for the crossing, the boatman takes us to his boat. He even gives us a life jacket. The sleepy official sees an opportunity and sends his niece along with us for free.

The boat rattles over the waves of the Río Muni and we have the wind in our hair. The man at the helm keeps nagging about money, but I worry mostly about the weather. Ink-black clouds drift through the sky over our heads and we see lightning over the land. The engine breaks down several times, but each time the skipper manages to repair it on the wide estuary. Left and right in front of us is Equatorial Guinea, to the right and behind us: Gabon. Just before we reach Cogo, the clouds can't keep it in anymore and it starts raining.

As we sail through the oil-covered water past a dirty, smelly and soggy patch of land, a woman in military uniform with a gun on her back comes running towards us. Her voice skips a beat as she shouts at me: 'Two thousand francs! Marina money!' I ignore her, pretending to be busy with my luggage and helping the passenger and her child get out. Marina money? There isn't even a marina. I'm already thinking about how I'm going to jump ashore with my luggage. Where is the mud less deep, so that I don't lose my shoes in it?

A few quick jumps through the shifting soil and I'm on drier ground. The female soldier keeps whining like a little child: 'Marina money!' I ignore her, walk straight to a small pink and blue office building, up the stairs to a balustrade, with next to it a proudly waving flag that I saw earlier at the embassy. Policía de Kogo y Aduanas is written on the blue wall of the office, Inmigración on the left door. I have arrived in Africa's only Spanish-speaking country.

Now that I'm here, I feel proud. It has cost an absurd amount of money, but my passport has an Equatorial Guinean visa and I have the blessing of Arsenia, who has assured me that I'm free to do as I please in this secluded country. There is a car next to the building: the last shared taxi to Bata, the only city in continental Equatorial Guinea. Apart from that, the country consists of an island, Bioko, where the capital Malabo can be found. Bata is at most a two-hour drive away, so it's still easy to reach today. I plan to go there immediately and to continue my visit to the country from there. I see no reason to stay in Cogo (the name is alternately written with a K or a C). But first, I have to get a stamp to make my visit official.

Just as I enter the building, huge shutters open in the black sky and it starts to pour. Large drops drum relentlessly in their thousands on the corrugated iron roof – compared to the luxurious embassy building in Libreville, this is a shack. It's a small miracle that it stays dry inside.

The woman with the child has concluded all the formalities, the niece who sailed with us for free gives a handful of francs to the officer and is also free to travel on and they take their seats in the taxi.

I put my passport on a rickety, wooden table. The graying man behind it doesn't even take a look and asks for twenty thousand francs. I open my passport for him, show him the visa and emphasize that everything has already been paid for. He repeats the price. I take out Arsenia's receipt and show him how much I paid for the visa. I also show him her card and tell him that she guaranteed that I would be able to enter the country without any problems. Even the luxurious business card of his own country's embassy doesn't impress. He simply keeps repeating his demand for money and leaves my passport untouched. Meanwhile, outside, I see the car with the ladies leave for Bata.

He understands that I'm stubborn and goes on a rant against me. He brings up all sorts of things and often uses bizarre logic. I could be a terrorist, a thief. He claims that Osama bin Laden also traveled on tourist visas on his twenty-four passports and a lot of other nonsense to convince me to give him those francs. When he stops shouting for a moment, the voice of the soldier outside cuts through everything. She too is still demanding her Marina money. No foreigner has come here for five months, the day is almost over: everyone here smells their chance. Hyenas circling a trapped animal, coming closer and closer, their heads in the air, howling, the mucus already dripping from their greedy mouths. They know that their prey can't escape and they have no clue when another opportunity will present itself.

Now, a new hyena enters. A drunk who can't make himself understood. He starts pulling at me. He must see in me an easy source of income to pay for his next bottle. I'm starting to get tired of it and push him away from me. Marina Money shouts at me that I should watch out: this is the customs official. When I take a closer look, I do indeed see a worn-out ADUANAS badge on his filthy shirt. Meanwhile, I snatch my passport and walk out.

The uniformed Graybeard now starts to quarrel with the customs man; perhaps he sees his share in this white windfall diminishing? They get into a fight and the old man pushes the drunk down the stairs. Now I see how drunk he is. He can no longer stand up, tries to work his way up the steps and helplessly reaches for the handrail with his right arm, but he misses, falls back and remains lying halfway along the stairs. Meanwhile, the rain that continues to fall mercilessly from the sky is making him soaking wet.

I sit down on the veranda outside. Graybeard comes up to me, I try to explain as calmly as I can what I think of the situation and ask him again for a stamp. Instead of answering, he disappears and leaves me alone. I'm left with a customs officer sleeping it off at the bottom of the stairs in his soaked clothes and a female soldier giving me vicious looks and continuing to shout her demands into the air until she eventually gives up and disappears.

This is the moment I have been waiting for. I'm going back into the office. I'm just going to stamp my passport myself, given that those appointed for the job are too lousy to do it. I open the desk's drawers and look under it and beside it, but unfortunately, I can't find a stamp among all the rubbish. As no one is here anyway, I sit down on one of the chairs and take a closer look around the half-dark room. A picture of the president, of course, on the blue wall. The same photograph as in the embassy in Libreville, but without the golden frame. A small cupboard. Two rickety chairs and the little table I'm sitting at. In the meantime, the rain continues to pound on the corrugated iron roof.

After a while, a new official appears on the scene. This one seems serious and offers to take me to the Comisario. Why not? We drive for a while on the road to Bata, but unfortunately, the Comisario is not home, so we return and I'm back at the now-familiar border building. A little later, the car comes back with Graybeard inside instead of the Comisario. Who knows, maybe the other one talked to him? He asks for my passport and says he is going to help me, but when I walk with him, he starts shouting again just like he did before. He claims that tourists cross the border here every day (does he really think I believe that?) and that he has never had these problems before. Well, who knows, maybe this is the same man who expelled Heinz from the country because he didn't have the right date on his stamp? He says that he and his colleagues have decided that they will throw me in jail unless I pay up and that the police have labeled me a rebel. When he sees that I'm not impressed, he disappears again into the semi-darkness.

Marina Money is now back too, she closes the door and windows of the office and sits down on the veranda. She takes the gun in her hands. She plays with the weapon: she points it to the left, to the right and back again. She shouts at the sky in a tumbling voice, but she must know that I'm here. I'm too far away from her to smell whether she is drunk as well. I'd be surprised if she wasn't.

When she unlocks the gun, I grab my stuff and walk down a side staircase. She realizes, stands up, points the gun at me, starts laughing hysterically and calls me a coward. Whether she's drunk or not, I don't want to be around this crazy lady playing with a loaded gun, so I walk away from the veranda. Again, I ignore her provocative words. Now I just need to stay calm to avoid accidents.

Then, a bright idea comes to my mind. Arsenia! Madame Arsenia Francisca Molina Mananga – Sécretaire Particulière de S.E. M. l'Ambassadeur, who has given me the visa in Libreville. Of course! I have her card and her numbers. She told me that I didn't have to pay anything here and that I could always call her in case I encountered any problems. This seems reasonable, given how much I paid her.

It turns out my phone doesn't have any service within Equatorial Guinea, but luckily I have just a sliver of a connection to a Gabonese mast on the other side of the Río Muni. While I look at my phone, for the first time since I stepped out of the boat, a good feeling comes over me. Why didn't I think of this before when Graybeard was still around!

'¿Sí?'

'Buenas tardes, Arsenia. How are you? It's Boris. I have now arrived in Cogo and have a question.'

'How do you dare to call me?'

'Wait a minute, Arsenia. Listen. I got a visa from you a few days ago, I paid a lot for it. You guaranteed that I could cross the border in Cogo and that I wouldn't have to pay anything more here.'

'Why didn't you fly to Malabo?'

'You knew I was going to Cogo, overland. I told y..'

'I told you not to go overland. Now you have to sort it out yourself over there.'

'I was hoping you could help me by talking to them.'

'No way. I'm not going to do anything for you. Don't you dare call me ever again.'

'Arsenia, ...'

Beep-beep-beep. I look at the phone – my last lifeline. Arsenia, with her golden iPhone, her stiletto heels, her caramel-colored breasts, her luxurious black car with tinted windows and her Luna. Arsenia, who defied her colleague at the embassy and granted me a visa on the advice of the man with the gold-rimmed glasses, even though it was in a sketchy bar in Libreville and not at her embassy itself. Arsenia, who, with a few words, could have helped me out of this predicament.

The staircase is empty: the drenched, drunken customs man has disappeared. I don't see Marina Money either, but it could be that she is hiding somewhere in a dark corner.

Outside, the short African twilight has set in; in ten minutes, it will be dark. The rain has stopped, streams of water dripping from the roof make a ticking sound on the concrete floor. Now that it's dry outside, I walk away from the office, sit down on a large stone by the side of the road and take a moment to calm down and survey the situation. And that situation is, simply put, hopeless.

I wonder how and where this day will end. I have decidedly few options left. Now that no one is in the office anymore, I could of course boldly walk away without a stamp, but I'm bound to get into huge trouble when I leave the country, or at any checkpoint on the way. Besides, I can't avoid traveling back to Gabon via this same border crossing. It's crystal clear that I can't expect anything from the authorities here: none of the officials I have seen give me the slightest reason to expect favors. I played my trump card, Arsenia, but it was an utter failure. Going back to Gabon is also impossible, and besides, if I haven't officially been in the country, I can't say I have visited. Then everything has been for nothing. Plus, I can throw away my very expensive visa.

There is nobody to talk to, nobody to help me, nobody to cheer me up. Traveling is fun when you're on the move, when you can enjoy the views, discover new places, make new friends. Problems along the way are there to be solved and usually give travel an extra dimension and juicy tales to tell later. But I can't see a way out now, it feels like I have thrown all my cards on the table and lost the game. I haven't felt this lonely in a long, long time. It has become dark and quiet and I have no idea what to do. Why did I have to go to Equatorial Guinea, one of the hardest countries to get into?

Then three white shadows sail through the lonely night into my field of vision. Where did they come from? Three lifebuoys are thrown at me from nowhere. I have to grab them at once. I get up from my rock, run after them and hope they aren't drunk. Only when I'm closer do I notice that they are European women. They look surprised. What is this white man doing here, in this remote corner of a forgotten land, all alone in the dark?

Now that I get a better look at them, I see that they are nuns. Gold chains with crosses dangle around their necks. It appears that these Spanish ladies emigrated here during Franco's era. In a flash, I think back to my intensive Spanish course in Madrid. I couldn't have imagined then that my Spanish would help me out here and now, in Equatorial Guinea, twenty-five years later. I hadn't even heard of the country at the time.

The women shake their heads when they hear my story and walk with me to the office. Moments later, a car arrives and the Comisario gets out, together with Graybeard. The most determined of the nuns comes with me into the locked room that turns out to be the Comisario's office. On the wall above his chair: the president, and the flag. UNIDAD – PAZ – JUSTICIA. Ah, well. On the sidewall is a picture of the Real Madrid team: each player looks taller than the President's portrait. Does he know that? Is that not sacrilege?

Since the nun is with us and I know that the border gang knows who she is, I have faith in this conversation. I assume they will stop shouting now and listen to this honorable Spanish nun. She starts by explaining that I have already paid a lot of money for my visa. I have been promised trouble-free entry into the country, I'm tired after a long journey, I'm here in good faith,

I'm a good person and I have come as a friend of Equatorial
Guinea. With the friendly request that the Comisario please
take this into account in his decision on the matter. She says it
all convincingly, calmly, in flattering, diplomatic language,
occasionally giving the Comisario an encouraging, friendly
smile but, as befits a good nun, without the slightest hint of
feminine charm. I couldn't have put it better. Surely the
Comisario will be convinced by her performance?

With an angry face, he immediately kills my hopes. He is
obviously not happy to be disturbed on his night off and has set
his sights on getting his money's worth. When he speaks, he
doesn't look at the nun but directly at me. He holds a long
discourse. Tourism is important to Equatorial Guinea (is it?),
the price of a stamp in a passport is twenty thousand francs and
he is not here to discuss anything. According to him, what
Arsenia told me has no value because she said it in Gabon and
they can say what they want in Gabon, but here the local law
applies (or, at least, that of the Comisario I think). A remarkable
assertion, because both Arsenia and the embassy in Libreville
are of course official representatives of the country.

The nun whispers in my ear that there is no point talking
any longer, that she can't help me either and that the only
option left is to pay. I realize that there is nothing more she can
add to her convincing story and her request for clemency. In
disgust, I throw two ten-thousand-franc notes on the table,
watching the wad slowly flattening out now that I no longer
have it clenched in my fist. They will surely be buying alcohol
to drink to victory over this foreign rebel.

I do finally get the stamp in my passport, have another good look to make sure the date and especially the year are correct and ask for a receipt. Surprise surprise: they are out of those. Oh, and photography is forbidden within the country. As soon as I arrive in Bata, I have to get a special permit to travel around: this stamp is only proof that I entered the country and doesn't allow me to travel through it. So, to all the questions I asked her, the lady with the stiletto heels just told me one lie after the other. And I was foolish enough to believe them all.

When I finally leave the building, I now know inside and out, it feels like liberation. The nuns invite me for dinner. Fresh fish on a terrace overlooking the darkness. One of the three sits quietly and doesn't look happy, but the other two immediately rise to the occasion and seem glad to be able to tell their story to a stranger. They talk endlessly and I slowly feel all the frustration and anger of the last few hours sink in.

They talk about the situation here, about their long years in this impossible country, about their fight against the local authorities, about the wealth of the country that flows in its entirety to the president and his family and about the poverty of the people. All the while, Equatorial Guinea is in the global top three in terms of oil production per capita, up there with the oil states of the Persian Gulf. They don't mince their words in their criticism of the situation. They invite me to come to their school the next day and take me to a guest house where I share a room with at least five rats (at least, that's the number I can see running across the room at any one time). The fan soon cuts out, leaving me to be steamed in this windowless room. Electricity only works a few hours a day.

The nuns take me to their school the next morning: two floors of pupils aged six to eighteen. All in green t-shirts and red shorts. Each classroom has about twenty pupils of the same age. The nuns invite me to go to all the year groups. I start with the youngest and end with the almost grown-ups. I end up staying for a couple of hours. In each class, I let the pupils ask me questions. I tell them about the Netherlands and my travels and show them where I'm from on a world map. Of course, I take my turn to interview the pupils as well, because I'm extremely curious about their view of the world. Of their world. One of my questions: 'What would you do if you were president of this country for one day?'

As I listen to the children's answers, anger and sadness well up inside me. Sadness when I hear how these kids would build a hospital, provide electricity and running water if they had it their way. Anger when I hear how the children are deprived of all the basic needs of a child: safety, hygiene, care. Anger at the lack of any perspective. And disgust when later, after I have seen all the classes, the nuns point to an island off the coast.

There, they say, one of the daughters of president Obiang is developing a golf resort. There, she will soon be flying her helicopters to bring friends to play golf on courses that are perfectly maintained and watered, and whose lawns are kept neatly short, while this village doesn't even have running water or electricity that works for more than a few hours a day. Her father is, according to Forbes, one of the richest heads of state in the world, in a country with only half a million inhabitants. Obiang's eldest son, Teodorin, former Minister of Forestry – another sector in which the country, or rather the Obiang family, makes lots of money – has now risen to the position of Vice-President. A few years later, he will be under investigation by the Swiss authorities for criminal activities, after which the Netherlands will confiscate his $100 million yacht. His Danish girlfriend, then Miss Universe, loses her title because she is linked to a criminal organization. She is an easy target: the Obiang family eventually stays out of harm's way.

Can't all those petrol billions, Mr Obiang, be distributed differently? Why did you have one of the most expensive yachts in the world custom-built for you? Why do you and your children have estates and huge houses, cars and private planes in Europe and the US, which are worth millions, or rather: billions? One of your Bugattis or Lamborghinis could vaccinate all the children in your country. Meanwhile, child mortality here is one of the highest on the continent. Maybe one less trip to Europe where you do your shopping in exclusive Parisian shops? Or perhaps stop buying Michael Jackson memorabilia worth millions?

Obiang is a dictator of the worst and most brutal kind. In 2003, he led his people to believe that, to prevent corruption, he was personally taking over the national treasury. He has officially made himself equal to God, which includes the right to control the country's inhabitants and affairs. He is therefore above reproach and is guaranteed not to go to hell, they say, even though there are rumors that he eats the body parts of slain opponents. There is no free press, opposition is almost non-existent. Meanwhile, the West lets Obiang do as he pleases by continuing to do business with him. Because, well, oil.

Talking to the students and the nuns and listening to their stories often brings tears to my eyes. Ah, what was yesterday's incident with a couple of drunk officials compared to the daily lives and futures of these young people and these women? The prospects of improving their lot are hopeless. Obiang's son is eager to pick up where his father leaves off. Even though he has aligned himself with God, Obiang will still die one day. The family knows how to play it well, for hardly anyone is familiar with this dreadful dynasty. Despite their wealth piled up everywhere, they manage to stay under the radar. Yet in recent years, various governments in Europe and the US have finally started investigations into the origins of all the extreme wealth of the Obiang family. Of course, other rulers in the world hardly have clean hands either and keep their people under wraps in all respects. But Equatorial Guinea takes the prize.

With a heavy heart, I get into the shared taxi that takes me to Bata. On the way, there are checkpoints and one of them even has a large sign saying that corruption is prohibited in the country. Right. After yesterday's frustrating hassle, I have decided not to enter another bureaucratic roller coaster and thus not to apply for a visitor's permit or photography permit. I have had enough. Instead, the first thing I do when I arrive in the city is to go to the Spanish consulate, the only European representation here in Bata. Seeing the European flag in this lawless place somehow gives me comfort.

A distinguished, middle-aged Spanish lady talks to me. She whispers imploringly through the glass of her counter and I put my ear close to the opening to understand her. 'Be extremely careful, as this is a very dangerous country. You are outlawed here, especially as a foreigner. The authorities can throw you in prison without mercy and without reason. The only way out is to pay a huge amount of money. Last year, a group of Europeans were arrested near Monte Alén. They were detained for a week; we could do nothing for them. So be very cautious about what you do and what you say. You need a permit to take photos. Give me your passport and I will make a copy. That way we know that you are traveling here as a European and we can contact the Dutch government if the need arises.' When she hands me back my passport a little later, I see a note in it with a phone number that I can call 24/7 should I get into trouble. I wonder if my phone would have any service if it did come to that.

The following days, I walk along the promenade of Bata, across the market, through the backstreets. I abandon my plans to go into the countryside – I would have liked to go to Monte Alén as well. I want to minimize the risk of being caught. It's clear to me that I'm at the mercy of the authorities. I feel strong lawlessness. Total arbitrariness. The lady at the embassy merely confirmed that feeling.

When I have had enough of Bata, I share a taxi to Mbini, a village on the coast, further south. The ferry that until recently provided the connection to the other side of a river lies slanted on the muddy bank like a carelessly discarded, huge, empty cigarette packet. The taxi takes the new road over the Benito Bridge, which has made the ferry redundant. The futuristic bridge stands out strangely in this otherwise barely developed rural area of the country. Lines of little flags are stretched between the lampposts: a flag of the country, one of the party and, inevitably, one with Obiang's photo on it. From hundreds of flapping flags, his face smiles at me. Now that I'm in the country and know the stories better, I can no longer look at his mug with an open mind, as I still could at the embassy in Libreville, in the room with the newspaper-reading official.

In this remote village, I feel freer and I finally get the chance to talk to people, to look around without immediately fearing reprisals. People here seem less afraid of the authorities, too. Children call after me: 'Chino!' They think that every foreigner is from China. The Chinese have also descended on this part of Africa to build infrastructure in exchange for raw materials, without posing any tough questions about human rights. Evidently, they also built that new bridge. Colonization 2.0.

A teacher tells me a story about her sister who lives just across the border in Gabon and how the last time she wanted to enter the country, she was forced by my friends at the Cogo border post to pay an amount equal to her monthly salary just to get out of the country for a short family visit. They, and others, tell me about the dictatorship, their fears, their poverty. Once more, I feel great hopelessness. One guy thinks I'm a journalist and begs me to publish about these abuses. The anger and disgust I felt in that little school in Cogo about this shameless regime only deepens. Oppression has rarely been more tangible for me.

After a few days of depressing gloom, I'm back in Cogo. I have promised the nuns I would visit them. I find them in their school, still dressed in white and with their golden crosses around their necks. After they finish their morning lessons, I wave at the girls and boys in green and red who are going home for their lunch break and the ladies take me to the house they share, higher up on a hill. It's surrounded by a garden with flowers.

The women are preparing lunch while I look out over the village and the bay from the veranda. The tension that had built up over the past few days, during which I always had the feeling that a sword was hanging over my head and that I could disappear behind bars at any moment for a completely arbitrary motive, is slowly slipping away from me now that I'm with the friendly sisters.

During lunch, I tell the ladies what I have seen, what people have told me. That I feel disgusted by Obiang and his family. I ask how on earth they can live here. The question is visibly uncomfortable for them. They say that they, too, see that the system here is rotten and that they are only staying to do something for the inhabitants of Cogo and their children. It doesn't look like they will ever return to their motherland. I can only admire their perseverance and their spirit of sacrifice.

The moment of farewell to my angels has come. The nun who had spoken well for me on that first evening implores me that I can always ask for their help if the officials try to make my life difficult again when I leave. With great reluctance, I go to the familiar building of the INMIGRACIÓN. There, Graybeard tries to extort money from me again, but this time I get away without paying anything and I still get a stamp. He refuses to keep his promise to give me a receipt for the twenty thousand francs. Even when I'm already in the boat that will take me back to my smiling border post friend in Cocobeach, he and his colleagues keep shouting curses at me over the dirty water of the little harbor. I don't hear Marina Money this time.

When we finally sail away from the stinking muddy shore, I feel an enormous burden fall off my shoulders. At the same time, the anger remains. Even though I have left this country, the inhabitants will have to continue living oppressed and poor in the clutches of a horrible, shameless and exploitative family for a long time to come.

Chapter 8
Bear in the Road

Tajikistan/Kyrgyzstan – 2010

Soon after I started applying for visas for my trip through Central Asia, I found that for each country, I had to indicate when I would enter and when I would leave again. I hate the idea of tying myself down in advance like that. For me, it takes away from the essence of travel: the ultimate freedom of adventure, on which you simply cannot put a timestamp. But what has to be done, has to be done. I tried as best as I could to estimate how long I would stay in each country before I left. Once the visas were glued to my passport, the possibilities of adjusting my travel plans were closed.

By the time I was in Turkmenistan, on my long journey east, it was much harder to keep abreast of what was happening in the world. The few times I was online, I saw that riots had broken out in Osh, Kyrgyzstan's second largest city. That was exactly on my route. When I wanted to enter the country from Uzbekistan, the Tajik official who examined my passport wanted to check where I would be traveling after I'd left his country. He saw my visa for Kyrgyzstan, asked me where I intended to leave Tajikistan and looked at me with wide eyes when I confirmed what he already suspected. That border crossing was less than 250 kilometers south of Osh. He made a grim gesture with his right hand across his throat. Kyrgyzstan? You shouldn't go there now, least of all to Osh. But that was precisely my intention.

After the overwhelming brilliance of Uzbekistan's restored monuments, I needed nature and I found it in western Tajikistan. Hiking along green lakes in barren mountains with caps of snow and tufts of trees dotted along the water's edge made it all picture-perfect: the Seven Lakes of Marguzor gave me exactly what I was looking for. From the lakes, I traveled on to the capital Dushanbe, but I didn't feel like visiting cities and traveled further east. One of the highlights of my trip was going to be the Pamir Highway. A road built by the Soviets through the Pamir Mountains, which connected Tajikistan and Kyrgyzstan when they were both still part of the Soviet Union.

This famous highway starts in Khorog, a small town in the southeast of the country, near the border with Afghanistan. From Dushanbe, I take a bus with Alberto, an Italian I met in Uzbekistan and with whom I decided to travel the Highway. The next day, we explore the town together. We notice that there is a lot of activity in the streets. Alberto speaks Russian fluently because he lives in Moscow. I can kick myself for not having done more work to learn this beautiful but challenging language, which comes in very handy in this region.

He asks around about what is going on and so we find out that Emomalii Rahmon, the president of the country, will be visiting a few days later. Khorog must, of course, look top-notch for this special guest. Planters are given a fresh coat of white paint, fresh plants are placed in them, dustbins are emptied, streets are cleaned and a new layer of asphalt is laid in front of the stadium where he will undoubtedly give a speech. This is the same president who, a few years later, would be awarded the title of 'Founder of Peace and National Unity, Leader of the Nation' by his parliament. You would want to polish your city for someone of that caliber.

In the regional museum of Khorog, we mainly see banners from the time when Tajikistan was part of the Soviet Union. The hammer and sickle are still on a pedestal here and the dominant color is red. There are also objects with special stories. Probably the most remarkable is the first piano of the region. Almost a century before, ten Russian soldiers carried it here all the way from Osh in two months, through the mountain range we would later be crossing in the opposite direction. Less surprising is the collection of busts of Lenin, displayed throughout the building.

After visiting the museum, we continue our exploration of the town. We see a few more statues of Lenin, which apparently also survive outside the museum. We cross the street at an intersection and to our surprise, we're immediately stopped by a policeman wearing one of those caps with a large, steep top. If you were to enlarge it, it could be a ski-jumping slope – but one for advanced jumpers.

'Passports!' he barks, with an implacability that suits his cap.

The tone immediately tells me that he means business. We have to quickly change our way of thinking after the endearing sight of people trying to get the town ready for the upcoming visit of their leader and the little museum with its curious collection.

'Why should we show our passports?' I try to play innocent, but I don't like his tone at all. Besides, I'm not aware of having done anything wrong.

'Passports!'

I consult Alberto for a moment. After all, he speaks Russian and can communicate best with the official. I point out to him that under no circumstances should we hand over our documents.

'Could you tell us the reason for your request?' Alberto asks cautiously. He translates for me in Italian what they are saying to each other.

'You have just crossed the street illegally,' says the man, still in a harsh tone.

'We don't deny that we crossed the street, but what exactly was illegal about that?'

'You don't see the zebra crossing over there? You didn't use it, and that is an offense. Passports!'

Even though Alberto explains what the officer said, I can hardly believe my ears. The zebra crossing the man is pointing at is still a work in progress. A stretch of road has been fenced off with rough stones that have been pulled out of the verge a little further down the road. Road workers are busy painting the stripes on the new asphalt. Seven stripes have been completed; I estimate that there are another five or six to go before they reach the other side. Cars slalom around the boulders. Does Mr. Skijump-hat truly believe that we're going to pay a fine for ignoring a half-finished pedestrian crossing? We might as well argue that we don't want to disturb the workers in their important job. After all, the president is coming in a few days and there should be an immaculate, white zebra crossing here and perhaps elsewhere too. Who are we to tarnish it in advance?

I notice that I'm getting angry and I'm glad that I don't speak Russian well enough, otherwise words would have come out of my mouth that the policeman – who is obviously fishing

for a bribe – could have used against me. Alberto is better at
this and explains in a calm voice that we were not aware of
committing an offense by ignoring a half zebra crossing, apolo-
gizes and grabs my arm to lead me away. To my surprise, the
officer and his ski-jump cap let us go.

That evening, Alberto and I arrange for a car with a driver. An
Irish friend of Alberto's joins us. The next morning, we set off
for Murgab, the last town before the border with Kyrgyzstan.
Six days straight, through the rugged landscape of the Pamir
Mountains. At the bottom of the valley, we see the wild Pamir
River carving its way through the rough rocks in its bed,
bordered by green strips and terraces where the land is culti-
vated. On the other side of the river is Afghanistan, where we
see shepherds walking through the mountains and hear them
occasionally shout at their small herds of goats. The temptation
to wade through the river and into Afghanistan increases as the
Pamir narrows.

On top of hills above the river, we see ruins of old
fortresses that Marco Polo must have seen when he passed
through the region on his way to China. And then, when I
crane my neck: majestic mountains rising above all this, with
glaciers and eternal snow. The valley is already above two
thousand meters, so these mountains are veritable giants, some
of which reach over six thousand meters above sea level. This
is scenery that stays overwhelming even after several days of
seeing it. The enormous crack running through the windscreen
of our dented and worn-out Lada does little to make the views
less stunning.

We sleep in simple yurts or in people's homes and drive
through deserted valleys without roads or villages, occasionally
seeing a lost yak along the way. We're lucky to see Marco Polo

sheep running around with their thick butts and huge horns. We get closer and closer to the snow line.

We stay in Bulunkul, a village near a lake, more than four thousand meters above sea level, where people have purple faces from living at such a high altitude and in the cold. This cold also strikes insidiously now, at the beginning of the short summer. Mostly at night, when the sun doesn't show itself, like a burglar making his move in an unguarded moment. In the morning, there is always a layer of delicate white crystals on the streams. To brush our teeth, we have to break the ice. When I go for a walk in the mountains, I get caught in a snowstorm and for a moment I don't know what's up and what's down. It's the middle of June and I wonder what the winters must be like here. I understand from the residents that they sit for months on end in their homes, cut off from the world, driving their Ladas on the frozen lake as their only entertainment.

Then, after six days of adventure and some of the most desolate landscapes I have ever seen: Murgab. The fact that we're approaching Kyrgyzstan is indicated by the large number of men wearing Kyrgyz black and white felt hats. Murgab has no Internet, but when I ask around about the situation in the neighboring country, the locals tell me not to cross the border. If I did, they say, I would probably be shot or robbed. It also turns out that there is no transport to the border because of the disturbances. So, I have to carefully consider my options. More often than not, nothing is more difficult than to assess the situation when you are on the ground.

After the long ride through the mountains, it's pleasant to stroll through the town. The market consists of containers placed in a row, with one side open. Some have signs on the exterior to indicate what is inside. I see one with a large dollar sign: the bank. Inside the containers, the goods are displayed and the owner sits on a folding chair waiting for customers, sheltered from the cold wind. Between these metal shops, potential buyers shuffle through the sand.

Murgab is dusty. The streets are dusty and the constant wind brings in new dust from far and wide. Cleaning is of little use. In the meantime, I wonder if the President will also come here after he has been in Khorog? In any case, no one is trying to make the town look any tidier. There are certainly no zebra crossings being painted here.

I meet several foreigners, which is surprising after days of driving through empty landscapes. Where did they come from? They turn out to be mainly Swiss and they too are on their way to the border. Most of them by car, one girl on a bicycle. They, too, are in doubt as to whether they should cross the border. One of them has a satellite phone and calls embassies in the region for advice. The conclusion after an afternoon of phone calls: do not cross the border. The Swiss decide to drive back to Khorog, from there to Dushanbe and then to fly to Bishkek. Alberto and the Irishman also go back. They try to persuade me to come along.

However, it isn't so straightforward. My visa for Tajikistan expires in two days and it's impossible to be out of the country before then if I turn back here. It's also impossible to get the visa extended in time, if only because the weekend is about to start. An expired visa in your passport is always annoying, but in these parts, it's something you have to avoid at all costs. Especially in countries where an unfinished zebra crossing is already a reason for a fine.

Apart from these formal concerns, there is my firm conviction that I want to make this trip overland. I don't want to see the inside of a plane for a couple of months, I just want to travel east and not backtrack anywhere. That night, I toss and turn in bed, waking up again and again, as the dilemma keeps echoing in my head. Should I continue and stick to my original plan, at the risk of driving straight into a war? Or go back with the others, with all the annoying hassle of my expired visa that will undoubtedly follow? And abandon my ambition to strictly travel east? When I wake up the next morning, the whirlwind in my head is gone. Somewhere in my restless sleep, I must have cut the knot and decided to move on. I also understand why. The first village after the border is Sary Tash. I assume I will get a better idea of the situation there than here in Murgab. If I hear that it's seriously dangerous in Osh, I can always travel straight into China on the motorway which leads past Irkeshtam. That is my plan B. With that alternative in mind, I'm ready for the adventure.

I explain my plan to the others, but they stick to their decision. They turn around. I wave them off and I'm the only foreigner left in Murgab. Now, it's a matter of finding someone who is willing to take me and that is not easy: the Sary Tash taxi stand is empty. In the end, the owner of my hostel finds someone willing to take me to Kyrgyzstan. To break the long ride, we will spend the night at Lake Karakul. After that, I will reach the border exactly on the day that my visa expires. I am, after all, a last-minute person.

Early the next morning, we leave Murgab behind. After we leave the last exit on our right and continue north, it turns out that we're the only ones on the road to Karakul. Once we have worked our way through a stretch of rugged mountains, over the Ak Baital, or White Horse Mountain pass, I look ahead and I forget all about the situation in Kyrgyzstan.

On the horizon, far above us, I see a white mountain ridge. The highest peaks, at 7134 meters and 7495 meters respectively, were once called Pik Lenin and Pik Stalin. The twentieth-century history of the Soviet Union can be captured here in a single glimpse of snow-capped mountains. The highest of the two was originally called Garmo but was named after the infamous leader of the Soviet Union in 1932. When Stalin fell from his pedestal under Khrushchev, the mountain was named Communism and a few years after Tajikistan's independence it was renamed Ismoil Somoni, after a 10th-century Samanid leader. The second-highest peak was named Lenin in 1928; in 2006 it was renamed Ibn Sina or Avicenna, the famous Persian polymath. Far below these giants, at the bottom of the landscape, lies a huge lake formed twenty-five million years ago by the impact of a huge meteor. For years it was called Lake Victoria by British cartographers with their relentless monarchical impact, whose traces can still be found in the most unexpected places. The Soviet cartographers renamed it Karakul, Black Lake, which is much more appropriate, if only because it lacks any political or ideological connotation.

Once I arrive in the hamlet at the edge of the lake, I find a basic place to sleep. After leaving my things there, it's time for a walk along the Karakul coastline. I'm at just under four thousand meters here. The few people I meet on the street also have those deep purple veins running through their faces – a thick blush, marked by altitude, cold and wind.

The wind blows incessantly. It comes down from the mountains, dives into the lake and finds its way around the hills and other obstacles. It laughs at the few white houses in the village, blows around them, or rather, right through them. If a door or window is closed, the wind rattles it until it swings open. The wind is the boss here and it constantly makes itself known. I dip deep into my jacket, even though it's the end of June.

I had wondered about it at Yashil Kol, the other high lake near Bulunkul where I was before. Are the people who live here brave, or just foolish? Such empty land, so much space to live in, and then to choose one of the coldest places in Central Asia, where it's forty degrees below zero or lower for months in winter and the nearest village is many hours away. They must truly love their country.

The next morning, I'm up in time to see the sun rise from behind the mountain ridge that marks the border with China. On the other side, the full moon sinks over the mountains of Tajikistan. According to the visa in my passport, this is my last day in the country. Once the sun rises above the mountain ridges, it immediately begins to warm the cold land. It has become my tradition to skinny-dip in the mountain lakes I encounter and today this seems like the ultimate challenge. Here and there, I see pieces of ice. A few weeks earlier, the lake was still covered by a thick ice crust that always lies here from October to the end of May.

The water is indeed icy, but that's not the problem. Only when I come out of the water do I notice how cold it is – I feel that eternal wind blowing around me. I sprint along the beach, back and forth, waving my arms, until I'm dry and I feel the warmth coming from within. That is my body's reward: a wonderful, tingling warmth that expels the cold.

Back in the village, I walk to the lovely little white mosque. There is nobody around and the wooden door is closed. The wind has apparently forgotten to open it, so I push it. The inside turns out to be a mess. Prayer mats are scattered across the floor, there is a dusty bag and a few pens on a wobbly table. I wonder how often the mats are rolled out here to pray. A blue wooden board with a red line around it has five clocks that stopped ticking a long time ago. They all show a random hour. Once upon a time, they must have indicated the five prayer times, but I wonder when was the last time anyone prayed in this mosque.

A few hours later, we're on the road again, driving north to the border. I start feeling some tension inside. The border crossing is the first obstacle today. More importantly, what is the actual situation in Kyrgyzstan like? Will I be able to travel on and stick to my original plan? Or will I have to escape to China after all? The driver works his old white Lada uphill, ever closer to the answers to my questions. We travel further up the dirt road into the mountains, bend after bend, higher and higher, although the huge white peaks in the distance remain as unreachable as before. The road we're driving on is the only evidence that there must have been people here before. Otherwise, it's eerily empty. The other proof that humans have been here was, of course, the piano I saw in the museum in Khorog. I try to imagine how ten Russian soldiers carried it over this same road almost a hundred years ago. All so the daughter of the fort commander of Khorog could practice her play.

Then, a few turns above us: buildings. That must be the Kyzyl-Art Mountain pass. The border. After the driver manages to get the small but strong car up the last stretch of this mountain pass, I see a red and white pole hanging across the road between the buildings. A little closer still, I see a padlock securing the barrier to a metal post.

Soldiers come out of one of the buildings, playing with their dogs. They laugh: today is Sunday 27 June, the president is on tour in the region, southern Kyrgyzstan is at war and so the border has been closed for four days. How bizarre that nobody told me about this in Murgab. My youngest niece Roya turns 9 today, but the Tajiks don't know that, although they would undoubtedly appreciate her Persian name. The Tajik language is closely related to Persian. We're invited inside and offered a cup of tea. I laugh along with the soldiers, trying to hide my nervousness: the visa that expires today is burning in my passport like a ticking time bomb.

The driver runs off with my passport and comes back saying that the border will open for twenty dollars. I tell him that I'm not in a hurry. This is a bluff of course, but it seems to work, because again the driver disappears. I drink another cup of tea. The soldiers make it clear to me with hot-tempered gestures that I mustn't go to Osh and that I should stay in Tajikistan. I know the story by now. To my surprise, the driver comes back after a while and tells me to get into his Niva. One of the soldiers walks up to the barrier, takes a key out of his pocket and opens the padlock. The border swings open and when we're past the barrier, the soldier lowers the pole and reattaches the lock. I will never know how the driver managed to pull this trick. He doesn't say anything about it and doesn't ask me for money.

A little later at the Kyrgyz border post, I'm welcomed with open arms. The officials assure me that I can travel to Osh and wish me a good stay in their country. Finally, a more hopeful message. The quality of the road is now extremely bad and several times the driver must steer our car over hardened mud streams running straight across the road. In the end, the car breaks down. While the driver lies under the car with the bonnet open, I walk around, looking at the red-brown-green-gray mountains around me. The tension of the past few days is slipping away and I feel at peace. I trust that the car can be fixed, although we haven't seen any vehicles since we left Karakul. Help is not to be expected on this officially closed road. The most important thing is that the Kyrgyz border guards have put me at ease.

My faith in the mechanical capacities of the driver proves to be well-founded and less than an hour later, we drive into Sary Tash. After saying goodbye to the driver and finding a simple place to stay in the village, I get my first taste of Kyrgyzstan. For the time being, it seems very peaceful. The snow on the mountains is only slightly higher than the wide, green valley in which the village is situated: a few weeks ago, the snow must have reached up to here. Something that immediately catches my eye: the yurts and the horses. The black and white felt hats I had already seen in Murgab. Signs in shops, in the Cyrillic-like Kyrgyz script and also in Chinese – the border with China is only seventy kilometers east. There are the colorful clothes of the women and their golden teeth. I also see young people playing volleyball in thick clothes over a net that hangs limply between two poles.

When I ask people about Osh, no one makes a morbid throat gesture anymore. Yes, I can continue my way north. No problem. Organizing transport turns out to be easy. The next morning, a white Volga, the classic Russian car, drives up to take me to the troubled city. We pick up another woman with two children and a live goat is put in the boot, next to my backpack. During our ride over the unpaved road, every once in a while we hear a violent kick from the poor animal. We encounter herds of his kind and leave the snow-covered mountains behind us. The landscape eventually opens up, we see green meadows, the air becomes denser and people walk in summer clothes. There is more traffic on the road as we approach the second-largest city in the country. Osh.

Just by looking at the map, you can see that this is an extraordinary region. The Uzbek border lies some ten kilometers to the northwest and Uzbek enclaves west of Osh have taken bites out of Kyrgyzstan. Weeks earlier, Anneke and I were on the Uzbek side in the Fergana Valley. Ethnic Kyrgyz and Uzbeks regularly clash: the collapse of the Soviet Union and the independence of former brother states from that communist union have reanimated old animosities. The skirmishes two weeks earlier cost about two thousand lives and resulted in an enormous flow of refugees into Uzbekistan.

The mother and her children in the back seat had been talking at the beginning of the ride, but they are silent when we enter the outskirts of Osh. When I look back, I see them with their noses pressed against the windows of the Volga. I realize that they know as little as I do about what we're going to encounter. At first, nothing seems wrong. People are walking in the streets, cars are driving, it looks like daily life as you would imagine it to be in a southern Kyrgyz city.

Then, I see a blackened house. Windows have disappeared. A burnt-out car wreck. Another house that has gone up in flames. Several more car wrecks. Black tree trunks whose branches and leaves have been devoured by a relentless fire. The closer we get to the center, the more burnt-out houses we see, until we drive past entire streets lined with ashen houses and cars. Witnesses of blind violence and destruction. It's quiet in the car. Even the goat is no longer kicking.

A little later, I walk through the streets looking for a hotel, which I find quickly. Getting hold of local money turns out to be difficult. All ATMs seem to have fallen prey to pyromaniacs. I expect that in these difficult times, foreign money should be in demand, but it turns out to be hard to exchange dollars. Once I have finally sorted out the practical matters, it's time for a walk through what feels like a war zone.

I head to Jayma Bazaar, the city's main market. Osh is the oldest city in the country and for centuries it was the principal city on the Silk Road within this region. I was curious about the Lonely Planet's description: *'The thunderous daily Jayma Bazaar is one of Central Asia's best markets, teeming with Uzbeks, Kyrgyz and Tajiks dealing in everything from traditional hats and knives to pirated cassettes, horseshoes (forged at smithies in the bazaar), Chinese tea sets and abundant seasonal fruits and vegetables. It stretches for about 1 km along the west side of the river and crosses it in several places.'* On the way there, I see a building with large, white letters written on it: MIR. Peace. Well, well.

When I arrive at the place where Jayma Bazaar once was, I see a large open area with only charred buildings. The smell of fire is in the air when I walk onto the field. Twisted steel, black houses, vanished walls. I can still see where stalls used to be. Stuff lies scattered on the ground. Kyrgyz men are walking around with looks of astonishment and bewilderment in their eyes. What happened here? They seem to have the same questions as I do. But who has the answers to those questions? Where are the traditional hats, the locally forged horseshoes, the knives, the Chinese tea sets, the fruit, the clandestine cassettes and all the other things that were traded here until recently?

Later that afternoon, I visit the country's only World Heritage Site: Solomon's Throne, the mountain that towers over the city. It's named after the prophet Solomon, who is said to be buried there. The prominent mountain is also probably the Stone Tower mentioned by Ptolemy, which supposedly marks the halfway point of the Silk Road. This mountain is normally a place of pilgrimage, but today there isn't a pilgrim to be seen. I'm alone on the mountain: the inhabitants of the city are busy clearing the ruins of the riots and don't have time for a stroll. I come to a tiny cave through which, in normal times, women would wriggle in order to have healthy children. As in more places in Central Asia, where hopeful women often roll down hills to get pregnant, I wonder what locals actually learn about reproduction. I see clothes hanging in trees, serving as prayer flags. There is a sprawling cemetery, but no fresh graves. Where did the thousands of war victims go?

At the closed museum on the other side of the hill, I run into a Kyrgyz TV team. As soon as they see me, they come running after me. A foreigner in Osh is a sight to behold during these difficult times. After gestures and words of English and Russian back and forth, I'm interviewed about the situation. I try to convey a neutral message as carefully as possible, saying that it's a pity that such a beautiful, historical city as Osh has suffered such great losses and that I hope peace will return as soon as possible.

That night, far away in South Africa, the Dutch national team plays the eighth final of the football World Cup. In my hotel, I find the match on Uzbek TV. There is no commentary during half-time, but instead a speech by Islam Karimov, who has ruled the country since 1991. After 15 minutes, the speech continues. The second half is never shown. However, the wifi is working and that's how I find out that the Netherlands have beaten Slovakia 2-1 and are through to the quarter-finals.

On the way to Bishkek, I make several excursions. In bad weather, I climb a mountain to see the waterfalls higher up and walk through the world's largest walnut forest near Arslanbob. On the way back, I see an Australian and an Austrian who look familiar. Suddenly, we remember: we saw each other a few months earlier on the Rocket boat in Bangladesh. For a short while, the world seems very small.

The country gets greener the lower and further north I get and when I finally walk around the capital, I feel the heat of summer after all. For the first time in over a month, I see women in miniskirts. Bishkek and the north of the country are Russian Orthodox and there is no strict dress code here. Coincidentally, I see some of the Swiss from Murgab sitting on a terrace. They say they have been worried about me and are happy to see me. According to one of the Swiss who once worked for Swissair, the flight from Dushanbe to Bishkek wasn't devoid of danger due to a faulty aircraft and non-compliance with regulations. This puts my decision to travel through Osh into perspective and shows once again that risks are often hard to assess beforehand.

After Bishkek, I continue my journey further east, along the huge Issyk-Kul Lake. By now, I'm often approached by people on the street and find out that they recognize me from the item about Osh they saw on TV. Looking south, I see gigantic, snow-capped mountains rising before me from the green landscape: the Tian Shan or Heavenly Mountains, which the country shares with China. In Karakul (yes, another village with that name, yet another Black Lake), I watch The Netherlands beat Brazil in the quarter-finals: 2-1. The Kyrgyz are clearly supporting my home country.

The next day, I take a taxi together with a policeman. The driver drops me off at the beginning of the Altyn-Arashan Valley, which I want to hike until I reach the Palatka Glacier. I check with him several times and he confirms just as many times that he dropped me off at the right place. Only after the officer has disembarked does he suddenly ask for ten times the amount of money we had agreed on. I keep the peaches that I had wanted to give him as a present and give him the agreed amount.

I don't have time to waste and I walk at a fast pace along the mountain path into the valley. The dew is still thick on the grass and in no time, I have soaking wet shoes, socks and trousers. After walking for an hour, I meet a couple of men and a small herd of cows. Young women come out of a house with a full bowl of milk in their hands, which they proudly give to me. It's made of metal and feels warm to the touch. As if the origin of this milk weren't already clear, they point at one of the cows and then at the bowl.

Exactly what I was afraid of: I don't like drinking milk from a carton at all, let alone the hot drink with lumps and strings of fat that I'm now being served. I can't refuse, so I decide to empty the bowl as quickly as possible, hoping I won't gag. To my surprise, the milk has a sweet taste and I keep it down. Before they can offer me a second bowl of milk, I ask if I'm on the right track to Altyn Arashan. They look at me with pity. No, that valley lies further east.

There is nothing to do but to walk back to where I started as soon as possible and enter the next valley. There, I find an unpaved road with coarse rocks. When I finally arrive in Altyn Arashan, I leave my bag in one of the six houses. After having eaten and drunk something, I hike further up. Around me are green meadows, a stream and pine trees on either side of the valley, with mountains reaching for the blue sky above. After a while, I come across a herd of horses on an island in the stream. When I approach, they run away, startled. Wild horses. Occasionally, I cross a tributary on a pair of tree trunks lying side by side. These makeshift bridges are the only sign that there must have been people here. There are no houses, no signposts, no rubbish. This area is pristine.

The valley splits: one branch bends to the east and I go along with it. The mountains around me get higher, their peaks covered with snow. There are no more logs crossing the tributary streams: every time I have to take off my shoes and socks, glide through the icy water over slippery stones, dry my feet, put everything back on and continue hiking. Sometimes the path is hardly visible. I see thick layers of ice and snow stuck to the steep slopes on the other side of the valley. Narrow waterfalls cascade down dozens of meters. But there is no trace of the Palatka Glacier, other than the flowing water in the small river next to me.

Meanwhile, my stomach starts to rumble. Have I eaten too little or did I move too much and too fast? In sports, you would call this hunger pangs. Every extra step I take, I will have to walk back and I also have to walk further on to Altyn Arashan. I set a deadline for turning around. When I reach it, I can't even see a glimpse of the glacier in the distance. I eat my penultimate Snickers, have a drink and turn around. It's at least another three hours of hiking. My legs make the movements necessary to go forward, as if they were automatic. My window of consciousness is getting smaller. The impressive images of this forgotten valley with its snow-covered mountains get lost on me. I am now walking in a daze. There is a boulder on the valley floor that I walk around without even giving it a thought.

And then it happens.

A brown bear appears from behind the big rock. He is coming straight at me. My eyes are drawn to his monstrous claws. My hair stands on end and goosebumps shoot up my arms. My heart skips a few beats. In a split second, a sharp burst of adrenaline spurts through my body. In a reflex, I throw my arms up in pure fright.

He stops a few meters in front of me. Every fiber in my body is awake now, my head is working overtime. Only later would I learn that you must never look a bear in the eye, but that is exactly what I do. I want to examine his expression, I want to make contact with him, I want to let him know that he has nothing to fear from me.

But before I can think what to do, the bear has already made his decision. The enormous beast turns around and walks away from me. His dangling tail looks whimsical. Maybe the raising of my arms gave him the impression that I looked bigger than I am? He is evidently not as hungry as I am.

For a moment, I'm still watching, aware that my right index finger is on the shutter button of my camera. In all my consternation, I forgot to take a picture of the predator. As I continue my descent, I keep repeating to myself: 'I've just seen a *brown bear!*' A few hundred meters further down the trail, my knees start to buckle and I sit down on a large stone. I allow myself to let everything sink in.

You hardly stand a chance against a bear, because it can do everything better and faster than people. You can run, you can climb, he's bound to get you. I know little about bears. Are they solitary creatures? Is it possible that there are others here? Are they staring at me now, from the occasional tufts of pine trees stuck against the slopes? Has this animal ever seen a human before?

The realization that I have to hurry to get back before dark makes me get up again and continue, after I have eaten the last Snickers. It's beginning to get dark. Behind all the rocks and under all the trees I can see shadows that look very much like bears. When I finally get back to the little house where I left my bag, I feel an enormous sense of exhilaration. I have made it! The only thing I want now is to eat and sleep a lot. What I also want is to shout from the rooftops that I have just seen a bear, but that seems a bit strange here, in a village of a few houses where nobody speaks English and a bear isn't as special as it is to me.

Eating turns out not to be so easy. After waiting a while for someone to come (they must have known I would be coming back because I had left my luggage behind), the owner of the homestay arrives. He tells me that the cook is drunk. It's no longer possible to eat. I go to the kitchen hoping that this is a joke, but the guy wasn't exaggerating. Not one sensible word is uttered by the cook who, leaning against the kitchen sink, is putting a bottle of vodka to his mouth with drowsy eyes.

I'm very upset, pack my stuff and walk off into the night. I don't want to spend the night here anymore. I have a choice of five houses, but there is light in only three. In desperation, I knock on the neighbor's door, even though it's dark inside. A young woman with an innocent smile and shining eyes opens the door and my little Russian language guide has enough written sentences to cope with situations like this. We manage the rest using gestures. Yes, I can sleep here if I don't mind sharing a room with five others. Yes, she can make sure I get something to eat.

When I step into the dim room, I see a bluish glow on the ceiling. In the middle of the room, a man is sitting at a table. His head is completely wrapped in white bandages. He supports his head with a fist. He is listening to bad, tinny Russian pop on his phone, which lies on the table in front of him. He is smoking a cigarette. When he sees me, all kinds of gibberish comes out of his mouth. Even if I spoke Russian, I wouldn't understand a word, because the man is even further gone than the cook who couldn't make me any food.

Meanwhile, the young lady starts cooking in a large pan on the stove. The bear is still on my mind – it will be for weeks – and I want to share the story with her. After browsing through my little language guide, I find the words to tell her that I have seen a brown bear. Funnily enough, there is no standard phrase in the 'Emergencies' chapter to make this clear. She looks at me in disbelief. I show her the words in the booklet: bear, see, me. She keeps staring at me with big eyes as she continues to stir the well-filled pan of soup.

That night, as soon as I close my eyes, the bear comes back to haunt me. I keep seeing an image of me walking around a rock and suddenly, a few steps away, seeing the bear coming towards me. I wake up regularly. The man with the bandage turns out to be a loud snorer; time and again I get up to turn him on his side. When I finally fall asleep, the bear comes back. The next morning I'm still far from rested and the bear is still haunting me. I wonder whether he is also thinking of me now?

The next day, I meet a local mountain guide who speaks reasonable English. When I tell him the story of the bear, he looks at me in surprise. He hasn't seen a bear for more than ten years. He usually guides groups in the region, but the chance of seeing a bear is much bigger if you're alone and you don't make any noise.

I clamber around for a day in the snowy mountains above Altyn Arashan, before returning to Issyk Kol. Further west in the green country, I go hunting with a *bürkütchü*, an eagle hunter. I can feel the iron grip of the mighty bird around my arm, even through the leather glove. The magnificent eagle has fabulous eyesight and catches a rabbit that runs a few hundred meters away. It brings it back to us and tears the furry animal apart. In a matter of minutes, little is left of the poor creature.

In Naryn, in an otherwise dark and empty room, I watch the semi-final of the Netherlands against Uruguay: 3-2. This time, no long speeches from the president. I would go on to see the lost final a few days later from a sterile hotel room in Hotan.

I manage to get a special permit to travel from Naryn to China. With a car and driver, I ride into the Tian Shan mountains. On the way, we stop in Tash Rabat, the last caravanserai of the Silk Road that I would see on this journey. Completely deserted. It's been a long time since travelers and horses stayed here on their long journey to the west. Once more, I'm at a high altitude. This time it's the Torugart pass that marks the border with China. The day ends in Kashgar – the legendary starting and finishing point of the Silk Road, a city I have looked forward to visiting for so many years that it has acquired a mythical status in my imagination.

But alas: I'm too late. Much too late. The Chinese have efficiently demolished the old city and only the old core remains, which has been set up as a place for sightseers. Around it, the prefab flats you see everywhere in China have been erected. It reminds me of how they raped Lhasa. Instead of enjoying a historic marketplace, a melting pot of traders from the surrounding countries, the variety of colorful hats and caps, instead of summing up my long journey through the fascinating cultures of Central Asia and experiencing the beginning and end of the Silk Road, I feel indignation and anger.

I manage to slip in early in the morning before the old city opens, pursued by Chinese ticket ladies who shout at me that I must pay. Paying to see how the Chinese are destroying this traditional city: I cannot and will not do it and I run faster than the desperate women who aren't used to such disobedience. When they finally leave me alone, I see what the houses look like from the inside. In many places, the walls have already been demolished, while the furniture is still in the rooms and a forgotten shower curtain flutters in the open air.

Chapter 9
The Iron Lady in the Jungle

Gabon/Congo – 2013

As he walks away from the car, the policeman carelessly holds my passport between his thumb and index finger, as if it were a dirty piece of junk that he wants to dispose of in a dustbin as quickly as possible. The driver of my *taxi-brousse* urges me to go after him. Drizzle whirls down silently from a solid gray sky through the thick tropical air as I get out and walk towards the man with my passport. Am I mistaken, or is there a waft of alcohol swirling in the air behind him?

I catch up with him and when I ask for my document, he takes me to a shabby little office by the side of the road without even looking at me. Calling it an office would be an exaggeration: it's more like a shed with a rickety wooden table inside. He turns around so that I can see him for the first time. I look into a paunchy face, from which two eyes seem almost to be squeezed out from the inside. They are more like the eyes of a crocodile than those of a human being. They radiate infinite stupidity, boredom, laziness, contempt. His green and brown spotted uniform is like a corset around him. A fat belly tries to force its way out: two buttons are about to pop. His body altogether lacks the elegance of the crocodile.

This discussion sounds familiar.

'Three thousand francs.'

'Why should I pay three thousand francs?'

'If you pay me, I will give your passport back.'

'Could you tell me why I should pay you? Is my visa not valid? Is there a problem with the passport? Are my vaccinations not in order? If you can tell me what the violation is, I am of course willing to pay the corresponding fine.' I try to sound as ignorant as possible.

'Three thousand francs and you get your passport.'

Here I am, hitting that same wall again and hearing the same childishness. Not even attempting subtlety while trying to extort money from me. First, seize something, then ask for a ransom, as if he were holding a hostage. *This passport is the property of the State of the Netherlands*. It says so unambiguously: even I have it on loan from my government. Yet here in Central Africa, it's confiscated time and again and used as a means of extortion. At the dozens of previous checkpoints, my blunt refusal to pay had caused doubt, or surprise, or indifference, so that I eventually got my passport back, or I could snatch it away in an unguarded moment. But this time it feels different. Outside, a dark green Toyota pick-up truck with more than ten people inside is waiting for me. My luggage is piled up with a whole load of other stuff in cardboard boxes, tied up on the back of the Japanese car that is almost falling through its rear wheels.

The officer knows that all factors are lined up in his favor. The car won't wait forever. I also won't wait indefinitely. The afternoon is drawing to a close, the short twilight is approaching and the first suburbs of Libreville are still more than an hour away. Three thousand francs is, well, a few euros. So, with complete confidence, he lays my passport on the far corner of the table, looks out of the glassless window, pretends not to see me and waits for me to throw three crumpled thousand notes on the table with contempt.

I have just come from Equatorial Guinea. I'm glad to have left that country behind, where a dictator begrudges his people the light in their eyes, steals everything there is to steal and thus sets an example for all the lesser gods of his government apparatus to do the same on a much smaller scale. Back in Gabon, I'm reminded that here too, cops are a visitor's worst enemy – and for that matter, the enemy of the vast majority of its residents. They see every passer-by, and certainly the foreign kind, as a walking ATM from which you can withdraw money without a PIN code.

So, am I going to pay to get out of this and get my passport back? No way!

Just as the officer ignores me, I pretend not to look at him either. In the meantime, I keep a close eye on him from the corner of my eye. When he looks away for a second, my moment has come. In a flash, I dash forward and grab my passport. The crocodile is faster than I thought. He stands closer, his arm reflexively snatches at the table and his fist clasps around my passport a millisecond before my hand. He holds it in an iron grip. While I hold his fist, he does his best to do as much damage to my passport as possible. Fortunately, the plasticized page containing my details is strong enough to withstand his violence; I can hear the other pages crumpling under his force. I can't tear the passport from his hand, no matter how hard I try.

It's practically arm-wrestling without a table and then, suddenly, we're lying on the ground. The policeman on top of me, me on top of him: we roll over and over, the passport in the middle, neither of us intending to let go. As we spin around like this, I try to see if there are any witnesses and I notice that he is wearing a service pistol around his belt. But my anger at his attempts to kidnap and then destroy my passport, making my stay here much more complicated, is greater than my caution. We growl, we scream and we roll on. Now that his face is close to mine, I know for sure. He has been drinking and is determined not to give up.

Meanwhile, a group of Gabonese watches this unannounced spectacle. Their respect and sacred awe of authority prevent them from taking action, from intervening. This has often surprised me in these parts. No matter what a policeman does, a Central African almost always resigns himself to his fate, continues to show respect and eventually submits to what the authority demands of him. I'm beginning to wonder how this will end. The policeman won't let go of what may be his last chance of the day to contribute to his next bottle of whisky. I can't go on without a passport and I'm not going to pay for it. A classic Catch-22.

Then the officer stops rolling and turns his head away, towards the road. I follow his gaze: a line of brand new, white suvs drives past, slows down and stops. A distinguished-looking gentleman opens his window and gestures for us to report to him, one by one. In the confusion about the procession of cars, I have managed to get my passport out of the merciless fists of the officer. The policeman goes first and I hear him ranting and raving, occasionally gesturing at me with his sausage-like arms. When he has finished, I report to the car. It turns out that I'm talking to the Minister of Justice, who is on his way back to town. I show my passport to the Minister, with the rumpled pages: proof of the traces of the fight, proof against the police-man. I think. I hope.

He gives orders through his phone, asks us to wait and drives off. Another policeman arrives and scolds me. What am I thinking, as a foreigner? You rich white guy, why do you come here? Why are you going against the authority of my colleague? Why do you travel by shared taxi? You are rich: hire a car with a driver! I'm startled by his tone, his aggression, his words. I hold my passport tightly.

I feel a lot less confident than when I took back the passport and wonder how this will end. Which auxiliary troops has the minister called in? Are they favorable to me, or not? When a couple of hotshots show up in their flashy cars and shiny suits, I still don't know the answer and as we climb a hill to a larger building, I feel a knot in my stomach. Who knows when I will get out of here. Who knows if my Toyota will still be there and where my luggage, which I left in the boot, will be. For now, miraculously, the car is still there and the passengers are still in it, waiting for me. Nobody objects. The only question is how long their patience will last.

Once we're in the building, the gentlemen direct us to a room with a desk. Soon after we're seated, it becomes clear which way the wind is blowing. The high-ranking gentlemen exhaust themselves in apologies. They claim that Gabon wants to attract more tourism, but what has happened here is surely not an advertisement for the country! Did the officer really ask for money? More apologies: corruption is strictly forbidden in Gabon. This must have been an unfortunate, exceptional inci-dent. I don't tell them about the countless other checkpoints in this country where, although less aggressively, they were defi-nitely after money. About the awful witch in the Gabonese embassy in Yaoundé who shrieked through the marble hall against all potential visitors to her country who had got it into their heads to apply for a costly visa. Not much of an advertisement for the country either.

When they look at the policeman, their gazes are toxic. Surely, they will have smelt his alcohol breath. After a while, he starts to cry softly. Still, I just can't manage to feel sorry for him. He doesn't look like a crocodile anymore, but like a pathetic human being. Even his service pistol suddenly looks helpless. I accept the apologies of my rescuers, cast a last glance at the huddled man in uniform who almost literally kicked me out of his hut half an hour before and quickly head for my taxi.

Fortunately, it's still there, with my fellow travelers and my luggage. I get in as if nothing has happened, nobody asks me anything and we drive on towards the city. From the station of the *taxi-brousses*, I take a bus to the train station. There, I discover that someone has managed to steal some change from one of my pockets in the dark. A little later, I plonk myself down on the night train to Franceville, in the southeast of the country. A real railway: the pride of Gabon, proof that it wants to belong to the vanguard of African countries.

Franceville. Gabon is one of the few former French colonies in Africa where France still has a good reputation. So good, in fact, that they have named their easternmost city after it. It turns out to be a quiet provincial town, much more pleasant than the capital, Libreville. It's lovely to walk around, if only because the temperature is much more pleasant than at the coast. I visit the wide Poubara waterfall and the ancient liana bridge in the dense jungle an hour south of the city. As in so many countries in Africa, the Chinese have come here to build a hydroelectric power station – who knows what resources they will get in return for their everlasting hunger for African raw materials.

I make a two-day excursion to the jungle with a guide. As so often, I'm struck by how friendly and honest the people are, and how much they contrast with the authorities, who more often than not, cause problems. The same goes for this guide: he has a sense of humor, is eloquent, patient, knows his stuff and is keen to show me the best of his country.

We're looking for forest elephants. The longer we walk through the dense wilderness, the more unlikely it seems that we will see them. Apart from the fact that they are difficult to spot in the abundant vegetation, they are, after all, heavily hunted in these parts, where borders are porous and it's easy for poachers to escape. Moreover, it's virtually impossible to patrol this practically impenetrable jungle and there is always the possibility of bribing the rangers.

After spending the night in a tent, followed by a long morning walk, the guide suddenly stretches out his arm, turns his head and urges me to be quiet. In front of us, in the middle of the river, I see ripples in the water and then – still unexpectedly – the water breaks. The gray mass of a forest elephant rises from the creek. The water drips from his tusks as his legs push the bulky body up out of the gooey mud. He walks through the water slowly enough for us to keep up with him along the bank. We follow him for a while, sitting silently behind a rotting tree trunk to observe him as best we can, while he sprays himself with his trunk. We decide to follow his example, take off our shirts and freshen up in the river, at a respectful distance from the juggernaut.

The next day, I arrive at Léconi, the last town before the border with Congo. I visit a deserted canyon with red-white-brown colors. In other parts of the world, hordes of people would be standing here to see this extraordinary landscape. But I have it all to myself. This is my last stop in Gabon: from here, I will travel to Congo. The former French Congo: Congo-Brazzaville.

I still have to find transportation and that turns out to be difficult. On my walk through Léconi, I see only a few cars parked alongside the dusty streets. The only petrol station in the town turns out to be lacking in petrol. I think it's better to wait at the border post until someone passes by who is heading east. Someone takes me to the border crossing on the back of his moped over an excellent asphalt road. The official in the small building proves to be extremely helpful, offers me a chair and lets me sit there for hours. Every once in a while, I hear a motorized vehicle approaching and go outside. But no one is crossing the border.

Meanwhile, I'm watching a tiny TV. Margaret Thatcher passed away a few weeks earlier and I'm watching a documentary about her political career. Outside, the afternoon light shines in ever softer and warmer tones over the undulating African landscape. I hear French around me, while the black and white images on the screen throw me back to the eighties. Images of the Falklands/Malvinas, of political intrigue in London, of speeches, triumphs and betrayals. One of the remarkable political leaders of my youth, remembered in a booth of the Gabonese immigration service. Narrated in French by a Gabonese journalist. The Iron Lady, or Dame de Fer as the French call her, with her inseparable handbag, demanding that the United Kingdom should get its money back and should have an exceptional position within Europe. Who says 'No, no, no' to proposals to further integrate the EU. How was Brexit unexpected? It was already on the cards back then.

Then, the officer on duty enters and pulls me out of the eighties. A car has arrived that will cross the border. The driver's name is Kemajou, a Cameroonian from Bafoussam. I immediately hit it off with this tall, bearded man, if only because I had been in his city a few weeks earlier, which he is delighted to hear. Of course, we don't leave right away. He first has to gather enough freight before he can leave. We negotiate a price: he would have been carrying only goods and no passengers in his Toyota pick-up, so he is doing me a favor. He takes me back to Léconi, where I can stay in the hotel I had previously checked out of, until my departure. On the way, he has a loud argument with a Gabonese man who has a load of tomatoes for him. I can't quite follow what it's about, but I do know that there is a lot of shouting back and forth.

Officially, I have already been stamped out of the country; I hope we can leave before midnight to avoid any awkward questions. Finally, it's half-past ten in the evening when Kemajou comes to fetch me. His pickup is full of round barrels containing petrol. They are tied together with worn-out rope, with fuel dripping here and there. It's puzzling: the petrol station is dry, so where did he get it? I always have the same amazement at how things work in Africa – despite having traveled around the continent extensively. The tomatoes didn't make it.

Kemajou has a co-driver, which I'm glad about because it will be a long ride through the night. There is room for me on the back seat, where a man from Benin also appears to be sitting. Of course, I'm not the only passenger and the inside of the car is packed with all kinds of things that have to cross the border. We squeeze ourselves in between the piled-up boxes and after five minutes we stop and people jump on top of the barrels of petrol in the boot. When I look back through an opening, I see more than ten guys sitting on the barrels, some of them lighting cigarettes. I remember the leaking petrol, have visions of a huge explosion and feel like we're sitting on a moving time bomb. I hold my breath.

Shortly after passing the post where I spent that afternoon watching images of Thatcher and where my friends wave me goodbye, we leave the lovely black tarmac behind us. It will be a while before I see asphalt again. We drive through dense vegetation over a loose sandy path, the people on the containers are constantly hit by the overhanging branches of trees along the road. When we stop somewhere to let someone else climb onto the fully loaded pick-up, I urge Kemajou to ask our fellow passengers not to smoke. I can't let go of my vision of an explosion, but he doesn't see any risk. Not much later, we stop at a house. We can only see what the headlights are shining onto, everything else is pitch black. The passengers jump off the containers and disappear into the night – the risk of an explosion has now diminished considerably, and I feel a bit safer.

We continue our way, the lights of the car piercing through the complete darkness of this rough no man's land. Kemajou has unquestionably done this before: he steers us without hesitation through the deep sand of the winding road. It's impossible to sleep, if only because the car is shaking constantly. Have we already crossed the border? I may have been stamped out of Gabon, but I still haven't seen a Congo border post, even though we have been on the road for hours.

I get into a conversation with the Béninois next to me. Daniel. He tells me about the message he received yesterday: his mother has passed away and will be buried within a few days. According to him, the quickest way is via Brazzaville and although it seems completely illogical, I suppose he is right. Even today, the shortest connections in Africa, in terms of travel time, are often very different from what you would expect based on geography because of the lack of infrastructure, transportation, or a combination of both. The fastest connection between neighboring African countries may even be through Europe.

Just when my head starts to nod, Kemajou slows down and we drive into an insignificant village. It's half-past three. All I can see are silhouettes of huts. Only the trajectory of light from our headlights shows a few seconds of the buildings before they dissolve into darkness again.

'La frontière,' says the driver.

He knows what he's doing: he drives straight to one of the huts and gets out while letting the engine run. In the bright light of the lamps, I see a man, barefoot and dressed in a T-shirt and shorts, come out. He holds his hand in front of his eyes so as not to be blinded, walks to the car and climbs onto the remaining barrels of petrol.

We drive on for a few hundred meters and all get out. I'm glad to be able to stretch my legs. We walk behind the man. He opens the door of a hut, walks into the darkness and lights a candle. In the flickering light, he beckons us inside. I now see that his T-shirt is faded and worn, with dark brown stripes. He asks Daniel and me for our documents. Not the driver and his co-driver: they are crossing the border undocumented and will undoubtedly pay for it in some form or other.

When he has put our passports on a table, the man takes a phone from his khaki trousers, switches on the light and shines over the pages. He inspects all the pages of my passport and I help him find the visa for Congo that I obtained a week before in Libreville. Then he demands money to enter the country. He also claims that I need a separate permit for this border area. Here we go again. I had already asked the embassy about this and they assured me that my visa was valid for the whole country and that I could cross any border. My refusal to pay brings a deep frown to his forehead: he expects to be compensated for this nightly bureaucracy. To my surprise, he says he will check my words with his superior. He switches off the light of his phone, turns it around and keys in a number. If he is upset about the unwanted disturbance of his sleep, what will his boss say about his calling him in the middle of the night? Where is this superior, by the way?

It seems hard to believe, but his boss actually answers this night-time phone call. Even more surprising: he agrees with me on all points. With visible reluctance, the official switches the light of his phone back on and stamps my passport. He tries to ask for money for the stamp and a permit from the Béninois as well. I stand up for my travel companion out of compassion for his deceased mother and ask the man with the power of the stamp to treat him the same way he treated me. After all, we both have similar visas and we are both on the way to Brazzaville. Daniel's passport now gets stamped as well. Kemajou seems surprised that we got away so easily when we get into the car a little later and drive on, after we have taken the man back to his hut so he can continue sleeping.

When dawn breaks a few hours later, we find ourselves driving under a gray sky. It has been raining here: Kemajou is steering our car over slippery mud tracks. He is doing all he can to keep the car on the road. Then, all of a sudden, we find ourselves half capsized in a bush. The co-driver, Daniel and I manage to push the car back onto the road while our feet disappear into the dark red mud. Fortunately, all the petrol drums have been delivered by now. Otherwise, it would have been impossible. We skid off the road again and once more we manage to put the car back on the dirt track. We lose so much time because of all the slipping and sliding that when we arrive in Ewo, a small town in the midwest of Congo, we find out that we have missed the once-daily bus to Brazzaville. I don't feel like staying here and Daniel also wants to move on. We manage to charter two young lads to take us east to Oyo on their motorbikes. That is where the tarmac starts and from there, buses depart regularly for Brazzaville. We agree on a price, based on their estimate that the journey will take a few hours.

After our luggage has been firmly tied to the vehicles, we can just about squeeze ourselves in between the luggage and the rider. Before we even leave the village, I wonder whether we made the right decision. We ride eighty kilometers per hour on a gravel road, without helmets: every pothole is a potential killer. The guys are still at the age of overconfidence and making an impression, steering their bikes from left to right to catch the fastest part of the track.

But this speeding doesn't last long. Before we know it, we're sliding through the mud. Sometimes I sink to my knees in the wet muck while my rider pushes the bike through it. I often have to dismount. In no time, all four of us are covered in clay. To my amazement, the riders manage to get their bikes started again every time we get stuck. Soon I hope the road consists of mud because whenever the surface is hard, the guys try to make up for the lost time by racing far too fast over the bumpy road.

On the way, we're overtaken by a pickup truck whose driver tells us to stop. It turns out to be the immigration officer from Ewo. He wants to check our documents and warns me that terrorists from the north are targeting foreigners here. When we hear that he is on his way to Boundji, which lies in the direction of Oyo, our bike riders ask if he can offer us a ride. Unfortunately, this is out of the question, so we get back on the bikes and plough on.

The rainy season has begun early: we encounter long stretches of all but impassable roads, where we have to dismount and plod dozens of meters through the goo. When we reach a clearing in the forest, I see three four-wheel-drives stuck in the thick brown mire. The occupants are trying with all their might to get the stranded vehicles going again. One of the cars belongs to the immigration official and our brave bike chaps explain that, given his position, they should help.

When a truck arrives, I hope it can solve the problem, but alas: it too sinks into the unforgiving mud. The men try everything. Parts of a tree are put under the wheels, the cars are pushed, the strongest men try to lift one of the cars out of the mud while the driver hits the pedal. In the end, it takes more than four hours before all vehicles are freed from their misery. As a gesture of gratitude for our help, we're now allowed to ride in the back of the immigration official's pickup truck. We pay our riders, who still have a long way to go before they are back in Ewo. They may not have brought us to Oyo by a long shot, but they have already spent much more time on the road than we had imagined beforehand.

It gets lighter as the day draws to a close. A late afternoon sun breaks through the low gray cloud cover, the landscape opens up, the road gets harder. I'm beginning to enjoy the vast vistas, the villages we pass, the children who call out to me. Sometimes we plough through deep pools of water like a boat, the bow wave hitting the rear wheels so that the worst of the mud cake is washed off.

We're dropped off in the main street of Boundji. We see a taxi-brousse to Oyo and have already confiscated two seats in the shared taxi when a policeman shows up and tells us to come with him to the station. There are three more policemen inside. At the sight of us and our passports, a glow of greed slides over the faces of the men. A stroke of luck. Two foreigners, that will make up for a day of boredom! They lock our passports in a drawer of the office (again, taking our travel documents hostage) and start looking for as many clues as possible to make money out of this. Did the immigration officer who just dropped us off know about this? Why didn't he immediately help us into the taxi-brousse?

The European is, of course, the most interesting. I have to open my luggage and I watch powerlessly while they turn every-thing they find inside out. Clothing, clean and dirty. Shoes, wash bag, book, electronics: everything is taken out of my bag as a trophy and held up in the air. With every object, they say: 'Un cadeau!' Every time I respond, 'No, it's not a gift.' They are so insolent, they even want to take away my mosquito repellant, my malaria pills, the last drop of water I have left behind, yes, even my condoms are considered possible booty, although they themselves laugh about their attempt to confiscate them.

Fortunately, my money belt with the cash in it remains unnoticed: it's invisibly tied around my waist. I stand my ground, trying with all my might to contain my anger, demanding not only my luggage, but also my passport. I'm amazed when they eventually give everything back. I pack everything again, close my luggage and remain seated. They turn to my traveling companion. I'm convinced that now they have blown the whistle on me, they will let him go for the simple reason that I'm white.

The opposite turns out to be true. First, Daniel is also subjected to an impudent baggage check. Then, they ask him to pay because his visa isn't valid in this region. At that moment, I stand in for my over-tired and sad friend. I explain as kindly as I can that we have had a long night of traveling, that we have the same kind of visa, that we're traveling together and if they could please let us through because our car is waiting outside. This interference isn't appreciated: an officer escorts me outside. There, I tell him without beating about the bush that the poor man is on his way to his mother's funeral, far away from here, and ask him for clemency. The man shrugs his shoulders and orders me not to come in.

After ten minutes of waiting, my patience is exhausted. When I step inside again, I see in a flash that the Béninois' wrists are bound together with handcuffs. His head is bent forward and when he looks up at me, I see tears running down his cheeks. His mother is dead, he hasn't slept for at least twenty-four hours, he helped push our pickup out of the mud, survived a perilous ride on the back of a motorbike, and now he is being handcuffed when his only crime is not wanting to give money to the cops.

I can't restrain myself any longer and I ask what on earth they are doing, to which the men reply that he hadn't confessed how much money he was carrying. One of them adds that I have nothing to do with it and orders me to leave. When I make it clear that I have no intention of doing so without Daniel, two policemen lift me up, push me outside, shove me and my luggage into the car that's still waiting for us and instruct the driver to leave with an empty seat. Daniel's seat.

I protest, try to get out, try to make it clear to the driver that I want to stay, but he starts to drive, spurred on by the cops outside and the people in the back seat. Around me is still that peculiar early-evening light of equatorial Africa, even warmer than before. I don't notice it anymore: a deep feeling of disgust runs through my body. I feel like a traitor and I'm afraid that Daniel will be picked clean now. No one knows he is there, they can do what they want with him without ever having to account for it. Even though I did what I could, the feeling that I let Daniel down leaves a bitter taste in my mouth. Will he be in time for his own mother's funeral? I will never know.

The driver of the car turns out to be a nice man. I tell the story of Daniel and the greedy, inhumane police to him and the other passengers. They are all upset: handcuffing a man on his way to his mother's funeral for money – you don't do that. That is too far. For the umpteenth time, it strikes me how honest and human the 'ordinary man' is and how this contrasts with the behavior of the authorities. A few days later, a Ghanaian Muslim in Brazzaville will confirm this image. He tells me how the police regularly come to the mosque during evening prayers. How the Muslims, as soon as they walk out of their house of prayer, are surrounded by policemen who take their money from them in the darkness.

When we finally drive into Oyo, the night has long since fallen. Driving on to Brazzaville is out of the question. The driver somehow feels that he has something to make up for and wants to give me a better image of Congo. He offers me a bed in his house and then takes me out to dinner. Soon, an attractive young woman joins us: his *cousin*. When I walk behind the restaurant to pee behind a tree (there are no toilets here), she suddenly stands close behind me. Before I know it, she grabs my right hand and puts it on her left breast and her other hand slides to my crotch while she whispers sensual words in my ear.

Later, when we drive back to the driver's house, he can't understand why I don't want to take his *cousin* to my room. He still seems disappointed when I retire alone to let all the events of the last twenty-four hours sink in. He had wished me a wild night to improve his country's image. But the vision of Daniel sitting on a bench in handcuffs and bent, surrounded by policemen who are after his money, is still burnt into my mind. No lascivious Congolese can change that.

CHAPTER 10
THE PACIFIC SOLUTION

Kiribati/Nauru – 2012

I had managed to get three months off, so I could start planning a trip to the South Pacific. A gigantic region, unknown to me, with countries I had hardly heard of: Vanuatu, Tuvalu, Kiribati and particularly: Nauru? For years, somewhere in the back of my mind (and I admit, not hindered by any relevant knowledge), I had had the image that the whole region would be a boring affair and that all those little islands would look alike. White beaches, a few palm trees, turquoise water and people frolicking in reed skirts through an idyllic but ultimately dull landscape.

Once I started reading up, I soon realized that I could throw those stereotypes overboard. It turned out to be a region of atolls, certainly, but also of enormous islands with mountains and volcanoes, ruins of ancient cultures, recent remains of man-eaters and many relics of the Second World War that played havoc there in a much more gruesome way than we realize in faraway Europe. The more I read about it, the more I realized that for some countries, a few weeks would be the minimum to do it any justice. Three months suddenly seemed far too little. It would turn out to be the most surprising region of all my travels.

I soon found out that it would be quite a challenge to travel between the different countries. I had to forget about my naive dream of sailing from one island to another. That was only possible if you had a lot of time (or even better: a private yacht). Three months was far too short for that. For the most part, there were only supply ships that sailed irregularly. It was also not easy to fly: flights sometimes went only once or twice a week and logical routes were often non-existent. For instance, there were no flights between Tuvalu and Kiribati in the north, even though they are neighboring countries, and you had to fly via Fiji, which lies some distance to the south.

However, reaching Nauru proved even more difficult. Two flights a month. I soon realized that I had to plan my three months around Nauru. When I finally put the puzzle together, I ended up with over thirty flights between the nine countries I wanted to visit. I couldn't avoid booking all of them in advance. While I normally prefer not to book anything at all, in order to retain as much freedom as possible, I couldn't afford to miss any of the rare flights available. Fiji was to be my base: Air Pacific (later renamed Fiji Airways) had a monopoly over the region.

In my preparation, I saw that Nauru was also the only country in the area for which I needed a visa. That seemed a formality: a ticket and hotel reservation were sufficient. Since I already had the ticket, I only had to book a hotel. Just to be sure, I started looking for one well in advance, even though the task seemed simple: there were only two hotels in Nauru. I wrote to both of them but got no response. A follow-up email went unanswered, and I didn't hear back from a third one either. When I phoned them, no one answered the call. I approached the consulate in Brisbane and they once again underlined the strict condition of a hotel booking for the visa. My argument that it's difficult to book a hotel when none of them react fell on deaf ears.

In desperation, I started emailing Fabiana, the representative of Our Airline. This was the cute name of Nauru's national airline, which was called Air Nauru until it went belly-up in 2005. A curious service: it's based in Brisbane, with a fleet of exactly one Boeing 737. Fabiana tried her best but couldn't help me out either. She could confirm that there were indeed only two hotels on the island and advised me to keep trying.

My South Pacific journey started in September. Through Hong Kong, I flew to Auckland, where I went hiking for a few days to get used to the ten-hour time difference. Then I flew on to Fiji, Tonga, Fiji again, Tuvalu, Fiji once more to end up in Kiribati. Pronounced: Kiribas. Meanwhile, I still hadn't managed to make contact with the hotels and I was beginning to get worried. On the way, I sent another couple of emails, I bought a telephone card in Tonga to call from sandy telephone boxes, but no matter what I tried: no response. After Kiribati, Nauru was the next stop on my complicated itinerary and the pivot around which the rest revolved. Getting the visa was becoming an urgent matter.

Meanwhile, another problem came up. A few months earlier, Australia had relaunched the *Pacific Solution*, the controversial program to receive boat people on various islands in the Pacific. Nauru was one of them. The country was in serious need of hard currency and had opened its doors again to asylum seekers, mostly coming from the Middle East. They had traveled halfway around the world in an attempt to build a new life in Australia – far from the misery they were fleeing. But they had gone in the wrong direction, for Australia was ruthless and threw these people into camps on Nauru and Manus Island, in appalling conditions and without any prospect of leaving in whichever direction. The last thing Nauru wanted was prying eyes. With only two hundred visitors a year, tourism is negligible; any visitor in this politically sensitive situation is suspect from the start.

Eventually, Fabiana managed to put me in touch with an employee of one of the two hotels, the Od-N Aiwo, and he sent me a confirmation of the reservation within a few days. There were only two days to go before my flight to Nauru and I emailed the consulate in Brisbane with relief.

Nevertheless, it was not enough. The consulate official replied that only a letter printed on the official paper of the hotel would be accepted. An email wasn't enough. Now the penny dropped. The consulate had no intention to issue me a visa at all and kept posing new conditions that were impossible to meet. I sent another desperate email to Fabiana and to my surprise, a few hours later I received an email from the consulate that I could get a visa upon arrival at the airport. Fabiana had been able to pull the right strings after all. I was extremely relieved: the last missing piece of my Pacific puzzle would now be laid, whereas a day earlier I had almost given up. All the tension that had built up over the previous weeks suddenly fell away.

That relief, however, turned out to be short-lived.

The day before my planned departure, I go to the office of Our Airline in Bairiki, the part of Tarawa that serves as the 'capital' of Kiribati, to confirm my flight. A formality. While I wait my turn, I look at the employee on duty who is sitting at the desk under the Our Airline advertising posters. She is seriously over-weight. This region is notorious for its obese population. The first ten countries in the international ranking of overweight people can all be found in the Pacific.

When it's my turn, I sit down at the desk, pull out my ticket and ask the lady behind the table to confirm my flight. She looks at the date and says in passing that the flight has been canceled. I'm shocked and ask her what that means.

'That means, Mr. Kester, that we will rebook you on the next flight. That flight leaves in a fortnight.' She looks at me as if she is doing me a huge favor and expects gratitude, turns back to her screen and continues typing on her keyboard.

My head is spinning. Yesterday I was in a jubilant mood after receiving the confirmation that I would get the visa on arrival. All I had to do was fly to Nauru. Now, everything has been turned upside-down. The flight canceled? My carefully constructed row of dominoes, with all the flights in the region, is about to be sabotaged as she removes the piece in the middle. Waiting two weeks is simply impossible.

'Wait a minute, I have a ticket, I have follow-up tickets from Nauru to Fiji and then on to other destinations. Everything is organized around this one flight. How can we solve this problem?'

'There is no solution. I can offer to accept you for the flight in a fortnight.' She is no longer looking at me and goes on to other things.

I feel light-headed. This can't be true! After going through so much trouble for the visa, after planning my whole three-month journey around this one flight, it's canceled and the airline isn't even attempting to help me, to see if there is another possibility? Frustration, anger, disappointment and powerlessness rush through my body. I leave the office, wanting to cool down first.

When I go back in, the lady has disappeared. She turns out to be in another room. I walk up to her, explain how important this is to me and ask if she really can't find a solution. She still isn't looking at me and I'm not even sure if she's listening. When I have finished talking, she says nothing. She is busy working at her computer. When I take a closer look, I see that she is chatting with friends. I put my ticket next to her: maybe she needs my details? She immediately pushes it away, says without looking that I can take the flight two weeks later, free of charge, and continues messaging her friends. I understand that I can't get any further with her and ask if I can speak to her manager.

Finally, she looks at me, telling me to go away. I ask for her manager again, but now she starts screaming: 'Go away!' I tell her that I'm staying until she takes action, whereupon she grabs her phone and starts calling. She speaks in Gilbertese, so I don't understand a word. When I hear my name, I know she's talking about me and decide to record the call on my phone. Then she turns around, sees the phone I'm holding in my hand, immediately understands what I'm doing and loses the little decorum that was left.

Her face distorts into that of an inflamed, rotund witch. She wriggles out of her chair and staggers towards me, her huge legs rubbing together with every step she takes. She sits down on me with her full weight, clutching for my phone with her sausage-like arms. The huge mass on my body forces the air out of my lungs. I'm just about able to stretch my arm out far enough so her gripping hands can't reach it. But I have no idea how to get out from under her or how long I can keep this up. Growling sounds coming from deep within her indicate that only one thing matters to her now: to take my phone and make the recording stop. Until now, obesity was a meaningless number to me, a BMI of over thirty. Now, for the first time, I feel what that actually means. My lungs have already been squeezed dry and I don't know how much longer my muscles and bones can take it. Besides, is the chair I'm sitting on designed for such a heavy load?

To my relief, two policemen appear in the office. I don't know what they are doing here but consider them my liberators. In a way, they are, because when they enter, my attacker stands up. It soon transpires that they haven't come to rescue me, but to take me to the police station, with phone and dented body. So that's what her phone call was about.

At the police station, I make a statement and file a complaint against the Our Airline employee. Now that they have heard my side of the story, the officers understand that it's different than they had thought based on that phone call. Who knows what the lady made them believe?

They advise me to go to the Australian High Commissioner for assistance. I walk straight there and am received as if I had an Australian passport. Allison, the lady in charge, takes the time to listen to me. She is shocked by my story and offers all possible help. She invites me to use the consulate's swimming pool to relax, but that's not what I'm after. I do enjoy her fascinating stories about Nauru, where she has lived and worked for years. She gives me the book *A Pattern of Islands* by Arthur Grimble, who lived here for decades after the end of the First World War. It's a fascinating book that gives me an insight into the time when Kiribati was still a British colony and was called the Gilbert Islands.

When I pass a school on the way back to my hotel, some of the pupils are running into the schoolyard. I stop to have a look. One of the teachers beckons me through the gate and before I know it, I'm surrounded by screaming kids. I take pictures of them, which only adds to the cheering. They jostle with each other to get to the front of the queue and now even more children are coming out of the school towards us. I talk to the teacher, who introduces me to the headmistress. She asks me to come inside, rummages around in her desk and pulls out a decorated handmade dagger with dozens of tiny shark teeth on the cutting edges. She proudly hands it to me: a memento of Kiribati.

As I walk on, with the special souvenir in my rucksack, I find not only peace but also the good feeling I had since arriving in this island nation. In the previous days, I felt exciting energy that made me very happy. People waved at me. Children ran up to me and posed for photos. I saw a traditional dance with Kiribati women in reed skirts. I received coconuts from a few kids on my long walk across the east end of Tarawa atoll when I was severely thirsty and had to keep walking to avoid being trapped by the rising tide. I was greeted with openness and a touch of surprise by everyone. That solid serpent from Our Airline is an exception here.

Back in the Utirerei hotel, Nei Maseta, Nei Taam and Apaula, the friendly girls at the reception, listen to my story and sympathize with me. I send another email to Fabiana. Now that I think about it again, I realize the nature of the problem. If the only aircraft of Our Airline does indeed have a technical defect that can't be fixed, it's simply impossible to carry out the flight.

Especially if the airline isn't willing or able to lease another plane or have another airline operate the flight. It's difficult for me to sleep. On the day I was supposed to fly to Nauru, I decide to go to the other side of the atoll. I want to get away from it all, away from all the hassle or, if you like, bury my head in the sand for a while.

On the outrigger canoe that takes me to the other side, the Pacific breeze blows through my hair and I finally find peace. I leave my bag in the only accommodation and rent a bike, but the chain breaks after riding ten kilometers on sandy roads. After the major setback of the previous day, this is precisely what I do not need. I trudge back over the sand, trying to assess whether I will make it back before sunset. Then, a small lorry comes up behind me, its loading bay full of women.

Fortunately, my bicycle and I still fit in. The women are cheerful and sing the whole ride back to the village. I have no idea what they are singing about – probably love. I feel an energetic lust for life. Meanwhile, they look in amazement at the stranger with his broken bicycle and their laughter is so infectious that in the end I can do nothing but laugh with them. I even have time to go for a walk on the dry seabed to watch the sun sink into the immense ocean. That night, during a restless sleep in a primitive room, my mind can't let go of Nauru and Our Airline's timetable, until I get a flash of inspiration. I suddenly sit up straight in my bed. I can still go to Nauru after all!

Although Our Airline is the airline of Nauru, Brisbane is its home base. They fly Brisbane-Kiribati-Nauru-Kiribati-Brisbane and Brisbane-Fiji-Nauru-Fiji-Brisbane twice a month. Instead of flying directly to Nauru, I have to fly back to Fiji, then take the flight to Nauru, stay there for five days and then fly from Nauru back to Kiribati and back to Fiji again to pick up my original itinerary. But along with the excitement about this plan come the doubts. Who says that all these flights will operate, and that they have seats available? What if I get stuck on Nauru because a flight is canceled? There are no alternatives – Our Airline has a monopoly. But the glimmer of hope that this idea gives me eventually makes me fall into a deep sleep.

From the Utirerei, I call Fabiana to share my idea with her as soon as I'm back the next morning. She doesn't understand my plan, so I send her an email to explain what I had thought up that night and go for lunch. A little later, I receive a message that makes me ecstatic. She has had a meeting and will make the necessary reservations. I can fly to Fiji the next day, so I still have a few days there before my flight to Nauru. 'A birthday present from Our Airline', she says, referring to my upcoming birthday, which I will celebrate the day before I arrive in Nauru. I send a message to Allison to share the good news with her.

 The next morning, the High Commissioner's limousine, with flags of Australia and Kiribati, pulls up and takes me to the airport. At the check-in counter, it soon turns out that no reservation has been made at all. I can't call Fabiana: it's still night-time in Australia. I talk and talk, showing Fabiana's email with the flight details and my original ticket. Allison puts in a good word for me, but obviously, she doesn't have enough influence here. A little later I'm back in the Utirerei hotel, where the receptionists can't believe their eyes. I find consolation in the delicious food of their chef.

As soon as the office is open, I call Fabiana. She says she doesn't understand a thing and a little later sends me a ticket to Fiji. This will leave a few days later and it's going to be tight: I will have one day in Fiji before my flight to Nauru. All my plans for Fiji can be thrown out, but I quickly get over it. Fiji is easy to reach and I can always return there. I must now hope that nothing more will go wrong. I decide to take the boat to Abaiang, an atoll to the north. Suddenly, I have five extra days in Kiribati and it's time for a change of scenery.

The boat trip on the wooden catamaran takes me across the waters of the South Pacific – which are as blue and green as I had imagined in my wildest dreams – to the southernmost tip of Abaiang. A small canoe takes me to the beach. I walk north over the snow-white sand. I soon realize that this is a very different island compared to the main atoll. There, most buildings are made of concrete, there is an asphalt road with cars on it, people walk around with mobile phones, there are shops and the wrecks of American and Japanese war machines that have been rusting away just off the coast for seventy years. Here, the houses and even a church are made of pandanus leaves, there is a loose sandy path, families live in compounds with everything: sleeping house, eating house, kitchen, sitting room and a few graves of their ancestors.

I quickly turn into a spectacle here. Children shout out to me: 'I-Matang!', run to me and pose for my camera. Their parents sit in front of their houses, either wrapped in a cloth, wearing a t-shirt or topless. They wave at me, call to me and gesture at me to come over. Before I realize it, they send a son who, without a rope or any other accessories, fetches a coconut for me from the crown of one of the many palm trees in their back garden. They fire their questions at me, bewilderment in their eyes at this stranger from a land they have never heard of.

Everyone laughs at me with a beaming face. They show me their gardens. In one hut, I see a second floor with a big bed, surrounded by a mosquito net. Another building is open and used for storage. One section of the garden is marked by coral stones; it's used to dry coconuts. There is a hut without walls, from which they can enjoy the views over the sea. The sea, which decides everything for them and which provides food. The sea, which gives them barely enough space to live, precariously, on a meager strip of land. Yet I feel absolute peace here. Pure bliss.

The sun has already set considerably and I have drunk several coconuts, when I start to get worried. When I ask how far it is to walk to Taburao, the main village on the island, I always hear: 'Two villages further on.' Finally, a man on a motorbike catches up with me and takes me to the Women's Council of the island. This is the only place to spend the night and they turn out to be great cooks – what else but super-fresh, soft and briny fish?

The next morning, I jump on a truck that drives to the northernmost tip of the island. From there, I will walk back and explore the rest of the island. The driver seems to be having a good day, smiling all the time and infecting me with his cheerfulness. At one point, he loads a complete prefab roof made of pandanus leaves onto his truck. I wave at all the I-Kiribati on the way, feeling a lump in my throat. So much hospitality, so much joy, all under the tall palm trees and on the spotless white beaches. Life seems so straightforward here. Very, very far from the rest of the world, with its breakneck pace and corrupting influence. I should have been in Fiji by now, but I'm thoroughly enjoying this unexpected adventure.

At the end of the sandy path, I get out. I walk to the tip of the island. There, a man emerges from a hut and walks the last bit with me. We stand on the blindingly white beach. He scoops up a handful of sand and asks me to look north. He smears the sand on my cheeks, then on his own face. We walk to a shrine, where coral rocks have been placed in a rectangular shape, with one piece of coral standing upright. There, he takes some branches from a tree and braids them into two garlands. He places one as a crown on my head and the second crown on his own. He explains that from this moment on, for the rest of my stay on the island, I have the protection of Nei Arauri: the goddess born from the sea.

I chat for a while with the man, who asks where I am from. No, he has never heard of the Netherlands, nor of tulips, cheese or even football players. I try Germany or France and that seems to ring a faraway bell. I tell him that my home is close to both countries. He seems to understand and then he asks how long it would take to sail from Holland to Germany. The question surprises me. I patiently explain that there is a border between the two countries and that you can just walk, ride or drive from one to the other. He doesn't understand. But how long is the boat ride to France? Again, I explain that you don't have to cross any sea from the Netherlands to get to France. I don't make it any more complicated by saying that you have to go through Belgium first. I see that he is struggling with my explanation. I estimate the man to be in his thirties, assume he has been to school and wonder how he can't know that there are many countries whose borders have been drawn by all kinds of historical developments.

Then, suddenly, it dawns on me. This man lives on one of the many islands of Kiribati. That country covers an area the size of the United States and lies in all four hemispheres. In this region, your island determines your identity. Even the larger countries further away, such as Australia, New Zealand, Japan, the Philippines, and Indonesia, ultimately are all island nations. He can't imagine that different countries can be attached. I try to explain to him that I can travel from the Netherlands to China by land, crossing many countries without ever having to cross any sea. From his face and questions, I gather that he can't understand that there can be different languages and cultures between countries, which are defined only by a seemingly arbitrary, man-made line. Come to think of it, he might have a point there.

On my walk to the south, I have the sea on my right. I encounter village after village on my long journey back to Taburao. On the way, I see a couple of *maneabas*: large community buildings with very low entrances, so that every visitor has to bow his head when entering and automatically shows respect for those who are already inside. All kinds of ceremonies and gatherings take place under these enormous roofs. These, too, are of course made entirely of whatever can be found in nature: huge tree trunks and leaves are woven into a herringbone pattern, although to my surprise I also see one with a corrugated iron roof.

I walk past Tebunginako, which is a clear example of global warming. Only half the village is above sea level and the inhabitants have fled to higher parts of the island. Higher is a relative term here: the atolls of Kiribati are at most a few meters above sea level and are considered among the most threatened by rising sea-levels in the world. The government even has bought pieces of land in Fiji to be able to evacuate the population if the trends continue and there is no land left to live on.

In Koinawa, the next village, I see a rectangular, white tower rising above the palm trees: the hundred-year-old Cathedral of Our Lady of the Rosary. Decorated with shells and with brightly colored windows, it's an anomaly on this island of huts and other wooden structures. A little further on, I hear loud music coming from a *maneaba*. Someone invites me in. Only after I duck under the low-hanging roof do I see that a village festival is in progress.

Women with shawls and flowers in their hair dance barefoot on reed mats. Around them, men sit on the ground and watch. Soon, one of the women grabs me and drags me into a wild dance. I only just get the chance to kick off my shoes and throw off my daypack. A few minutes later, another woman takes over, and so I go from hand to hand and from woman to woman, seeing all corners of the *maneaba*. The men and children laugh with their beautiful white teeth at that strange *I-Matang* who swings and swings with their wives and daughters and mothers and sisters. I am given food and drink, pulled up on the mats again by women with whom I haven't had the honor of dancing, until my shirt is soaked and I have to drink more. I get away with great difficulty: after all, I still have a long way to go, back to my Women's Council.

After all the walking, dancing and sweating, it's time for a dip in the sea, which has been seducing me all day with its turquoise brilliance. I dry off as I walk further south. A family living in a hut on stilts just above the surf invites me in. Their shed is only accessible via two long beams, hanging diagonally above the water. Apart from getting the inevitable coconut, I'm shown family photos from a weathered envelope that they conjure up from behind the only piece of furniture in the hut. How often do they look at them? Again, I need to move on: it's getting late. Families walk with nets through the sea, their silhouettes standing out black against the orange sky of the sunset. Just before dusk, I make it to my sleeping place.

That evening, some men who work for the government invite me in and I try *kava* for the first time. This is the drink made from the roots of the kava plant that everyone in this region loves. At the end of the afternoon, you can hear the pounding of wooden poles in bowls to pulverize the root. Subsequently, it's left to boil with water for a prolonged time. It's said to have both sedative and euphoric effects. After a while, my mouth goes numb and I feel light-headed, but apart from that, the drink tastes mainly of earth. I would rather have coconut. The gentlemen just can't get enough of it and keep on replenishing my bowl. It's a pity that in the Women's Council building, no women are drinking with us. I have heard that kava sends them into uncontrollable fits of giggling.

The next morning, everything is different. There is rain, there is thunder and outside is a mud pool. The Women's Council owner's son takes me on his motorbike to the bay where the catamaran is moored, which should take me back to Bairiki. We leave after two hours of waiting, but twenty minutes later, the engine breaks down and a couple of men climb into the hold for repairs. They get it going, but a bit further on it cuts out again. They try to repair it once more, but this time in vain. We're still in the bay of Abaiang. My plane leaves in two days – my last chance to reach Nauru.

The boat that should take us back to the shore also breaks

down and a man swims ahead with a rope to tow us. Before-hand, I had spoken to a yacht owner in Betio, on the main island, who had promised to keep an eye on things. He would come and get me if he heard I was stuck. When I call using the telephone at the Women's Council, he doesn't answer and no matter how hard I stare at the horizon, I don't see his boat. The catamaran won't be repaired today, I'm stuck on the island, and I have no choice but to sleep at the Women's Council again. Where is my protection, where is Nei Arauri now that I need her so badly?

Early in the morning, the engine has been repaired sufficiently and we sail back to Bairiki at the slowest pace. It takes us more than twice as long as it did on the way there. I'm very glad when we finally arrive that afternoon and when I return a little later to good-old hotel Utirerei for the umpteenth time. Then, everything goes more smoothly. I fly to Nadi without fail and on time, rent a car and drive to Navala, a traditional village in the highlands of Nausori. After the atolls of the last few weeks, it takes some getting used to driving up hairpin bends on a gravel road, not being able to see the sea and being surrounded by completely different vegetation. I celebrate my birthday with a mother and son who show me around their traditional village with rows of huge, straw huts. In their house, a dog and a young cat peacefully live together and I watch in fascination as the cat snatches crickets from the air and leaves them strug-gling on the ground, so that the dog can give them the fatal blow with his paw. He is under the impression that he can still hunt, although he is far too old for that.

Back at the airport, the next day, apprehension kicks in: will the Our Airline flight depart? When I arrive, I see the plane parked at the gate, which is a good sign. I show them my hotel reservation when I check in, get a boarding pass and even an upgrade to First Class. My neighbor turns out to be Fabiana's sister: a taste of tiny Nauru where everyone is related to each other in some way.

But I mustn't rejoice prematurely. Who knows, we might break down and have to fly back to Fiji? It's only when we're over halfway through the flight that I feel an enormous amount of tension lift from my shoulders. A bit further on, I see the island through my window. It's so small that one end of the runway is built into the ocean. I get goosebumps on my arms and tears in my eyes. It can't go wrong anymore, I'm about to land in the country that seemed unreachable for so long and which I had given up all hope of visiting less than a week before. Whether, and when, I will get out of here is a matter of later concern.

Nauru is the second-smallest country and the smallest island state in the world, with the second-smallest population after Vatican City, and it lies less than sixty kilometers below the equator. The more I read about the country, the more incredible the story seems. Once completely overgrown with jungle, it has been inhabited for some three thousand years, for centuries solely by Micronesians and Polynesians. At the end of the eighteenth century, whaler John Fearn was the first European to land here and immediately named the island Pleasant Island. It became a source of drinking water for other Europeans and less than a hundred years later, it passed into German hands. Then came the Australians, the League of Nations, Germany again,

Japan and the United Nations, until it became independent as Nauru in 1968.

Meanwhile, around the beginning of the twentieth century, phosphate had been discovered and this not only turned the country upside down, but also nearly destroyed it. It brought Nauru so much wealth that on paper it was the richest country on earth, per capita, in the 1980s. When the phosphate ran out, it turned out that the funds from the proceeds were so badly invested that the country could no longer meet its basic expenses. Nauru went bankrupt. Within a generation, the Nauruans had gone from being the richest people on earth to being one of the poorest. Nothing is left of the original jungle: the island I now see below me is gray, with a minuscule green fringe of vegetation on the coast.

At the immigration counter, my passport is immediately confiscated. I can collect it in the afternoon from a small office on the other side of the runway. By that time, the Our Airline plane has left, so it's already certain that I will be here for another five days. No commercial flights are coming before then.

To my surprise, someone calls out my name when I step outside. A huge woman smiles at me, points to the back of her scooter and before I know it, we're whizzing towards Boe, the village west of the airport. Another thing: Nauru doesn't have a capital. Yaren is a district where government buildings are located and serves as the *de facto* capital. But what is a capital in a country that totals less than ten thousand inhabitants?

After the unanswered emails, the non-functioning phone lines and the endless frustration of booking something here the previous months, the unexpected lift from this lady and the welcome at the Od-N-Aiwo is surprisingly warm. I'm glad that

I have ended up here because the only other hotel is on the east side of the island, too isolated to be a good base for exploring. I leave my belongings behind and walk back to the airport.

A gray Australian Hercules flies by. Could it be asylum seekers or Australians who come here to help shape the Pacific Solution? I stand at a fence to watch. A policeman apologetically points out that I'm not supposed to be here. Indeed, I have ignored a sign. The plane is too far away to see who is coming out and I walk to the little office where my passport should be.

The same man who seized the document a few hours earlier lets me into his office. He asks what I have come to do in Nauru. I answer that I'm here as a visitor to discover his country and I tell him about my journey around the South Pacific and my ambition to visit all the countries in the world. He fiddles with the papers on the table and his eyes dart back and forth. They finally rest on the camera hanging from my shoulder. He speaks to me in a preachy tone.

'Don't behave like a journalist here. Don't you dare go near the detention center. We don't want any prying eyes here. You have a tourist visa: behave like a tourist.'

There, that much is clear. My suspicions about why it was so difficult to get a visa have just been confirmed. I promise him that I will 'of course' behave like a tourist, even though I don't know exactly what he means by that. It seems better not to ask difficult questions now. On the stamp in my passport, he writes: *as a tourist visitor*. It's valid until 31 November, which makes it even more special.

Even for a small country like Nauru, five days is hardly enough. To begin with, I want to walk around the country in a day, if only because there are very few countries where that is possible. The next day, in the dark, I walk along the runway towards the east coast and watch sunrise over the jagged limestone rocks sticking out of the surf. In the northeast of the island, I come across a cage with frigate birds: the Nauruans have developed a method to lure and catch these enormous animals. An elderly man comes out of the nearby cottage and proudly shows me his feathery friends. To my surprise, they aren't shy and I can look straight into their beady eyes. What is the ancient fascination of the islanders with these birds? Is it their link to a distant outside world? Their symbol for a possible escape? How much have these animals contributed to the phosphate that has irreversibly changed the island?

As I continue walking towards the northern tip of Nauru, a young woman on a scooter stops. Under a blue baseball cap, I see a light brown face with freckles and a lovely smile. She introduces herself as Ann and asks what I'm doing here. Walking around the island, I say. She offers her luggage carrier but understands when I explain that I don't want to miss out on this opportunity to walk around a whole country.

When I reach the west side two hours later, she is waiting for me at the side of the road. She takes me to the hospital where she works and gives me a short lecture on obesity. Nauru has been ranked number one in the world for obesity for some time now and it's determined to move down from that spot. As I write this, years later, it has still not managed to do so.

A bit further south, Ann shows me the ruins of the buildings where guest workers lived in the heyday of Nauru's enormous wealth. The grass has grown tall; here and there I can see vague slogans, spray-painted onto the crumbling walls many years ago. She walks me back to my hotel and offers to show me the island the next day.

At the agreed time, nothing happens. An hour later, there is still nobody. In the meantime, I eat some of the mangoes I brought from Fiji. Nauru doesn't have its own supply of fruit and has to import almost all its (canned) food from Australia. Since they are a rarity here, they taste even better than they did in Fiji.

But Ann doesn't turn up. I give up waiting and go outside. Later, someone tells me that the Nauruans have a reputation. 'In Australia, if you have an appointment with someone at four o'clock, he will be on time. In Fiji, he comes between five and six; in Nauru, there's a good chance he won't show up at all.'

The stern words of the official who issued my visa have inevitably made me curious and I walk inland. Apart from the main road around the island, several dirt roads lead to *Topside*, as the Nauruans call the area. The islanders all live by the sea; *Topside* is the gray wasteland I saw from the plane. Now that I'm walking through the landscape, I see up close how little of the country is left. I find myself in a landscape of jagged, white-gray limestone rocks, with only the occasional green sprig. The island has been turned into a bed of dead coral pushed up from the ocean. When I arrive at a barrier, I'm surprised they let me through. At the end of a side road, I see a more serious check-point with an Australian flag over it. I judge that it's probably best not to take this turn, but I do wave to the soldiers on duty there.

Behind that high fence, under that flag and the unforgiving equatorial sun, refugees from Afghanistan, Iraq, Syria and other countries are being held in an open space without shelter.

They were picked up from the sea by the Australian Navy. Years later, a report would be made about this camp that would paint a chilling picture. Child abuse, rape and suicide attempts – some successful, some not. One thing is certain: if Nauru still had its phosphate and wasn't reduced to begging, it wouldn't have to prostitute itself to rake in strong Australian dollars on the backs of people who will never have heard of Nauru in their lives.

Over the next few days, I explore more of the island. I nose around the batteries of rusting, Japanese anti-aircraft guns, which reminds me once again how much of a battlefield this whole region was during the Second World War. Even on this tiny dot in the gigantic Pacific. I wander around the village looking for a postcard. When I finally find some, the shop-keeper has no change, but he gives them to me as a present. I rent a bike, as I want to cycle around the island, but halfway through, the pedal breaks when I push a little harder as the road is slightly uphill. So, I walk the western side of the island for the second time, this time pushing a bicycle. The day before my departure, I'm briefly in my room when there is a knock at my door.

Ann.

Before I know it, I'm in a car with her friends, while a guy is following us on his motorbike. We have long conversations about the country and its history. I ask all sorts of questions, curious to know how this generation is doing. Their parents were very rich. I now remember that Allison, the High Commissioner in Kiribati who lived here in the heyday, told me that back then, when your suv broke down, you parked it by the roadside and immediately bought a new one. Having it repaired was too complicated.

The new generation is poor and will most likely remain so for the rest of their lives. They call the whole phosphate story a curse for the island. They would rather have kept their old traditions and lived the life the Nauruans lived for centuries on an island covered in dense jungle. Now, they have become the playthings of greater powers, they have forgotten how to fish and look after themselves as the migrant workers always took care of that, they are only independent on paper, the country is in debt and they have been forced to tolerate an Australian detention camp on their island. Since the cutting down of the jungle, the rains remain absent, even though the country lies almost exactly on the equator. Where once Nauru was used by European ships to fill up with water, now they have to import water, by boat – from Australia. No way to say no to a refugee deal with that same Australia.

We see thin walls of sharp coral rock, climb on them, discover small lakes, walk through the last remaining part of the forest and feel completely out of this world until we crawl through a hole in the rock and suddenly find ourselves on the tarmac of the ring road again. After dinner, we drive around the island once more, but this time on the back of a motorbike. My fourth tour of an entire country in just as many days: I have never managed this anywhere else. The walks, the conversations, the rides, the peculiar history: the last few days have taught me that Nauru is an outsider in the Pacific. A special people. Food for psychologists. At the end of the evening, my new friends embrace me but tell me: no, you don't have to say goodbye. That comes tomorrow.

The next day, I check in and walk around the little airport. The plane isn't there yet, nor are my friends. When the Our Airline plane lands, everyone on the south side of the island must have heard the noise of the landing. My friends still haven't shown up. It's only when I'm the last passenger to climb the stairs, as the flight is about to depart, that I remember. In Nauru, there is always a good chance that someone won't show up at all.

Chapter 11
Operation Pepernoot

Somalia – 2014

I f there was one single country that I was reluctant to visit for years, it would have to be Somalia. Since 1991, there has been a civil war in which various warlords and (later) an African peacekeeping force have been active. Al-Shabaab, a self-proclaimed sister organization of al-Qaeda, has also entered this complex mix of unrest. Their logo: an opened Quran with two crossed Kalashnikovs in front of it. They take this logo quite literally. They frequently stop buses and anyone who can't recite a few verses of the Quran gets a bullet through the head, on the spot.

The capital Mogadishu is formally in the hands of African Union troops and what is supposedly the country's federal government. Al-Shabaab is trying to show, by carrying out irregular attacks, that it has no intention of giving in. Besides, they are taking revenge on the Kenyans, who are part of the international forces in the country, by carrying out major attacks in neighboring Kenya.

The Americans suffered a humiliating defeat in the early stages of the civil war when they intervened in 1993. Together with Malaysians and Pakistanis, operating under the UN umbrella, they tried to eliminate warlord Aidid and ensure that humanitarian aid ended up where it was intended and not in the pockets of the warlords. The Cold War had just ended and the hope was that the UN would be able to play a more active role in protecting vulnerable people around the world and improving their lot. But *Operation Gothic Serpent* ended in colossal failure. This bad start on the international scene by the then newly elected President Clinton contributed, six months later, to the fact that he, along with the rest of the world, looked on passively when the massacre in Rwanda took place. No one dared to mount a humanitarian intervention after the Mogadishu debacle. Warlords now ruled, unchallenged. Somalia was left to itself and slid into an unstoppable spiral of violence, death and destruction.

According to the travel advice of Foreign Affairs, you absolutely should not go to Somalia. But if your goal is to travel to all the countries in the world, you can't escape going there as well. While most other travelers choose to go to Somaliland, the safer north part of the country, I decide to travel to the 'real' Somalia. It's clear that this will be an unusual journey. Traveling around on your own is impossible in Mogadishu, there are no guidebooks for the country, and travel organizations don't include it in their packages.

While researching the possibilities of visiting Mogadishu, I came across Ahmed, a Somali returnee from London who offered tours of the city. His website was full of sunny pictures and promotional texts: if you didn't know better, it looked like a city trip to Madrid instead of Mogadishu. Besides showing you the city and its surroundings, he could also take care of all the hassle. In Somalia's case, that meant not only a visa and a secure hotel, but also armed guards. I had arranged everything online and through emails. Sometimes, I got restless when I didn't hear anything for a while. Occasionally, I would receive answers every day, but often I wouldn't hear from him for weeks. When I closed my front door to go to Mogadishu, I wasn't at all sure I would be allowed to enter the country.

Given the country's bad name, the lousy security situation and the strongly negative travel advice, my strategy for the trip to Somalia is entirely different from all my other travels. Because of all the practical limitations and impossibilities, this trip wouldn't be how I would like it to be. I will fly there, try to see and do as much as possible in as short a time as possible and then return. I approach it as a military operation and name it *Operation Pepernoot*, because I'm arriving on 5 December (Pepernoot is a ginger nut which people in The Netherlands eat on that day to celebrate Sinterklaas).

I also decide to make it a secret operation: I inform almost nobody about my upcoming trip. My father, girlfriend Anneke, colleague Martin and neighbor Eric are the only ones who know about it. They are sworn to secrecy because I want to prevent other friends and relatives from getting overly worried during my absence. While I'm packing the day before my departure, I hear that there has been a serious attack near Mogadishu airport. There have been so many victims that it's even on the news back home.

The phone is already ringing. 'Hi, it's Martin. Have you seen the news?'

'You must mean the attack in Mogadishu? Yes, I saw it.'

'I take it you're not going anymore?'

'Uh, my plan still stands. I leave tomorrow morning, on the 11:30 flight.'

'Are you sure? A car with explosives crashed into another car. Ten dead, many more injured.'

'Yes, I saw. That can happen there. Of course, going to Mogadishu is not without risk, but I'm going anyway. The chance that tomorrow another car with explosives will be driving by and target exactly my car, isn't high.'

'But aren't you afraid?'

'No. I think it's intriguing of course, but afraid: no.'

'Pff, be careful. I think you're crazy.'

'You're probably right. I count on my luck. Without that, you don't get very far in life. Especially if you want to travel to all countries, you must take risks now and then. See you soon!'

'Keep me informed. Hope to hear from you!'

Five minutes later, the phone rings again. Eric. Same conversation. Then, my father. Anneke doesn't call. She had said before that she wasn't happy I was going, but also that she knew she can't stop me.

It's time for some introspection. Am I really not afraid to go? Certainly, it feels different from when I went to East Timor a month earlier or, before that, to Ukraine, Cape Verde, or most of the other countries I have been traveling to for years. Somalia is exciting, or should I say: intimidating? It could go wrong and the chance of that is greater than in most other places. But fear: no. I haven't been afraid to travel for as long as I can remember. I'm convinced that you shouldn't embark on these kinds of journeys if you're afraid. It would drive you crazy. At the same time, I'm extremely curious to see how I will fare if I put my fate in the hands of Ahmed and my guards. To see what Mogadishu looks like in real life and what kind of life its inhabitants lead.

The next question I ask myself is: why am I doing all this?

Am I indeed crazy? When, years earlier, I made a list of the countries I still had to visit to reach my goal, Somalia was the country par excellence I had no idea how to visit. Even less, how to get home safely. Of all the other countries that could be called dangerous, this was the one I had dreaded the most at the time. But if I want to reach my goal, I can't escape going to Somalia as well. For the first time, I will be visiting a country just to cross it off my list. Besides, it doesn't look like the situation on the ground will improve soon, so there is no point waiting for better times.

Although the contact with Ahmed wasn't always smooth, I'm confident that I'm in good hands with him. Or do I want to convince myself that I have that confidence? I read reports of others who have gone out with him, and they all came back safely. My curiosity about the country that has been in the news in a negative way for so long is greater than my concern about what could go wrong. In deciding to visit all the countries in the world, I have set myself a challenging goal. You have to be a little crazy to set such goals. So, I continue packing.

When I arrive at the gate at Istanbul airport the next evening and see the word MOGADISHU flickering in yellow letters on an old monitor, some anxiety sets in. My secret mission is now about to begin. To my surprise, the flight is full. There are quite a few people at the gate, typical North-East Africans. Tall and slender, athletic, light-skinned, narrow faces, frizzy hair, women with cloths around their heads and men in long robes. This is evidently not a holiday destination. I'm given a boarding pass at the last minute and sit by the window. The flight departs just before midnight and has a stopover in Djibouti. Conversations with people around me make it clear that, apart from those who are disembarking in Djibouti, there are mainly

Somali expats on board. They have lived in the UK or the US for a long time and are now going back because the situation in their home country is improving and they want to start a new life there.

It's still dark when we leave Djibouti. Now that we have taken off and are on our way to Mogadishu, there is no way back. It's getting light outside. Just when I start to get tired, I see the city and the adrenaline starts to kick in. We fly past the airport, further south, out into the Indian Ocean. We're still flying pretty high. Now we're descending in circles, above the innocent blue water below us and only fly towards the coastline when we're already very low. While taxiing, I see several aircraft wrecks lying on the grass. There are white UN planes and helicopters on the platform. When I descend the stairs a little later, the heat hits me and wakes me up. In the small arrival hall, the usual African chaos reigns. Men walk through immigration to acquaintances and back again, people shout, laugh, greet and embrace each other. To my surprise, everyone leaves me, the only European in the hall, alone.

Now, it's getting down to the wire. Is my visa ready? Will the papers that Ahmed emailed be accepted and will I be allowed into the country? More importantly, will he be there to pick me up? I don't even know what he looks like: our Skype conversations were without video.

The officer at the Foreigners window asks 'Wherrr is yourrr escorrrt? When I reply that I don't know, he tells me that he won't let me through without an escort. Yes, of course, he knows Ahmed, he'll be here soon. He is often late.

Meanwhile, the heat of the hall envelopes me. I'm still in my winter clothes, there is hardly any ventilation and just when I'm considering whether I should dare to walk back to the platform in search of a cooling breeze, I hear: 'Borrris?'

Ahmed turns out to be a sturdily built man, smaller than the slim, tall Somalis on the plane and who I now see walking around here. He embraces me, has a chat with the official in the wooden shed who has just decorated my passport with a Somali stamp and takes me outside. In the back of the pickup truck are my four guards with various types of automatic rifles around their shoulders and a dark look in their eyes. I greet them, get in, shake hands with the driver and we drive to the hotel in twenty minutes. On the way, I wonder how my guards with their imposing weaponry will protect me if someone with a car bomb in his boot slams into our vehicle.

Through a gate, we drive into the courtyard of Hotel Sahafi International. My guards jump out of the loading bay with their weapons around their shoulders. Ahmed takes me to the lobby where I'm welcomed by the receptionist and Abdirashid Mohamed, the flamboyant owner. In the courtyard, I see only men, all adorned with the typical, long *djellabas*. I'm out of place in my winter traveler's outfit and seem to be the only 'international' component of this hotel.

Sahafi means journalist in Arabic. However, this hotel is mainly used by businessmen and government representatives and rumor has it that warlords and militiamen also visit the hotel. The courtyard of the heavily guarded hotel looks quiet and peaceful. I just have to hope that al-Shabaab isn't targeting any of the guests for their next strike. They regularly attack hotels and the formula is always the same: detonate a car bomb at the entrance, storm the hotel in the ensuing chaos and wage a battle. Even if most of the attackers are killed in the end, al-Shabaab has shown that they are still around. With a bit of luck, they will take so many people with them to the afterlife that they will make the global headlines. Nihilism can't get much more depressing.

I get a room on the first floor, at the back of the hotel. It's quiet and dark, the air conditioning is humming. I notice that I can squeeze myself under the bed, if necessary. I leave my bag, send a message to my four confidants, put on lighter clothes and off we go. Exploring Mogadishu.

My nose is pressed against the window of the Toyota to see what a country strangled by decades of civil war looks like. We drive through dusty streets, I see stalls with salesmen, I see women in colorful clothes with groceries on their heads and blue and green-yellow tuk-tuks navigating between the people. A stray goat. On walls, colorful paintings depicting what the shops inside sell. Televisions and toiletries, drugstores and dentists. Paper and plastic lie scattered everywhere in the streets.

Every time a car passes, the litter is lifted from the ground and flutters further down in an eternal turmoil of trash that becomes dustier and dustier. For the time being, it mostly just looks like an East African country. I see cranes pulling new buildings out of the ground. According to Ahmed, there is a positive atmosphere and a new future for the city is being built. That explains the large number of returning Somalis on my flight to Mogadishu.

Our first destination is the fish market. When our car stops, I want to open the door, but Ahmed stops me. A ritual takes place that will be repeated again and again during the next few days. First, the four bodyguards jump out of our pickup. Guard

One stays on my side of the car. Guard Two looks around and crosses the street. Guards Three and Four take positions on the road and signal to Ahmed that we can get out. While we do so, Guard One stays with the car while we walk to the other side, flanked by Guards Three and Four. In the meantime, Guard Two enters the market and beckons to us that it's safe to walk on.

Inside, once my eyes are used to the darkness, I see that there are counters all around with fish that has just been brought in from the wooden boats on the beach. Huge pieces of tuna lie for sale on gray-white tiles. The saleswomen behind them stand against a wall on which I can see numbers written in felt pen. Customers haggle over the price, looking and pointing at the chunks of fish, while flies try to find a landing spot on the merchandise between their swinging hands. No one seems to notice me, even though it feels strange to be looking at chunks of fish with two guards at my side, both with impressive machine guns hanging from their shoulders.

We drive on towards the old town, with the sea on our right-hand side. The closer we get, the more the white buildings show signs of battle. By the time we get out, we're surrounded by ruins. After the disembarkation ritual, I walk behind Ahmed. We step over lumps of rubble, walking past detached walls that were once part of a building. The ragged, stone tops hardly stand out against the gray sky. Boats lie on the scant grass between the debris. Fishing nets, oars, plastic bottles and other rubbish is scattered here and there as if a tsunami had thrown the contents of the old harbor onto the shore.

We're now in front of the remains of an octagonal tower. Once the proud lighthouse of Mogadishu, it was built by the Italians at the beginning of the twentieth century. At the time, it was one of the architectural jewels of the city. Even after more than twenty years of war, you can still see that this must have been a very special lighthouse – even though the building looks grayish and the walls have been blown apart. Instead of a slender, tall tower, this is a sturdy, plump structure. It looks more like the defensive tower of a castle than a lighthouse. It's precisely its strategic location and size that have led to its ruin. From the top, you have control of the harbor and there is plenty of room for large numbers of gunmen and their arsenal. For attackers on the ground, this is an unmissable target that needs to be destroyed as quickly as possible.

The closer we get, the more the decay reveals its cruel details. Where the plaster has disappeared, we see round stones stacked on top of each other. Here and there, pieces of the plastered wall remain. There are even a few fragments where it's possible to see that the lighthouse was once as white as the other buildings in this city, which in its heyday was called the White Pearl of the Indian Ocean.

Once I'm inside, I see a spiral staircase – or what's left of it. Large chunks of rubble are scattered across the floor. The walls are so eroded, more by battle than by time, that I can see reinforcing steel poking through the concrete everywhere. The round pillar, around which the spiral staircase is built, must once have been blue, judging by the few flakes of paint left.

We're welcomed by a man in gray rags, with a cap on his head. Is he a supervisor? Is a supervisor needed here? He indicates that I can go up and I hesitate for a moment, as the remains of the stairs look anything but reliable. One of the guards climbs ahead and when he has explored the first floor and found it in order, he gestures that I can follow. Ahmed doesn't dare to climb up and I understand why. Here and there,

I have to hold on to the iron reinforcement sticking through the damaged concrete.

Once upstairs, I see a rusty metal frame in one of the rooms, topped with torn up cardboard boxes. It turns out to be the man's bed. I now understand that he isn't a supervisor: he is a squatter who has taken up residence here. His shelter may be a ruin, but it probably has the best view in town and the sea breeze provides constant ventilation.

I walk around, seeing the old harbor below me, where a large number of boats bob up and down on the calm sea. Beyond the semi-circular beach at the foot of the tower, I see ruin after ruin. Across the small bay is a huge building, most of it shot to pieces. It once housed the Uruba Hotel. That was a showpiece on the boulevard of Mogadishu, but it has now degenerated into a skeleton where the troops of the African Union are housed. From there, they try to keep the city under control. At least they don't have to open a window when they want to shoot. The building hasn't had any for a long time.

We drive along the coast and stop near the former hotel. Surrounded by my guards, I get out. On the white beach, we find fishermen pulling their boats ashore, young mothers fully dressed in colorful clothes walking with their children through the surf, boys playing in the waves, men walking hand in hand, teenagers playing football. In no time, a group of youngsters forms around me. All smiling, fighting to exchange a few words with me and to get a good picture. Foreigners don't come here, no matter how beautiful the beach is. They stay far behind the high walls of their compounds. This automatically turns me into a curiosity. A connection to the rest of the world that seems so far away here.

Then, a ball rolls towards me. I give it a good kick and the boys scatter, shouting. In no time, I'm playing a game of football with Somali teenagers on the beach of Mogadishu, at the foot of the ruined Italian lighthouse and the carcass of the enormous hotel. My bodyguards run with me after the ball as if we were half a team, their AK47s dangling from their shoulders. People in the surf and on the beach stop what they're doing to watch the scene with puzzled smiles.

The ruins around the lighthouse are a foretaste of what I will see during our drive through the old city. We can't stop anywhere I want because Ahmed considers it not to be safe. Everywhere around me, I see destruction. Sometimes in the form of hundreds of bullet holes in drab walls, sometimes in the form of half-razed buildings, as if the demolition hammer had been wielded indiscriminately. Here and there, I see columns of rubble pointing into the air, like stubby, grotesque fingers of a desperate hand asking God how he could have let this happen. From the height of the rubble, I can tell that these must once have been sturdy buildings.

There is a triumphal arch in classical Italian style, complete with the year in Roman numerals: MXMXXVIII – erected for the visit of Prince Umberto of Savoy. The arch seems to have been restored. I don't see any bullet holes in it and the crowns on either side are largely intact, contrary to photos I had found before leaving, which made it look like the arch was an object of choice for target practice. In the 1920s and 1930s, Somalia was part of Mussolini's fascist Italian Empire. He had buildings put up in the city that looked as if they had been plucked right out of Italy and were intended to revive the grandeur of eternal Rome here in Africa.

We stop near the triumphal arch and, after the disembarkation procedure to which I'm becoming accustomed, we walk to the remains of what was once the largest cathedral in East Africa. It was constructed in 1928, again in honor of Prince Umberto's visit. In a blend of Arabic and European influences, this cathedral was modeled after the famous 12th-century Norman cathedral of Cefalù in Sicily. Pre-war black and white photographs show, in the best Italian tradition, a fountain in the square in front of the cathedral, palm trees, a stone staircase leading to the entrance and two square towers on either side of the church with a large cross above the entrance.

When I look up, I can only see a fragile pillar of rubble on the west side. A helpless, hushed cry of dismay, an absurdity: this is one side of the once-mighty bell tower. Nothing is left of the tower on the east side. The cross above the entrance is still there, as are the window openings in the façade. A huge amount of debris lies in front of the entrance, as if an earthquake had just struck. We jump over a pile of branches that are greener than you would expect in this desolate place. Are they supposed to keep visitors out? Once we're inside the nave of the cathedral, we see that the destruction is complete.

After Salvatore Colombo, the last bishop of Mogadishu, was murdered in this cathedral in 1989, no successor was appointed. At least he was spared the collapse of Italian splendor. The cathedral was set on fire and finally destroyed by al-Shabaab militants in 2008. It seems that they had a field day with the religious decorations in the church. High above the ground, a scene with Jesus on the cross is damaged, but still recognizable. Another decoration above the altar with St Francis is barely discernible. The saint's head was shot off, as was most of the rest of the artwork. What is still distinguishable, however, is that the background to this scene must have been sky blue.

The windows have long since disappeared. We can look outside unhindered. This has become an open-air cathedral and the tropical climate has been digging its ruthless teeth into the unprotected remains of the building for almost a decade. The columns, the walls and the capitals have a dull appearance. Where has all the luster gone? The frescoes, the statues, the stained glass? As we walk through the side aisles, the stench of piss hits us in the face. There is excrement and rubbish where believers once knelt in prayer. When I look out of the opening in the wall, I see makeshift shacks leaning against the sidewall. People in rags are scurrying about. I wonder if they have any idea what function this building had before it became a ruin.

The Italians haven't been in charge here since the 1960s. After their departure and especially since the start of the war here and the Islamization of the region, there are only a few dozen Catholics left in a country of eleven million inhabitants. The ruins of the cathedral are a symbol of the decline of Christianity in these parts. In 2013, the diocese of Mogadishu seems to have decided that the cathedral will be rebuilt. But the question is: for whom?

Despite street after street of completely ruined houses, despite its desolate appearance, it's undeniable that Mogadishu once had style and flair. It requires imagination, but if you let your mind run its course, supported by old photographs, an image of an elegant city on the coast of the Indian Ocean will develop in your mind. Wide boulevards lined with palm trees, buildings in white and pale-yellow colors, a mix of Italian and East African architecture, where a cathedral stands a stone's throw from a mosque, where squares with monuments and fountains light up the city. Mogadishu is like an old lady who, if you look past the grooves that time has mercilessly carved into her face, was once a desirable young woman for whom passing men turned their heads.

Having had lunch at our hotel, we drive to another part of the city that afternoon. We see wrecks of armored cars, partly filled with rubbish. Goats are gnawing on plastic scattered everywhere; they scurry away when my guards jump with a thud onto the sandy street. A little later, I poke my head through the opening of the dented, partly burnt out, rusty and piled-up remains of a failed American intervention.

As I look into the cramped space of an armored car, I imagine an American eighteen-year-old, just signed up for the army, being sent here. No idea where Somalia is. No idea what he is going to accomplish so far from home. No idea if he will make it out alive. He is made to believe that he is going to do good work, that he is going to help poor people in Africa, that locals will have food to eat because of his efforts. That he will be welcomed as a hero.

And then a mission that was supposed to last an hour degenerates into hell. Hundreds, perhaps thousands, of people will die, mostly Somali fighters and civilians, in what is now known as the Battle of Mogadishu. Two Black Hawk helicopters are shot down. Dozens of Pakistanis and Malaysians are killed, and nineteen Americans. The corpses of fallen American GIs are tied behind pickup trucks and dragged through the dusty streets of Mogadishu, cheered on by an animated crowd. It's the painful end of the operation and just one of many battles that have taken place in the city since. The foreign mission dropped out after the debacle, but for the city's residents, many more long, violent years followed.

A little further on, we walk through Bakara Market, the place where the battle was fought. We find stalls with merchandise, shy salesmen waiting for the next customer and cafés where people chat and laugh. Men on a terrace immediately invite me in for a coffee. They want to know everything and ask questions in poor English. Sometimes, Ahmed helps with translation. Somalis hardly have the opportunity to make contact with foreigners. If they see any at all, it's the military in heavily guarded vehicles, or sporadically, representatives of NGOs who also prefer not to come into the city and stay behind the high fences of their fortresses. It feels like they have a serious thirst. Thirst for expanding their world, thirst for stories from outside, thirst for a life in normalcy, thirst for recognition of the rest of the world. For a short while, I am that world to them.

I want to reciprocate their hospitality, so I take out a bag of *pepernoten*. I try to explain what they are (a kind of ginger nut), why this day is special for me as a Dutchman, that we eat these only on this day and I pass the bag around. They are all curious, try to taste it carefully, digging their yellowish teeth into the Dutch delicacy. Some don't like it, others ask for a second one, but I don't know if that is out of politeness, or because they actually like it. Sitting on a terrace in the afternoon sun, chatting with Somalis, I wonder why I still have those armed guards on my side. I suggest to Ahmed that I walk around without them, but he laughingly dismisses my idea.

According to him, there are snipers on the roofs and gangs looking for hostages, so it's unthinkable that I could walk around here without guards.

What a pity.

Normally, when I'm preparing to leave for unfamiliar places, I try to read about what I want to see and do there. At the same time, I really try to avoid seeing images. I want to go with as open and fresh a mind as possible and let myself be surprised as much as I can by what I'm going to see and experience. In this world with endless streams of photos in brochures, guidebooks, the Internet and social media, this is an increasingly difficult task.

In this respect, too, this trip was different: I tried to find as much information about Mogadishu beforehand and to collect as many images as possible. There are only sporadic sources of information and there certainly is no *Lonely Planet City Guide for Mogadishu*. It was only years later that I got my hands on an Italian travel guide from 1938, with a description of the city that turned out to be remarkably accurate after all those years. Apart from the photos on Ahmed's site, the only images of Mogadishu I had come across were YouTube clips from other travelers who had gone before me. Several of these showed the devastation just after a bombing, in which you could sometimes still see body parts lying in the rubble.

One of the rare images I found was a black-and-white drawing from 1882 of the thirteenth century Fakr ad-Din mosque. The pointed cone next to the dome immediately caught my eye. I saved the picture on my phone. When I asked Ahmed if we could go to the old mosque, he looked at me, not understanding what I was referring to. Even when I showed him the photo of the drawing, it didn't change his expression. No, he had never seen or heard of it. He showed the photograph to the driver, but he too shrugged his shoulders. An old mosque? There was no such thing in Mogadishu. Not anymore, anyway.

Still, the war and destruction began in 1991. Even if the building is damaged, there must be something left of it, like the other buildings I see all over the city? A strip of wall, with debris all around? The cathedral may be a ruin, but it's surely still visible. As we drive through the old city, I see a small group of older men sitting under a tree, chatting. They are old enough to have prayed in the medieval mosque, so I ask Ahmed if we can stop.

Surrounded by our guards, I get out and show them the black and white photo of the old drawing. The men look at me in surprise and nod immediately. Yes, they know this mosque; it's just around the corner! They stand up, order us to follow them and indeed: less than a hundred meters further, I see the prayer house towering over a narrow alley. The wooden door is closed; the men say that the imam is in hospital. A passing boy is sent to fetch him. The men invite us to drink tea under their tree.

A quarter of an hour later, a man with a reddish goatee, gray curly hair and a stately appearance in his spotless white *djellaba* and a dark brown *taqiyah* on his head, appears around the corner. The imam has escaped from the hospital especially for me. His eyes reveal that he must be old: the edges are blue, cataracts have set in. What have they seen in this city of devastation and ruin? I exhaust myself with apologies, but he dismisses them with a gesture of his arm. He is obviously delighted that a Westerner shows interest in his mosque. He urges us to follow him and so we do, back into the alley.

The old man opens the door and gives us a short tour. It's dark inside and the imam takes a torch out of a closet. In a corner, two massive, old, wooden door sections stand on their sides, with empty jerrycans, cardboard boxes, flat plastic bottles and other rubbish in between. The *mihrab*, the niche that indicates the direction of Mecca, turns out to be a gem. A gold-colored rectangle with flowing, blue Arabic calligraphy above it. The imam urges me to take as many photos as I want – who am I to contradict him?

This mosque is the seventh oldest mosque of Africa. It was built seven decades before Ibn Battuta, the famous Moroccan explorer, visited the city in 1331. He described Mogadishu as a 'very large city with rich merchants'. He was here in its heyday. I try to imagine how this mosque must have looked back then. How the same Ibn Battuta must have prayed here, in front of this very *mihrab*.

We climb the roof. It looks exactly like the picture of the nineteenth century drawing on my phone: now I can finally add color to the black and white image. The structures are painted in a fresh green. The paint is peeling off on all sides. A rusty pot of paint has fallen over and lies on the roof next to a half-full bag of cement. The hexagonal cone has a blue base and the dome has a red and white checkered border at the bottom. As we look towards the sea, the imam explains that the Italian governor, De Vecchi, had part of the mosque demolished to build the road by the tree where I met the old men before. According to him, the mosque extended to the waterfront. Indeed, it's now a small place of worship, hidden away in the oldest district of the city. So small and hidden that even Ahmed didn't know of its existence.

The next morning begins with the news that a minister has been killed in an attack during the night. Just as there are attacks here every day. The rest of the world only hears about the more serious cases; the daily killing here is too insignificant and too mundane to span countries, continents and oceans. I'm just glad that the minister wasn't staying in my hotel.

After all the blasted glory, the desolation of a city that has lived under the scourge of war and attacks for more than twenty years, we now drive on a bypass road to the southwest. We take an exit and the driver parks the pick-up near a ramshackle corrugated iron wall. Ahmed and I walk inside: we have arrived at one of the large refugee camps built around Mogadishu for people seeking protection here from other parts of the country. Who knows what they have endured on the way from lawlessness and war?

What follows is a walk around unsightly, fragile huts, made of old linen cloths and sticks, with holes everywhere and floors of sand. People walk around in rags. No laughter here, no children playing, no energy. A heavy feeling of hopelessness and inhumanity falls over me and I notice that Ahmed feels the same when I see the tears running down his cheeks.

We listen to people's stories. They are stranded here, fleeing from the extremists who are destroying the country. They have been living in this camp for years without any prospect of improvement in their situation. The way back home is cut off. A man with a deep wound in his leg comes to us – we listen to him and feel powerless. I don't have anything on me that could help him.

There is a small school, where young children learn the Quran by heart using old wooden panels. They seem to find it exciting to see a foreign visitor, they stare at me and pose for photos. But they don't radiate any energy, there is no open-mindedness, enthusiasm for life, or the playfulness that a child should have.

With a stomach full of stones, we walk back to the car. I consult Ahmed: he promises that he will call in a local organization to do something for these people and I make the first donation. But the miserable feeling can't be bought off.

Today is qat day. Twice a week, a plane from Kenya lands, full of the green stuff that can't be grown in Somalia's scorching climate. We drive to an open spot in the city. Trucks arrive here, directly from the airport, loaded with burlap bags containing the valuable leaves. As soon as a truck stops and the cargo box opens, men jump on it to put the bags on the backs of others, who then haul them off to the many stalls nearby. After a while, they come back to get a new bag. Around the square are stalls where you can buy bundles of qat. In poor, hopeless Somalia, the narcotic effect of chewing qat is a welcome distraction for many.

We drive back into the city, stop somewhere on a corner and Ahmed gestures for me to shift over to the left of the back seat. To my surprise, a lady dressed entirely in black gets in, sits next to me and partly unwinds her headscarf as soon as she has closed the door. She gives me a seductive look and I realize this is the first Somali woman whose face I have seen. Ahmed asserts that it's his niece. She is coming with us to Jazeera, a village south of the city.

On the way, we pass the wreckage of a plane that was shot down just before landing. Now I understand why my flight approached the airport with a large diversion over the safe sea before landing. For someone with an RPG (rocket propelled grenade) on his shoulder, it's not too difficult to shoot down an aircraft just before landing if it approached the runway over land.

Jazeera turns out to be a fishing village, named after the little island just off the coast. The old mosque that we can see from the beach is unfortunately closed. Ahmed arranges a boat, we sail around the island, see the fish in the crystal-clear water and enjoy the beach and the sea on our return. When I look towards the south, the beach seems to stretch into infinity. In the distance, I can see the dunes of the desert reaching the sea. I regret not being able to explore this cursed country further. To just travel around here carefree and independently. Take a local bus, without armed guards, talk to locals, sleep in small hostels in villages on the way. Who knows, maybe one day?

Meanwhile, I don't know what the intention of the young woman is. In the boat, she sits close to me and I end up throwing my arm around her shoulders. When, out of the blue, a Somali man appears on the beach with a stall selling souvenirs made from shells, she buys one for me. She also goes back with us to the city. We walk along Lido Beach, the most popular beach there, where the wealthier Somalis stroll and play in the surf. In a café, we smoke a water pipe and chat. Years later, al-Shabaab will also cause death and destruction here with an attack on the frivolous beach bars, the only place where the inhabitants of Mogadishu still have the opportunity to get away from it all.

By the time we return to the hotel, it's pitch dark. My Somali girlfriend has disappeared just as suddenly as she had emerged beside me a few hours earlier. Once I'm in my room, I read worried messages from Anneke: Ahmed had said we'd be back at six and it's already half-past eight. I realize again that I'm not in an ordinary destination and that there are four people who, far away from here, are concerned about me.

Ahmed doesn't turn up the next morning and after waiting a while, I get nervous. My flight leaves in a few hours; we had agreed to drive into town for the last few photographs. I can't afford to miss this flight. I'm completely dependent on him and my security guards: I can't just hail a taxi on the street. The receptionist tries to call Ahmed, but can't reach him. When he finally arrives, he has a vague story about a sick daughter and problems with his phone battery. We drive into town anyway, I take photos through the closed window of our car and we walk around one of the city's markets. For the last time, I'm surrounded by my bodyguards.

Once I'm at the airport, the ground staff looks surprised at my standby ticket and, to my relief, immediately hands me a boarding pass. I struggle through the five security checks: unpacking and packing my luggage, searching and searching again. All those checks only give me a marginally safer feeling because I know that first, we must safely take off from this airport. The images of the plane wreck from the day before are still on my mind. I walk across the runway and up the stairs, and then I'm back in the familiar surroundings of an aircraft cabin. After take-off, the aircraft makes a sharp turn to the east, out to the ocean, even though our first destination is Djibouti. It's not until we reach cruising altitude that we change course and head north.

The tension of the last few days, of the last few years that I had been dreading traveling to Somalia, falls away and gives way to relief. I have succeeded! Not only can I now say that I have been to Somalia, but I also look back on special days in the most devastated capital city in the world. I have seen that, in the end, it's mainly populated by ordinary people who try to lead a life and build a future amid the ruins, in a seemingly hopeless situation. To celebrate the fact that this adventure is behind me, I open the second bag of *pepernoten* that I have kept especially for this purpose. Before I arrive in Istanbul, the bag is empty. *Operation Pepernoot* is complete.

Postscript

Less than a year after I visited Mogadishu, the news on TV reports that Hotel Sahafi was attacked by al-Shabaab during the night. Two car bombs heavily damaged the front of the hotel. Aid workers who rushed to help were shot dead. The ensuing battle lasted a day. Fifteen people were killed, dozens wounded. The hotel's security personnel were killed, as well as its owner. People I shook hands with. Guards who were in the back of my pickup. Alarmed, I try to call Ahmed. The phone is answered by someone who speaks enough English to tell me Ahmed is in hospital. Wounded in the battle at the hotel.

The hotel is rebuilt and the son of the owner takes charge. A few years later, al-Shabaab once again attacks the hotel. This time, the son gets a bullet through his head. The cycle of violence hasn't ended, the Somali tragedy continues and no one knows how, or when, it will ever end.

Chapter 12
Doomed Tuesday

Liberia – 2016

Tuesday, 1 March

The chain rattles off the sprocket. I jump off my bike and run to the station through the chilly, dark morning. No matter how hard I run, I miss my train to The Hague HS and with it, my connection to Brussels. Without really thinking about it, I get on a slow train to The Hague Central. I am lucky: when I get there, a tram is just arriving to take me to The Hague HS. A little later, I can just about jump on the train to Belgium.

A few hours later, I'm walking through the center, past the huge Berlaymont building, the headquarters of the European Commission. Opposite, I walk into the stately building that houses the Embassy of Liberia. Immediately, I'm in another world. In Africa. There are posters of the country on the wall, wooden statues on tables, Africans walking around. After a while, a lady appears and takes my forms, passport photos and passport. Without so much as glancing at me, she tells me that I can collect my passport a week later. After a quarter of an hour in Africa, I'm back in Brussels and walk the same route back to Central Station. A few hours later, I'm home.

Tuesday 8 March

My bicycle has been repaired and the journey to Brussels goes off without a hitch. The same lady at the embassy smiles at me now and this time around, my stay in Africa only lasts five minutes. My passport has a new visa. Number 00073. It seems that not many visas are issued for Liberia. The prolonged civil war and then Ebola have kept most visitors away from the country for years.

Tuesday, 15 March

Once again, I'm on the train to Brussels. This time, I get off one stop earlier: at Brussels Airport. I check in, walk past a replica of Tintin's red-and-white checkered rocket and wait at the gate for my boarding pass. The Brussels Airlines crew is happy with my caramel waffles. After a stopover in Freetown, we land in Monrovia, where it's already dark. I have been here a few times before, a long time ago, but I never went beyond the airport; I always flew on to other destinations.

James is waiting for me. He is a guide for Barefoot, a local travel agent. I have decided to travel with a guide for a change, because I'm only here for a week. We have emailed each other several times. He will show me his country, although we only have vague ideas of where we will go. We will discuss that later. He takes me to a noisy, shabby, expensive hotel: there isn't much choice in the capital.

The next day, James invites me to stay at his home: a better option than sleeping in the overpriced hotel. The added advantage is that it will give me a better idea of life in Monrovia. His wife turns out to be a generous, sturdy and smiling lady, who proudly gives me a tour of her simple house. Her kitchen is on the veranda. The *marmites* are particularly striking: large metal pans, one of which is always simmering on a wood fire for most of the day. She proudly shows off one of her giant snails. When I take a closer look, I see them crawling across the yard here and there, with enormous shells on their backs.

We start exploring the city at the monument to the founders of this country. We see a prominent statue of Joseph Robert, the first president of Liberia. James takes the opportunity to tell me about the exceptional history of his country, for Liberia is a unique part of Africa. In 1816, the *Society for the Colonization of Free People of Color of America* was founded in the United States. The purpose of the society was to give freed slaves a new future in Africa, rather than having them emancipated and integrated within the United States. Slave owners in the USA were afraid that freed slaves who remained in the country would set an example for black people who still worked as slaves. There were several other organizations with the same aim in the first half of the 19th century.

Eventually, thousands traveled to West Africa, many of whom were forced to leave. They found pieces of land on the Grain Coast that hadn't yet been annexed by European powers. They also bought territory. They were the first African country to declare independence in 1847, more than a century before the other African colonies broke away from their European rulers. The Americo-Liberians thus became the dominant class and ensured that the original inhabitants were denied their rights. The division into Americo-Liberians and natives still exists today and explains, at least in part, the internal unrest and civil war of recent decades.

We walk up the steps to the ruins of the nearby Ducor Palace Hotel. Once upon a time, this was luxury accommodation, beautifully situated on rocks high above the sea and the city. It used to be the location of excessive parties held by high-ranking officials, rich people, pop stars and foreign heads of state. However, a combination of war and the onslaught of the tropical climate have wreaked havoc.

Oh, the swimming pool is still there, and even the diving board – but there's only a little murky water left in the deep end. The sunbeds are gone and the surrounding tiles have turned green. The lift shafts are still there, but to get to the top you have to take a crumbling staircase, as the shafts are empty conduits. Hovering lifts have not been seen here for a long time. We see all sorts of artistic drawings and paintings on the walls of what were once the five-star rooms of Monrovia. The surrealistic art reminds me of Escher. In the lobby, a spiral staircase leads upwards. Cracks have slowly split the concrete and moss grows on the sides. But it's not difficult to imagine that ladies in beautiful dresses, flanked by gentlemen in dinner jackets, were once walking down a thick, red carpet here in their shiny high-heeled shoes. Transience and Liberia's recent history fused into one building.

Later, we meander through West Point, the largest slum in the city. The poverty there seizes me by the throat and the dismal living conditions bring tears to my eyes, while the people do their best to make something of their miserable lives. But they are at least as proud and strong as they are poor. They greet, wave, smile and engage in conversation. Ebola has wreaked havoc here in recent years, but the last case was diagnosed some time ago. On the beach, I see the first hammerhead sharks of my life – so many times I hoped to see them while scuba diving, but now they are here, lying dead on the dark yellow grains of sand. The only question is: in which *marmite* will they disappear tonight?

After visiting the museum of Monrovia, we walk along the beach. James teaches me recent history. This is where ministers were executed in 1980, after being paraded naked through the streets of the city. A few days earlier, Samuel Doe had staged a bloody coup and killed President Tolbert and his supporters. In doing so, he broke the monopoly of authority that the Americo-Liberians had exercised in the country: more than a century of oppression and backwardness came to the surface in a gruesome day of reckoning. Doe himself would be killed ten years later in an even more horrific manner by Prince Johnson, one of Liberia's warlords. After his ears were cut off, he was beheaded. His naked torso was paraded through the streets of Monrovia. His last hours were caught on tape and circulated, shocking the world. After this coup, the country would sink into civil war and all the pent-up tension between Americo-Liberians and the natives would result in continuous fighting.

The next day, we share a taxi and drive to Bomi, in the west of the country. We charter two boys on motorbikes to take us to the blue lake of the same name. There used to be iron ore mines here; one of them flooded and became a lake. You can see from the cascading hills around it that this landscape was shaped by human hands. James tells the legend of a huge boa constrictor that lived in the lake so deep, no one knows if it has a bottom. On the other side of the lake, we find the ruins of what must once have been a restaurant. There is a white four-wheel drive from the United Nations, with a couple of Jordanians who have come here to relax. Their mission in Liberia is almost over.

James appears to be particularly used to guiding with a

rental car. Traveling with shared taxis is much more difficult than he had thought. Despite all the uncertainties and the lack of comfort, I maintain that this is the best way to experience a country and to get an idea of the life that people lead. In the meantime, I can also easily encounter Liberians. The fact is that James often makes bad estimations of the travel time. A journey in a shared taxi takes double the time it would a four-wheel drive. Or (much) more.

It has already been dark for a few hours when we arrive in Kinjor. Built for gold diggers, this new village exists because of the proximity of the gold mine. The streets are buzzing with dynamism, everywhere there are small shops that hope to siphon some money away from the profits of the mine. The owner of a guesthouse thinks he can benefit from the gold craze and asks far too much for his simple rooms. After some looking around, we end up in the home of a lady. Before I know it, we're sitting on her bed watching DVDs of music videos from the eighties, while eating an indeterminate stew. The bed we're sitting on turns out to be my bed for the night. Only when the others leave and I lie down, do I notice that I'm sleeping under two clotheslines full of bras and wigs. As soon as I switch off the light, I can hear clattering on the floor. It sounds like the rats are finding plenty to eat here.

The next day, I learn to cook with palm nuts, which are thrown into a huge pot together with water, a lot of peppers, smoked fish and pork, where they will simmer for hours until the spicy taste of the peppers has saturated all the other ingredients. Meanwhile, it turns out we need a permit to visit the gold mine, which can only be applied for in Monrovia – James' mistake. I get the supervisor on the phone, but he is not to be persuaded, no matter how hard I try to talk him into it. I won't get to see the mine.

Some distance outside the village, we see a place where a few men are cutting down trees and making charcoal. This is tied together in packages and taken to the village to be sold. After all, everyone needs charcoal for cooking. Slowly but surely, the woodcutters also ensure that the clearing in the jungle where Kinjor lies continues to expand. When we return to the big pot a few hours later, the stew is ready. It has an identical taste to all the dishes here. Every day, the same ingredients are used to prepare the same dishes. The only variation is the type of meat that is added.

As is so often the case in Africa, it appears that the European company running the gold mine is doing little to allow its employees to share in the wealth extracted from the earth here. Injustice revisited. A deal between the company and the government, which undoubtedly gets paid handsomely, while the people whose soil this is and who do the real work are fobbed off with a tip and a life in the margins.

We walk to a small village nearby, where the situation is even worse. The inhabitants show me their water source. It's clear that in the past, the water level was much higher: there is almost no water left. It's extracted for the mine and agriculture for the miners. These people, who have lived here since time immemorial, will have to find a new place to live within a few years, simply because the water from their well will be diverted to the mine. Needless to say, they won't get any compensation.

James has once again made a serious time miscalculation. It turns out that there are far fewer cars going to Robertsport than he imagined. After waiting for a while at the roadside, I calculate that it doesn't make sense and decide that we should take the first taxi back to Monrovia. At least there we can sleep at James' house. By the time we arrive, it's long since dark. The electricity is down, so we use torches to light our food. There is a surprise on my plate: although the taste is the same as the previous meals in Liberia, I can feel a new texture between my teeth. Now that I look more closely in the light of my torch, I see what I'm eating. As it's my last meal here, James' wife has decided to treat me to the giant snails from the garden.

The next day, we set off for the north of the country. We're lucky. Next to the driver of the *bush taxi* sits a distinguished lady, who repeatedly urges him to drive carefully. Where has she been all these years? All those hundreds of times my drivers have taken enormous risks, only to arrive a few minutes earlier? They often overtook where they couldn't, failed to brake, veered off the shoulder and sometimes off the road, and despite all their frantic attempts to crash, to my amazement, they did eventually bring me to my destination in one piece. No matter how many times I asked them to drive more carefully, it invariably had a short-lived effect, until the driver reverted to his reckless driving style. But this lady! She is constantly making comments and the driver obediently follows her instructions.

After a few hours of driving, we see flames coming out of the exhaust pipe of a car overtaking us. Our driver goes in pursuit. Big Mama now has nothing more to say, he has only one mission: to overtake the other car and warn them. Now the nature of the beast comes out. After a wild chase, he manages to overtake the car, still oblivious of the flames. We help to extinguish the fire. How badly I know Africa, I think when I enthusiastically grab the halon extinguisher that I had already spotted in our car. It turns out to be empty. Sheer decoration.

Many more hours follow that day, in various taxis and trucks. The road slowly transforms from good to bad tarmac until the tarmac has completely disappeared and we bump through deep potholes in unpaved roads. Where James thought we would make it in five hours, it ends up taking us more than ten. It's late in the evening when we arrive at Camp Four.

There are no hotels. We sit on a bench next to a house. We talk to a representative from Mount Nimba National Park and to other men who are in charge here about our options for the night. Everyone tries to think of a place we can sleep. The solution appears to be straightforward. We're accommodated in a house under construction, without windows or doors and of course without air conditioning, ventilation, electricity or a place to wash. It turns out to be mightily hot inside. Even in my silk sleeping bag, it's impossible to sleep, so I lie sweating on the ground in a bare room where the mosquitoes feast all night on the blood of our freely accessible bodies.

The next day will be the highlight of our journey through the country. The goal is to climb Mount Nimba, which we plan to do in stages. First, we ride up on motorbikes until we come across remnants of the mining era. Here, in the far north of Liberia, the infrastructure needed to mine iron ore was set up decades ago. Huge cylinders stand on the slopes. Ore was rinsed and then loaded from the cylinders into wagons, at which point, a locomotive pulled them to the coast. Since the civil war, the mines are no longer in use. Rust slowly eats away the containers, rails and all other metal parts, making these installations all the more impressive and photogenic. We walk up the slope to see where the ore was extracted before it went to the cleaning plant.

From this point, we were supposed to continue our climb to the top of Mount Nimba, but our Nimba guide, who is now dragging his leg, forgot to bring his gear. The guys who brought us on the motorbike have already left and James' phone has no reception, so the only thing to do is to walk down instead of going up. It's hours later when we finally find two other guys to drive us up the mountain again on their motorbikes. My driver may live in Camp Four, but he has never driven on this road. I have already forgotten my irritation at the clumsiness of the guide a few hours earlier, when I notice the sheer happiness in his eyes, seeing his village from a great height for once. How I would love to grant him a flight with a window seat, to see the world from the air.

We have lost a lot of time, so when we arrive at the start of the trail, I set off immediately. Off to the top of the mountain. The limping guide stays behind and James can't keep up with me, so I walk over the ridge of the mountain on my own. The sky is black. On my right: Ivory Coast, straight ahead: Guinea. A long time ago, I reached the top of Mount Nimba from Guinea, which shares the highest point of this massif with Ivory Coast a little ahead of me.

The rain drifts away and takes the black sky with it to Ivory Coast. An intense rainbow crowns the climb to one of the country's highest peaks, at 1362 meters. I enjoy this wide view of the threatening sky for a moment, take photos and turn around. I walk down as fast as I can and when I meet James and the guide, they turn around and walk with me. After all, we still have a long way to go and it's getting dark already.

After a while, a pickup catches up with us and takes us to a campsite. Henry, the driver of the car, turns out to be a jovial, well-educated, intelligent Liberian with a great sense of humor. Below us, we see the lights go on in Camp Four and Yekepa, as well as those of Bossou and Lola in Guinea. Henry calls his wife to give orders, leaves for Camp Four and returns an hour later with food and drinks. In the meantime, we have been able to put up our tents.

A long evening talking about the world, economics, politics, the upcoming first female president of the US (as it seemed back then), traveling, Liberia and our lives in general. Henry works as an engineer at the mine, which was reopened some distance south after the civil war. He asks where we are staying. When he hears about our empty house in Camp Four, he calls Wing. She is a friend/colleague who is in Monrovia for work for a few days. She offers me a bed in her flat at the mining company compound the next day.

The next morning, we walk back to Camp Four. Henry takes us out to eat in the canteen and then suddenly I'm in an apartment with a shower, kitchen, washing machine, TV, Internet and a lovely bed. After a week of primitive traveling, this is an enormous luxury that I had almost forgotten existed. The deal is that I take care of her dog, who seems to enjoy running around with me outside. I try to tell him that his owner will come home the next day and I think he understands. I hear torrential rain hammer down on the roof all night and I'm glad it didn't come the night before, when we slept in a tent on the flanks of Mount Nimba.

Tuesday 22 March

I wake up early. This is my last day in Liberia: this same evening, I fly home via Brussels. After a week without any news, I'm ready for a little update on what is happening in the world. The first site I open mentions an attack on Brussels airport. I decide to check it out. There is nothing on the airport's website, all flights seem to be leaving on time,

I say goodbye to James and walk to the departure hall, which is small, warm and full of people. I quickly change in one of the toilets. When the ground stewardess sees my ticket, she looks at me incredulously. No, this flight is fully booked, impossible with a standby ticket. I understand. Due to the cancellation of the Brussels Airlines flight, passengers have been rebooked onto the sparse alternative flights. The flight to Accra and Nairobi is one of them. I talk like a man in shining armor and explain that I have a work flight a few days later and that there are very few options left. But she is unruffled: even a crew seat is out of the question. As so often in Africa, there is a solution in the end: the ground engineer takes a seat in the cockpit so that I can take his place in the cabin. As we take off, I feel some of the tension from the whole day's racing slipping away. But I also know that it's not over yet. It's still a long way home.

In Accra, it's even more chaotic than in Monrovia due to the Brussels Airlines cancellations, as they are a major player in West Africa. The flight to Amsterdam is also completely full. In the end, I'm lucky enough to be allowed on it and when we land at Schiphol the next morning and taxi to the gate, my arms are covered in goosebumps. A race against the clock of almost twenty-four hours has ended well. At the same time, my thoughts are with the horrific attacks on the Belgian capital, the lives lost and the surviving relatives who now have to live on without their loved ones.

Two days later, I'm watching kite flyers and elegantly dressed couples dance in Fuxing Park in Shanghai, one of the places in the city that hasn't yet been bulldozed away. After my adventure in Liberia, it's a completely different world. Another ten days later, at home, I suddenly feel miserable after exercising and I go to a birthday party anyway, but my body isn't up for it.

I feel dizzy and feverish. Strange: I'm never sick. When I go to bed, I hope a good night's sleep will solve it.

But things don't improve the next day. The dizziness increases rapidly and so does the fever. Soon enough, it reminds me of the severe malaria tropica I had many years earlier, which I barely survived. Then, I know it at once. That hot, mosquito-filled night in Camp Four has inflicted the damage. With malaria, acting fast is crucial because the disease can become life-threatening within a fairly short time.

It's a weekend, so my GP is unavailable: it's time to call the first aid department in the nearest hospital. I emphasize the fact that I have just been to Liberia. A region where malaria and ebola are common. I also tell them that I have had malaria before and feel just as weak as I did then. Still, the doctor advises me to just take an aspirin and to wait for two days. This is obviously faulty advice. After all, the adage for someone who falls ill after returning from the tropics is: treat the illness as malaria until it's proven otherwise. But I'm too weak to put my foot down.

Tuesday, 5 April

I feel much worse and my fever is still well over forty degrees. It's time to call my GP. Within half an hour, a young lady with a small suitcase arrives to take a blood test. Less than an hour later, the doctor calls to tell me that I need to be rushed to the hospital because I have an advanced stage of malaria tropica. By now, my body is tired of fighting, all my energy has long since drained away and I'm lying helplessly on the sofa. When it's time to go, Anneke supports me; it takes me a few minutes to stumble fifty yards to the taxi. At the hospital, I have to wait.

I can hardly keep my head upright, that's how dizzy I am at this moment.

Once it's my turn, the cheerful nurse tells me I'm lucky: I don't have malaria! I barely manage to say that this is impossible, but the nurse shows it on the computer: 'Negative.' At my insistence, she takes another test and it turns out that a mistake was made entering my data. It certainly is malaria; the nurse corrects the error in the system.

Then, there is no bed available.

Half an hour later, I can finally lie down on a makeshift bed in a tiny room. Rest, rest, and still more rest: finally, I don't have any obligations anymore and I can give in to my intense fatigue. Anneke is still there, sitting on a chair that only just fits in the corner.

Then, someone enters wearing a tight suit with a mask. I can only just make out a face behind the transparent plastic. I hear a distorted female voice saying that she wants to check if I have Ebola. It has been three days since I mentioned on the phone that I had been in Liberia and only now the alarm is being raised? Within a minute of leaving the room, she is back: 'What I forgot to ask: did you eat monkey in Liberia?' Ah, had this lady seen the large *marmites* in which the food simmers for hours: indefinable, heavily spiced sauces with all kinds of ingredients that make it difficult to determine exactly what you are eating. In my imagination, I see James' wife's giant snails crawling through the garden and can't help but suppress a smile.

CHAPTER 13
DZANGA-SANGHA

Cameroon/Central African Republic – 2015

A topless Pygmy woman watches me while my fingers claw with all their might at the wet, slippery net to find a hold and prevent me from sliding further down. There, a meter below me, lies the head of a cow slaughtered less than two hours before. Its skin lies spread out on the back of the pickup truck and next to it are two pale plastic bags in which most of the meat is packed.

Flies have discovered this delicacy and are hitching a ride with us. The smell of death reminds me of the carcass, even if I can hardly see it anymore: the tropical night is about to squeeze the last bit of twilight out of the sky. Almost all the light that remains comes from the headlights of the car dragging us through the jungle. Every pothole in the road makes me slide towards the cow, so I try to pull myself up by the net to hang on as high as possible before the next rut pushes me down again. I don't want to end this long day sitting in the lukewarm remains of a dead animal.

After hanging on to the net for a couple of hours, we reach Bayanga. My feet have stayed dry but I'm not yet at my destination. I still have to travel another ten kilometers on the back of a *boda-boda*. Why not, after four days of continuous traveling.

The young rider of the motorbike finally drops me off at a tributary of the Sangha River, where the track ends. A floating wooden platform brings me to the other side by pulling the rope attached to a tree I can't see. Total darkness. This is the entrance to Sangha Lodge, where I planned to sleep for a few days. I sent a text message before, but did it arrive? Is there anyone here at all? Illuminated by the faint glow of my phone, I walk to the entrance. I put my bags on the ground and feel a wave of pent-up tiredness surge through the filth that sticks all over my body.

Then, I see a feeble light moving my way from afar. When it comes closer, the head of a white-bearded man appears in the flicker above it. He puts down his oil lamp, holds out his hand and says: 'Boris Kester, I presume?'

A few days earlier, I walked past the Golden Pavilion and through the meticulously maintained gardens at Kinkaku-ji in Kyoto: I was in Japan for work. After the return flight, I slept at home for a night, unpacked and repacked to fly to Yaoundé through Paris the next morning. I was on my way to the Central African Republic (CAR), one of the countries I had looked at with some awe for years. It was permanently colored red on the travel advisory pages. It had been a turbulent place for years, with fights flaring up regularly between Christians and Muslims, which had cost hundreds of lives. Instead of going to the capital Bangui, where a curfew was in place, I decided to visit the Dzanga-Sangha National Park. In this southwestern corner of the country, it was supposed to be relatively quiet. Instead of hiring a private plane or four-wheel drive in Yaoundé, I chose to travel to the border with the CAR by public transport. Big disadvantage: transport to the far corners of Cameroon was surrounded by uncertainty. I hoped to be able to do it in three days, one way, but it remained to be seen whether that was realistic. Big advantage: those same uncertainties were a guarantee for adventure.

After a short night in a forsaken hotel in a suburb of Yaoundé, near the bus station, I find myself standing next to smoking buses on the main road. It's still dark when I buy a crusty baguette with egg and mayonnaise – the French have left behind some good things here. The bus for Bertoua departs shortly thereafter. It brings me, faster than expected, to my destination, on a smooth asphalt road – by Cameroonian standards. A cheerful lady sits next to me and we chat about anything and everything. After a while, she puts her lips next to my ear and whispers: 'I would like to meet you when we get to Bertoua.'

I have to laugh a little awkwardly at these open advances and suddenly feel incredibly white next to this Cameroonian woman. In the meantime, she scribbles something on a piece of paper and tears it out of her notebook, saying: 'Here, my phone number. Call me later!'

'Merci, Armelle.'

With the scrap of paper still in my right hand, I wonder what to do with her. I look out of the window and let my left arm hang down along the banister. After a while, I feel a tickle. The person sitting behind me puts a piece of paper in my hand. When I smooth it out, I see 'Sophie' and a phone number scribbled on it. I'm curious to know who this Sophie is, but when I look back, the backrest is too high to see her. Only when I stand up to get out of the car can I turn around and look into her smiling face. She purses her lips and sends a kiss into the air with her hand while giving me a challenging wink. If I had taken the private plane, I would already be in Dzanga-Sangha, but I wouldn't have had two notes with pretty women's phone numbers in my hands. Now I just have to decide what to do with them.

But first, I must buy a ticket for the next stage of my journey. At the almost deserted bus station of Alliance Voyages, the ticket office is closed. A lady tells me that the ticket seller is praying in the tiny mosque in a corner of the plot. When he returns, I quickly buy the bus ticket for Yokadouma. The number plate of the bus is also mentioned on it. Departure: seven o'clock.

The next day, it's still early when I return. I know that the bus won't leave on time, but I don't dare to be late. It's a coming and going of cars, mopeds with passengers, traders, women with large bowls selling food, people coming to say goodbye, travelers. I hand my backpack to one of the baggage boys and settle myself on a crumbling wall. I look at the scenes around the white, green, blue and yellow Renault-Saviem buses from the seventies. On the sides it says: 'Yaoundé Bertoua Yokadouma', or 'Libongo Lokoma Kentzou'. On one bus, I see: 'Toutes Directions' (all directions). I would love to take it, but the number plate doesn't match the one on my ticket.

Everywhere, muscular, tawny men are lifting luggage and goods onto the buses. Their helpers stand on the roofs, sort luggage, try to stack it as efficiently as possible, tighten sails, tie ropes, tie knots. Then, when a new package arrives, they untie it all again. The mountains of baggage on the roofs grow steadily until they are almost as high as the vans on which they are piled up.

Of course, the given departure time is not realistic. The

guys on the bus are still piling more items on the mountain of luggage on the Renaults well past seven. While the last chaps finally jump off the roof, a man dressed in a white *boubou* steps onto a wooden stool by the bus with the passenger list in his hands. He reads out the names one by one. When your name is announced, you may enter to choose a seat.

I turn out to be the very first one. Inside, the bus looks like a prison van: a barred cage with wooden benches on a half-corroded floor. I sit down on the second bench, as the first row is too close to the driver's cabin. To my surprise, everyone waits patiently for their name to be called, in order of how the tickets were sold. So, it can be as simple as this. No chaos, no pushing, pulling or shouting; the van fills up quickly. At around ten o'clock, the man in white slams the door and we drive eastwards on Bertoua's main road, with some bumps and jolts. We haven't even left the last houses behind us and the tarmac is already gone. I will only see it again at this same spot, on my journey back home.

The windows are open and red dust is blowing into the cage from all sides. Slowly but surely, it covers our hair, clothes, shoes and bags. There is no music, but everyone is chattering away: a sociable crowd. We pause in Batouri; I venture outside the bus area, walk down the main street, then turn back for fear of missing the bus. When I enter the grounds, the bus is on jacks and all the wheels have disappeared. Two pairs of legs are sticking out from under it, with a range of tools and screws spread out on the ground. Time enough for a tour of the market.

Despite this extensive maintenance, the van starts to show more hiccups on our way to Yokadouma. Every time we stop, we all have to get out. Here, the unsurpassed commercial spirit of the Africans shows itself once more. Before we know it, a child or woman (rarely a man) shows up with oranges, with pieces of roast chicken in a plastic bag, with a box of sweets, combs in a variety of bright colors, tins of ointment, curlers, soap, or what have you. Ready to do business. Or they come just to stare at that yellow van, which for a moment gives them the illusion that they are connected to a far-flung city, to another part of the country, to the rest of Africa and who knows, the rest of the large, distant world.

Later in the afternoon, it begins to rain heavily. The road soon turns into a brownish-red, slippery mud stream. The window next to the row in front of me turns out to be missing and the left side of my t-shirt and trousers are soon soaked through. I'm lucky because there are large holes in the ceiling on the right-hand side and the rain pours down straight into the bus. The tarpaulin protecting the luggage on the roof turns out to be anything but watertight. The unlucky people sitting under-neath try to stay dry by holding a plastic bag over their heads. In vain. The water mixes with the red dust that we had collected hours earlier. Now it's a good thing that the bottom of the van also has large holes: they provide a way for the water to wash away.

Perhaps driven on by the sweltering heat, a very vocal lady and a distinguished-looking gentleman get into a heated argument with each other. Because of the animated conversations around me, I missed what preceded this. But now that they are shout-ing, they can be understood very well, especially because everyone has shut up to allow them to follow what is happen-ing. I now remember that even before we left Bertoua, the woman could occasionally be heard above all the voices with piquant comments about others. The man tries to calm things down, which results in an increasing escalation: the woman snarls at him in a shrill voice with severe indignities. The others in the cage love this free entertainment. Their cheering and laughing excite the two ruffians more and more, until the woman's final salvo: 'Once we get to our destination, I'll find a doctor and ask him to remove your genitals. The world would be a better place if you were no longer a man.' In her precisely formulated French, this sounds both frightening and elegant. The audience loves it, especially because the man has no response, or perhaps he decides that it's wiser not to say anything back. Then, of course, she goes on to taunt him. I admire the man's control. His strategy works: the woman gets tired of insulting him. Tempers calm down and we are mainly occupied with the rainwater still pouring into the bus from all sides.

Meanwhile, the day is drawing to a close and I wonder how much further we have to go. The various repair stops haven't helped our progress; nor have the checkpoints along the way. Sometimes, we're allowed to remain seated and the officers put their arms through the bars to accept all identity cards. Sometimes, they ask us to get out, which always results in vendors (how do they always manage to be in the right place at the right time?) swarming around us and offering us *Made-in-China* junk.

It's long past sunset when we finally enter Yokadouma. It soon transpires that there is 'most likely' no bus the next morning to Libongo, the border town with the Central African Republic. I talk to a couple of motorcyclists hanging around the bus station. A heated discussion ensues between those who believe that going by motorbike is too dangerous because of elephants and other wild animals, and those who say that it is indeed possible. None of the young men have ever driven the route. Nevertheless, there is a lively debate in which proponents and opponents eloquently try to convince each other they are right. My conclusion is that it's not impossible, so I have my plan B for the next day ready. I walk through the streets of Yokadouma, lit only by little lights at the abundant stalls, waiting for customers. I had read beforehand that bushmeat is still eaten in these parts. Fortunately, I don't see it for sale anywhere and I manage to find a restaurant that is still open and serves food that I recognise.

After a night in a dingy room with a saggy bed, no sheets, no lights and a worn-out bucket of water in the corner (the five-star luxury of Japan three days earlier now seems very distant), I go back to the bus station the next morning. It turns out that there is indeed no van. I also understand that one alternative, hitching a ride with the World Wildlife Fund's four-wheel drive, isn't possible. The car won't be traveling to Libongo today. I head back to the motorcyclists. Now that they see me again, they smell an opportunity, especially because by now they know for sure that there is no bus and no WWF car. They have become my last straw, making my negotiating position even weaker. Last night's discussion about the dangers of the trip immediately flares up again.

In the end, I grant Benjamin the ride: he comes across as the calmest and most reliable guy. He says he needs some time to refuel and pack his things. I urge him to take all the papers he may need on the road with him. Within half an hour, he is back. But then, after a few hundred meters, he turns out not to be satisfied with the bike and asks me to wait. Half an hour later, he is back: he has found another *boda-boda*. He tells me that the problem with his own bike couldn't be solved. He proudly says that he now has a new one on loan from a friend. Well, new: the speedometer and the headlamp are missing, the brake cables are frayed, the carrier straps are inner tubes knotted together – and these are just the defects visible to my inexperienced eye.

We tie my bag with the inner tubes to the carrier, with a pump on top. I get on the saddle behind him and we're on our way. Even before we leave the village, Benjamin is already speeding. He has to go back today – a one-way trip is 260 kilometers – and we have lost another hour altogether. The bumps in the road launch me off the bike a few times, while my feet rest loosely on the metal pipe beneath me. I hold the bars of the carrier firmly on both sides and I can barely see in front of me, not least the potholes in the road ahead.

Within ten minutes, my hands are cramping, but more importantly, I can see a potential accident around every corner and in every pothole. I realize that if Benjamin loses control of his bike, or if I get thrown off, I won't be able to count on help. I'm not wearing a helmet: he hasn't been able to get one for me. But am I going to be afraid all day? I take heart and convince myself to relax, hold the bars loosely and let my worries go. If I want to reach the border today, there is no other option than to go with Benjamin. I can only hope that my guardian angels will hold on to my shoulders, which are constantly shaking with the sudden movements of the bike.

Within a few kilometers, the first police shack emerges. According to a handwritten note on a board, this is the *Securité de Route* or Road Safety. We haven't even come to a full stop when Benjamin hands over some money to one of the policemen, although I hiss in his ear not to do so. 'But this is Africa, you don't understand.' Yes, I know that people here often blithely give money to policemen, hoping in this way to avoid discussions and get through controls more quickly. And admittedly, I don't understand that. This automatism is precisely the reason why the system remains intact. Every vehicle here has defects and so it's easier to buy off a check in advance. Yet, by doing so, that money doesn't benefit society but disappears directly into the pockets of the officer. How many times have I had this discussion with people in this region?

'Why did you pay that policeman?'

'Well, that's how we do it here.'

'What would be a reason for not paying?'

'Not paying? You can't. If you don't pay, you don't know what will happen.'

'But if all your papers are in order, the officer has no reason to be difficult, right?'

'No, but he doesn't have a high salary.'

'What about you? Is your salary higher than the officer's?'

'No, it's not.'

'You told me you were a teacher?'

'Yes, that's right.'

'You have an important profession: you are educating the future of your country. You deserve to be paid for that. Why would you give up part of your salary to a cop?'

At this point, I often see a thoughtful face. They never looked at it like that. But Africans have an admirable respect for authority and the policemen take advantage of that. I'm a cheeky foreigner who isn't intimidated by a uniform, even less so if it's worn right down to the wire.

I join the Africans in everything. I eat their food, even though sometimes it's unpalatable. I juggle plastic bowls in a tub of water to wash myself, in the beam of a torch because there is no running water or electricity. I squeeze myself into their bulging vehicles that should have been discarded twenty years ago and where I sometimes must hold the door to prevent it from falling in the street. They have to stop every half hour or less for the umpteenth repair, so you always arrive much later than you thought. I wait with them for boats that don't arrive, trains that don't leave, border offices that are closed. I laugh with them at their casual sense of humor and admire their purity, their endless inventiveness and resilience. I shake hands and embrace them and have long since taken them to my heart, simply because they are who they are. How often do they call me the White African? But in situations with authorities, I'm not a White African, but a straightforward, principled Dutchman. The easiest thing would be to pay. But that is precisely the point: I'm not here to take the easy way out.

Benjamin has already paid, so the policemen are in a good mood and are now looking at me eagerly. That foreigner will have to give much more. But I don't give anything, so I wait. 'Passport.'

I hand over the document and see that the officer goes through it slowly, examining each stamp as if looking for spelling mistakes. Almost all sixty-four pages are already full. Stamps in green, blue, red, black, some still fresh, some already faded, so there's a lot to see and a lot to decipher. After a while, I notice that he is holding the passport upside down. I point it out to him, he pretends nothing is wrong and composedly continues to leaf through it. He asks for my vaccination booklet. Fortunately, I just had a new yellow fever vaccination. A year before, also in Cameroon, an agent kept emphasizing that my yellow fever would expire two months later, that it was no longer valid and that giving him money would solve everything. Creative corruption. Two documents are now in order. He has to look for something new. 'Where is the *Ordre de Mission?*'

Benjamin didn't mention anything about this, so I pretend not to understand. The officer explains: he wants to see a letter from the mayor of Yokadouma, permitting me to leave town. I argue, making it clear that I have a valid visa, that I'm on my way to the Central African Republic and that nobody in the village has told me that I would need special permission from the mayor to travel to my destination. He realizes that this is a dead-end, looks in despair at his mate. What now? 'Open your luggage.'

It's time to put an end to this. I don't feel like taking down the luggage that Benjamin has painstakingly tied to his carrier with the old, torn inner tubes threatening to burst at the touch, just for a useless inspection. I ask him as politely as I can what would be his reason for inspecting my luggage. After all, we're still a few hundred kilometers from the border. He doesn't know either. With my documents in hand, I tell Benjamin, 'Come on, let's go.'

We walk back to the bike, one of the officers reluctantly pulls down the rope and with a friendly greeting, Benjamin accelerates. In their haste to collect some money, the officers have forgotten that they are actually at a road safety station: they never checked the whole bike. They could have found a whole list of shortcomings there. Or wait, Benjamin had indeed already paid for that check and this is actually not about safety at all.

The road, which runs through the dense jungle like a brown-red ribbon, turns out to be used mainly by large trucks carrying sea containers and gigantic tree trunks heading west. The arrival of the huge oncoming vehicles is announced far in advance. The approaching behemoths blow red clouds into the air – you can only see the front of the cabs as they emerge from the clouds later. The juggernauts take up the entire width of the road, so we make sure to get to the shoulder in time, waiting for the worst of the dust to settle and trying to cover our faces as best we can with our hands. Nevertheless, our ears, eyes, mouths and nostrils are soon filled with fine brown-red sand.

Logging is the only thing this region has to offer. They are plentiful: giant trees so tall that their tops touch, far above our heads. I suspect that the Chinese are cutting down trees to their heart's content. I imagine that after a long journey by road, all these dusty trunks will be transferred to a ship for the much longer boat trip to China once they reach the coast. There, they will be turned into tables, chairs, beds and cupboards, which will be polished off in a shiny finish and end up in one of the gray uniform housing blocks in Shanghai or Beijing or one of the many other Chinese multi-million-inhabitant metropolises that we don't even know exist. Ah, if only the residents of those flats could look around here to see where their furniture comes from!

Of course, there are more checkpoints and more police officers ahead. I ask Benjamin several times how many more we are going to see, but every time he says we have seen the last one, another comes along. I keep forgetting that he, too, is navigating this road for the first time. At some stations, the officers are friendly and surprised to see a white man on the back of a motorbike. But most of them make my life difficult. Benjamin is resigned to everything, working hard today to earn money with an assignment he only partially knows about. For this reason alone, I can hardly bear the aggressive, greedy looks and the sometimes arrogant attitude of the officers, especially since they ultimately radiate total uselessness. Often, by the way, they aren't even wearing uniforms, but dusty t-shirts and faded trousers. Sitting in the middle of a jungle, where no one lives, with only the occasional large lorry transporting their raw materials at high speed to a distant country. And then holding up the rope and stopping a *boda-boda* passing by because there might be a few thousand francs to scrape out of it.

Benjamin no longer pays the men, so he is also checked. To my chagrin, at the sixth checkpoint, he turns out not to have his driving license with him. Now the policemen have a justifiable argument to be troublesome. This was exactly the reason I had urged him to bring all his papers. But perhaps he has no driving license at all? It just goes to show that these checkpoints aren't actually about checking anything, but only about cashing.

We drive for hours through dense rainforest, with an occasional clearing where huts stand alongside the red ribbon of the road. Women sit stirring huge pans on the fire. Men chat under a big tree. Children run after us, shouting. The question that arises is: why did these people start living here at the edge of the road? Far from everything, with the guarantee of heavy trucks that take away their only capital every day, for which they will never see anything in return, except an ever-thickening layer of red dust on the fragile roofs of their simple huts.

Benjamin sometimes makes steering errors, misjudges the depth of potholes, or simply overlooks them. When we're launched off the road, my heart stops and I hold onto the bike as tight as I can to avoid falling off after landing. I hope my little angels are still clinging to my shoulders because if things go wrong, the nearest hospital is very far away. Moreover, who would take me there in the first place?

Many dust showers later, we finally reach the turnoff to Libongo, a crossroads at a forest clearing. We turn left and soon come across a barrier. A man comes out of his booth, pulls a serious face and asks for money. I make a joke of it, whereupon a broad smile breaks through his face. He is employed by one of the companies that chop wood here. He says he never asks for money, but he thought he could get some from a foreigner. We shake hands and he wishes us a good ride.

This road turns out to be very different from the main road we have been traveling so far. It's a narrow red lane that runs straight through the green heart of Africa. No more controls, no villages, no people, no openings in the forest, no trucks, no dust showers. Hardly any potholes. I can relax now. Below us: red, beside us: green, above us: blue. The world reduced to its primary colors.

Then, suddenly, Benjamin makes an emergency stop. I'm violently pushed into his back. Excitedly, he shouts: 'Look!' When I raise my head from his back and look in front of us, I see them. A group of huge gorillas in the middle of the road, with the silverback as the proud center. Benjamin is scared, that much is clear. Who knows, maybe he has never seen them before? While we stand there and look at the gray-black hominids who make no move to leave, I realize that in Uganda or Rwanda you have to dig deep into your pockets to see them. Here, they come as a bonus during a drive through the jungle. When the group has finally moved a bit towards the verge,

Benjamin takes his chances. He speeds up, steers as much to the right as possible and drives partially through the verge on the other side of the road. The silverback raises his head and makes himself impressively big, but we have already passed him and I look back in awe, just as the silverback looks at me in amazement.

The African colors of red, orange, pink, blue and gray in the sky announce that the day is coming to an end. Along the road, for the first time since the turn-off, we see a human being. A Pygmy. He is holding a dead blue duiker in his hand. Benjamin stops to chat while the big black eyes of the little deer stare at me innocently. The man lives in Libongo: fifteen minutes later, we drive into the border village. It took us almost eight hours to get here and I'm afraid I'm much too late to cross the border.

Benjamin is beaming. For him, this was as much of an adventure as it was for me and he enjoyed it. I pay him more than we had agreed for all his trouble and ask him if he is actually going to drive the 260 kilometers back to Yokadouma. He would be on his own, less than an hour and a half before sunset, with gorillas and probably other animals along the road. Without a headlight. Not to mention the checkpoints. He nods. He doesn't heed my advice to stay the night. I will never know if he arrived home safely.

The immigration office is closed, but after some walking and asking around, I quickly find the officer. He decorates my passport with a fresh exit stamp. He is cooperative and even finds someone who can help me find transportation across the border so that I can actually leave the country. The Central African Republic is on the other side of the Sangha River and I would preferably like to cross that river today. I also ask around about buses back to Yokadouma, but nobody can tell me anything decisive. Sometimes there is a bus, sometimes not. Yes, I suspected as much.

A load of goods has arrived which also needs to be transported to the other side and has already been loaded onto a large *pirogue*, so I'm in luck. With all the tree giants of the rainforest around me, it comes as no surprise that this wooden canoe is also huge. Some passengers are already seated. There is a boy at the stern and behind him, a man in a military uniform with a cap and a woman in a bright yellow-blue-green-orange robe. I take my place behind them. Behind me lie boxes and crates and a recently slaughtered cow. The head is loose, the legs are still attached to the rest of the moist skin and the meat is in bags standing next to it. The bulge of Bayanga, to the south of the country, is so isolated and inaccessible from the rest of the Central African Republic that supplies come from Cameroon. And well, borders. For me, the CAR means a new stamp, another new country, another step closer to my goal – I still have fourteen to go. But borders here have been artificially drawn by European gentlemen in top hats who, with cigars in their mouths, stood bent over the map of Africa in the nineteenth century. Africans take a much more pragmatic view.

On the other side is Bamanjoko, where a man in a hut writes my name in a school notebook. I don't even get a visa – he says I will get one the next day, in Bayanga. For years, I have wondered how to enter this country and where to get a visa. The official doesn't even ask for money. That is the beauty of Africa: even if you have traveled here a lot, it never ceases to amaze you.

When I walk out of the hut, I see that a couple of boys are

busy loading the cargo of the *pirogue* onto a white Toyota pickup. Around them, a large group of people are inspecting the goods. Once everything is lifted and pulled onto the car, the rear bumper almost touches the ground. Everything is held in place by a large black net. The seats in the car were already taken before we came ashore, and the only place left for us is to sit on the net. That is quite a challenge because they have built the goods like a pyramid, with steep walls you have the tendency to slide down, especially when the car drags itself through the deep pits of the endless road to Bayanga.

Rod and Tam, the South African owners of Sangha Lodge, turn out to be sensitive, warm-hearted people who do everything they can to make me feel at home here. Immediately after my arrival that night, they even make a pizza for me. Lit by two candles and the oil lamp, we gradually get to know each other. I eat and listen. They have had a difficult time: while everyone advised them to flee the country's ferocious civil war, they have stayed in this remote corner of the country.

The few visitors who come here do so, almost without exception, by chartered airplane. Rod is curious about my experiences and hears me out about the trip that brought me here from Yaoundé. Then, we discuss possible activities for the coming days. After the long journey here, I can finally focus on my goal: discovering the Central African forest. Because of the myriad obstacles on the way here, I already know I will have that jungle all to myself.

As always, it's exciting to arrive in the dark and not see the surroundings until the next day. I wake up in total darkness. The loud sound of the awakening jungle around me isn't interrupted by anything. Outside, the cover of night is slowly being lifted. I sit down on the spacious wooden veranda. The water in the wide, brown river is flowing fast, towards the south, where it will flow into one of the biggest rivers in Africa: the Congo. Eventually, it will end up in the Atlantic Ocean. A low fog hangs over the Sangha and its emerald fringe. Every once in a while, the cry of an animal emerges from the jungle, which is all around me. From all sides, I hear the twittering of birds in an overwhelming cacophony. I have arrived in the dark, beating heart of Africa.

After a while, Tam comes walking onto the veranda with a pangolin hanging from her shoulder. The scaled animal looks around with small beady eyes, its pointed snout sticking up in the air. While we're talking, she puts the animal in my hand. It immediately rolls up and it's suddenly a lot smaller. Pangolins are endangered here. They are easy to catch and are therefore regularly on the menu. Tam and Rod have taken it upon themselves to buy the animals at markets and give them a second life at their lodge.

Meanwhile, the river comes to life. Several *pirogues* sail by, carrying fishermen looking for prey. After getting a visa in my passport a few hours later, I start hunting for something completely different. A comfortable one-and-a-half-hour ride takes a ranger and me to Bai Hakou, the center of gorilla tracking of Dzanga-Sangha National Park.

Two Ba-Aka Pygmies join us. One of them walks ahead of us, right through the jungle. He picks up the pace. Without stopping even once, he determinedly leads us through the dense jungle via a tangle of paths. Every few steps, he snaps a blade of grass: markers to find the way back. My guide and I walk behind him, followed by the second native. The longer we walk, the more I realize how vast this area is and how impenetrable the jungle. Because of the large trees and dense vegetation lower down, our view is never more than a few dozen meters. How are we ever going to find gorillas here? The age-old thrill of safaris: there are no guarantees, you have to be lucky and, apart from looking around, you have little influence on what you will see. Good guides often make the difference.

When the Ba-Aka finally stops, he points down. Gorilla droppings. We're on their trail, I think, and I can feel my heart pounding with excitement. My sense of direction tells me that we're constantly walking in circles, but without even being able to see where the sun is, it's very difficult to find your bearings. The guides are in radio contact for a while and then we see them.

Three people.

Is this it, after two hours of walking? The men say nothing. When they see us, one of them puts his index finger over his mouth, his fingertip against his nose. Then they step apart as if they were following a script.

Right behind them, I see four large black spots among the abundant greenery. When we carefully walk forward until we're a few meters away, we can see, hear, smell and almost feel them. This is the Makumba family, the guide whispers in my right ear. The silverback is in the middle, he seems to be completely absorbed. He is sitting on the ground, chewing on bright red fruit. He regularly frowns. He seems to be in a philosophical mood. Yet Makumba means speed: this colossus can shoot through the forest like a flash when circumstances call for it. His two children, a girl and a boy, live up in the trees, climbing, jumping, running, romping. Nothing is foreign to the young gorillas. The young lady especially seems to know no fear and sometimes runs right past us. The parents have long since outgrown this phase of play.

The men turn out to be researchers and whisper explanations in my ear. They do their utmost to put me in the best possible position to observe the primates and take pictures of them. They do their own observations themselves. All the behavior is coded and timestamped in a notebook. The disadvantage of this is that after exactly one hour they know it's time to say goodbye. One hour is the maximum time visitors are allowed to spend around gorillas.

Finding the way back is no problem for the Ba-Aka. Using the snapped blades as signposts, the Pygmy walks back to the world without any problems. That evening, there is even a dash of wifi in the lodge and from this dark heart of Africa, I call my father to congratulate him on his birthday. For a moment, the feeling of total isolation and distance completely disappears.

The next day, the guide and I drive to another place in the park for a different kind of safari. A Ba-Aka accompanies us and after a short drive, we walk for half an hour, partly through a small river, to a large wooden platform that lies on the edge of a *bai*. Water flows through this large clearing in the forest, making it the perfect place to admire the animals of Dzanga-Sangha. Once I get used to doing nothing but sitting and watching, I'm glad that Rod advised me to take the whole day for this. Not in a swinging and bouncing jeep, not in a kayak, not on a horse and not walking, but just sitting on a wooden bench. My camera and lenses are around me and a bottle of water is within reach. Sheer joy. As if I were sitting in the loge of a theater with an endless show where the curtains are always open and there is never a break.

In the jungle, it's very difficult to spot animals, but here you can't miss them. The large opening is full of water sources, which makes it irresistible to all the wildlife. We see dozens of elephants on the plain. They stick their trunks into the gray soil, slurp up the equally gray water and move on. The little ones blow bubbles in the small pools. Or they shower themselves. Aside from elephants, there are bongos, reddish-brown antelopes with white stripes on their sides, herds of water buffaloes and a wide variety of birds. My guide says that a few years ago, before the civil war, there were many more animals here. Poachers seized their chance in the lawlessness of the war. A wonderfully relaxing day in the middle of the jungle doesn't end until late in the afternoon. While we're wading through the river on our way back, I'm holding my camera bag over my head, when we see a lone elephant approaching us. The guide gets a bit nervous and finally manages to chase the mastodon away by having us all make some noise.

The following day, I go hunting with the Ba-Aka – with nets. To my surprise, our party consists mainly of women. After they have loaded their nets and other supplies, we drive on in our pickup through the jungle. The women are singing in the boot while the guide throws a dilemma at me. Do I want them to kill an animal after they catch it? If so, they will do this on the spot.

So, the question is: do I want to sign the death warrant of their prey and witness its execution? My decadent Western urban sentiment resists – I still remember that matted look in the lifeless eyes of the dead blue duiker I saw a few days earlier. The guide offers me an alternative: if I pay them the equivalent of an animal, they will set it free. But with this remorse money, they will still buy another animal on the market that will disappear into the *marmite* tonight. On balance, it doesn't matter what I decide: the dwarf people are going to hunt anyway, and an animal is going to die. The women's songs remind me of this. Or are they singing love songs? Whatever the case, the energy is palpable: everyone is in the mood. During the ride to the jungle, I'm torn between the women's lively singing and my guilt about the imminent death of an animal. When we disembark, I inform the guide that the kill will be for the hunters. It elicits a cry of delight from the leader of the group.

We walk into the forest, the hunters spread out with their nets and communicate with each other via shouts, which echo under the dense canopy above us. Net hunting is hoping for a lucky catch. The hunters spread out through the forest, unable to see each other, but knowing exactly what to do. They hang their nets low on the branches so that they touch the ground and eventually form a large circle. Then, within the circle, they systematically search for animals trapped in this cage of nets. It doesn't seem efficient because if there aren't any animals in the huge cage, the deployment of the nets has been for nothing. With the dense vegetation, the Pygmies don't have much choice because the animals that live here are smaller than the vegetation and therefore difficult to spot and catch.

The hunters' energy is infectious, and I watch with them as they hang up their nets and search the jungle for possible prey for the evening's dinner. We push deeper and deeper into the jungle. However, even after they have made five circles, the yield is nil. Meanwhile, one of the women I'm with shows me how they make the nets from plants they find here and how they drink water from tree bark. The Ba-Aka have lived in this jungle for centuries, it's their home and they know exactly what they can use and for what purpose. They go home without any loot: time for a vegetarian dinner. Or, at least, get an animal at the market, but I won't live to see that. Secretly, I feel relieved.

At the beginning of my long journey home, I visit an American writer who moved here years ago. He tells me about the recent crisis, how his documents were stolen by rebels, how he went into hiding from the violence, how he came back to this house and how he will stay in this remote corner in the heart of Africa that he has come to love. I leave my luggage with him and walk back to the village to find a motorcyclist who can take me to the border. The sun casts ever-warmer hues over the houses and the landscape as we ride towards the light.

I don't bat an eyelid when the rider is tearing along narrow paths. After a while, he tells me that I'm the first white guy who hasn't told him to slow down. Whether that is a compliment, I don't know. Apparently, I have become a bit more reckless. At the border, my details are written down once more in the notebook and the man behind the rickety table asks for a contribution to buy medicine for his sick wife.

At the river's edge, the men of the big *pirogues* know they have me in their clutches. I have to get to the other side and the sun is already almost touching the horizon above Cameroon. They demand a price ten times higher than what Rod had advised me. I refuse, walk away, talk to others and ask around if I can sleep somewhere in one of the huts. Then, I see a young guy with a small boat and offer him a few thousand francs. When he hears my proposal, his eyes light up. Much to the chagrin of the others who approach us menacingly, we sail away a little later, due south, past an island in the river, to Cameroon. Upon arrival, I immediately walk to the village square where the bus leaves. Next to the little office, with the sign *Alliance Voyages – la maîtrise de la route*, is the old prison bus that I know well, with the same familiar number plate. Luck is on my side.

The next morning, as the sun begins its climb into the sky above the dense jungle of the Central African Republic, where Pygmies will once again be casting their nets, strong men load all the luggage onto the roof, the bus fills up quickly and I'm even allowed to sit next to the driver. Better still: on my right-hand side is a soldier, who manages to talk me past every checkpoint without further ado. Gradually, the cow corpse, the dead duiker, the gorillas, the forest elephants and their bubble-blowing youngsters, the hunting Ba-Aka and all those other intensely lived and often raw experiences of the last few days become vivid memories. A new reality presents itself. I'm on my way back to electricity and running water, to asphalt, to cops who aren't after my money, to cities, to predictability, and finally: back home. Far, far away from adventure.

Chapter 14
Betel Nut Boat

Papua New Guinea – 2016

One of the last countries to visit before reaching my final goal was Papua New Guinea, which I will call PNG for convenience. I had deliberately saved it until the end. Seven years earlier, in Colombia, I traveled for a few days with the Australian Jake, who spoke lyrically about the country and urged me to go there one day. I had decided to visit every country only months before and I hardly had a clue about PNG. For some Dutch people, Papua is remotely known, but that is the western part of the island, which officially still belongs to Indonesia. The eastern part, once governed by the United Kingdom and Germany, became independent in 1975 and is under the radar for most.

Years earlier, I had been pretty close. In Gizo, one of the Solomon Islands furthest west, I saw boats that could take me to Bougainville. This is the easternmost island of PNG that would end up voting for independence a few years later. But I decided to resist the temptation and to save the country for later, when I would have more time for it. Shortly after I visited Gizo, I met a UN employee in Vanuatu. She regularly visited the PNG capital Port Moresby for work. According to her, it was so dangerous that the UN forbade her to walk from her hotel to her office, even though she only had to cross the street to reach it. And so, every day a car was arranged to take her to the other side of the road. It confirmed the general picture of the country: I had read more warnings about the insecurity in PNG. But Jake's words were ringing in my ears as well, so I had a strong desire to see the country with my own eyes.

Quite weary after a long journey and looking forward to the adventure that lies ahead of me, I walk through the security gate at Cairns airport. The attendant glances at my boarding pass and when she sees my destination says: 'Oh, you have to be very careful there! You must be traveling for work?' To my negative answer and explanation that I will be traveling around for almost four weeks, she gives me a stare of incomprehension. Indeed, a little later I only see a few businessmen in the small plane that, in an hour and a half, takes me to the city where you supposedly need to take a taxi to cross the street.

Except for countries where you have to apply for a visa at an embassy or consulate, your first impression is that of the immigration officer at the border. Sometimes, they make your life difficult and don't look at you at all, or they give you a grim face. You hope that this is because sitting in a cubicle at an airport checking and stamping passports day in, day out, while a line of waiting, tired people are looking at their watches, can't be much fun. The man behind the counter at Jacksons International Airport, in contrast, puts a yellow sticker in my passport with a big smile on his face, after which he welcomes me to his country. That's a good start.

It's time to improvise. As is almost always the case, I haven't fixed anything at all for my trip; I only have a few places in my head that I would like to go to. The infrastructure in the country is poor. There are hardly any roads. Unless you have your own boat, flying is practically the only way to cover larger distances. At the office of one of the local companies, I buy a ticket to Wewak in a few hours.

Before entering the ATR-72 of PNG-Air, I stop to enjoy the unusual livery. Even though I don't know the country yet, I immediately see that the designers have succeeded in capturing the essence of PNG: stylized black and white masks with a sprinkling of red and yellow. It gives the plane a very artistic, recognizable and characteristic look. This must be one of the most beautiful aircraft tails I have ever seen.

My boarding pass says 1 A and I walk through the back door into the ATR-72. When I arrive at the first row, I realize that the rows are numbered back to front. Row 1 is at the very back of the aircraft. With all the flights I have taken in my life, I have never seen this before.

PNG portrays itself as the *Land of the Unexpected*. So far, this seems spot on, since everything appears to be different here. What more could the traveler wish for? I'm rapidly falling in love with this country.

We make a stopover at Mount Hagen in the highlands, which gives me a glimpse of the country's diversity from the air. Once we arrive at the small airport in the northern town of Wewak, I walk off the property and see a homestay across the street. Before I throw myself into bed, I quickly eat something near the beach. I catch up on overdue sleep with a long night.

Early next morning, I go to the city to withdraw money from an ATM. While waiting for my turn, I strike up a conversation with a Papuan man next to me. When he hears where I come from, he looks at me with pity. Europe, well, it certainly is very dangerous now, with all those attacks: Paris, London, Brussels, Madrid? He wouldn't dare go there for anything! I try to explain that it's not that bad, that it's still perfectly fine to live in Europe, but he doesn't budge. Then I tell him about the image that PNG has for many foreigners. Better to avoid it altogether and if you do go there, only be outside during the day and sleep in hotels with good security. If you want to cross a street in Port Moresby: take a taxi! The man hears me with big eyes and then bursts out laughing. Dangerous, here? What a weird thought!

I can barely fit the huge pile of banknotes into my money belt and I look like I have a big belly when I leave the bank. I walk through the streets of the town and soon notice that I'm the only foreigner.

After some asking around, I find them: the PMVs that I had already read about. Public Motor Vehicles, the main means of transport of PNG. I will soon find out that PMVs are not only buses: they can be any vehicle. Cars, jeeps, trucks, boats: anything that can take you from A to B and in which multiple passengers can travel. The public transport of PNG, but of course: different. There are no numbers, no colors, no route network, no stops and certainly no timetable. You just go to where they leave from, ask around and someone shows you a vehicle that will go to your destination. And then you wait for it to drive away. No crimps, no tickets, no fuss: it's a straightforward system.

After all the disaster stories I have read which made me consider hiring a chauffeur-driven car for some parts of my trip, my first PMV turns out to be a pleasant surprise. Even though it's full, I have enough room to sit down, look outside, breathe and move my legs every so often. Much better than what I have experienced in many other countries.

After a few hours of driving on a bad road, I arrive in Angoram on the Sepik, the longest river in the country. I walk along a rectangular field into the village. This used to be the landing strip of the local airfield; now it's crisscrossed by tracks for people taking shortcuts. On the other side of the field, I find a guesthouse.

The stoutly built man sitting in the shade of a large tree turns out to be Francis, the owner. I sit down with him to shelter from the fierce heat of the sun. We immediately click and we talk for hours about anything and everything. Of course, also about my plans here: discovering the Sepik and finding a way to get to the sea. To do so, I have set my sights on a trip down the river, as there is no road.

Later, when we walk to the Sepik, everyone seems to know him. One person accosts him with a question, another brings him something, yet another talks about his personal situation. It's as if I'm walking through the village with the mayor. Francis is not only a host who understands exactly what I need; he also has all the contacts to realize my plans.

Two burning repellent spirals and a net ensure that I survive the night without being stung by the enormous number of mosquitoes. The next morning, I sit on the back of a motorbike with an acquaintance of Francis. We ride over the airstrip and across the grass to the banks of the Sepik River. We get off at a wooden house. I see jerrycans with diesel; this must be the local petrol station for boats. Someone fetches a hollowed-out tree trunk and before I know it, I'm on the river sailing upstream. A few more men join us in the boat. Whenever we have to slow down, the boatman lights a fire in a metal basket to chase away the mosquitoes. We cough our lungs out in the thick smoke – but indeed, the mosquitoes leave us alone.

We visit several villages on the way. Most of the houses are on stilts. It appears that many artists live in these parts. As soon as they see me coming, women and men dive into their huts and come back with enormous wood carvings, which they quickly wipe with a piece of cloth to get rid of the worst dust. Beautiful art, but impossible to carry all the way home. I also walk through a market and see the enormous damage caused by a flood a few months earlier. Before we sail back, we pass a crocodile farm in the middle of the river. The Sepik is so wide that when the wind picks up at the end of the afternoon, jet-black clouds sail towards us through the sky and heads appear on the waves, which occasionally slam over the edge of our canoe. Miraculously, we remain dry.

The next day, I wander through the village. Along the river, there are wooden canoes with carved figures on their sides and a bow made of carved birds and huge crocodile heads. When I walk towards Wewak, I talk to several people who tell me they are suffering from malaria. After having contracted falciparum malaria myself in Liberia a few months earlier, I have decided to take malaria pills and that proves not to be an overreaction.

Under a tree large enough to provide shade to the entire market of Angoram, I wait with Francis for his friends who can help me down the river. There are rumors that in the evening a few boats will go down the Sepik, in the direction of the sea. But no matter how much Francis asks and calls, he can't get in touch with the boatmen. We watch the people chatting, the children playing on the gnarled roots that emerge from the ground many meters from the trunk, like writhing snakes looking for prey. But no news of the boat.

After dinner, Francis and I continue talking in his guest-house. Since I'm still hoping to leave that same evening, it's time to settle the bill. He had vaguely mentioned a price for the room, but not for the food and certainly not for all the help he has given me. He now charges a fraction of what I thought it would cost. I protest, but he says he already finds it objectionable to charge at all because he considers me a friend. His genuine reluctance to present me with an honest bill touches me. I calculate for myself what a reasonable amount would be, hand it to him, turn around and walk away. At least the hump in my money belt has become a lot flatter now.

Halfway through the evening, three men walk in from the dark. They timidly ask if it's true that I want to sail down the Sepik. They are going out to sea in their boats and I can come along. So, everything turns out alright after all. We walk through pitch darkness over the muddy road to the river and sail to the other side. The men speak *Tok Pisin* (talk pidgin). PNG (Papua Niu Gini in pidgin) is a language maze, with more than 850 languages for only seven million souls, and pidgin is the *lingua franca* that enables people to understand each other. With some imagination, I can sometimes understand what they say, but mostly, it's just a joy hearing them speak.

They still have a few things to arrange, and I sit down to watch the activity. Several men walk back and forth with large, white bags which they lay in two sloops tied together. Then the three men invite me into one of the small boats. Aside from a few jerrycans, the bottom is covered with dozens of bags of betel nut. The porters come along too; they will trade the bags. Betel nut is every Papuan's stimulant; the betel or areca nut, with its intoxicating effect, is transported from here to other parts of the country. I'm basically on a drug smuggling mission.

We leave the sparse lights of Angoram behind and sail off into the night. I spread out on the bed of betel nuts. It feels surprisingly comfortable. Infinitely far above me, a starry sky stretches out that here, in this remote corner of a country in a remote corner of the world, shines and sparkles so immensely that the tiredness I felt when I left is immediately forgotten. There, the first falling star. Then, there's another one. The men murmur amongst themselves, barely audible over the tuff-tuff-tuff of the outboard motor, while my eyes shoot from left to right, up and down, and back again, over the heavenly roof of Papua. I soon lose count of the stars, which continue falling in droves. When I can think of no more wishes for the world, my loved ones and myself, a deep, inner peace descends over me.

I have sunk into a shallow sleep when the monotonous engine noise suddenly stops. It wakes me up and I see that we're in the middle of the river. The bright starlight allows me to catch a glimpse of the riverbanks. We drift with the current while the men untie the boats. We're going to take a shortcut through the jungle and each boat will do this using its own power. One of the men switches on a floodlight, another starts the engine. Then we sail towards the shore, where there appears to be an opening. We're now going at full speed through the forest, through the white tunnel that the bright light drills into the pitch-black jungle. It's almost impossible for this to go well: every ten meters there is a bend in this small tributary of the Sepik. We sail right under trees, swerving left and right, but the helmsman makes no mistakes and we blast through the dense Papuan forest.

Then suddenly, something flies into the boat. It lands right on me – now I'm wide awake. I try to see what it is with my torch. A frog? A small bird? Another animal? I can't work it out and I forget about it. Only when we emerge into the wide Sepik again does the helmsman switch off the engine and we float on, waiting for the second boat. As soon as it arrives, the boats are tied together again and we cruise along towards the river mouth. I drift back into a shallow sleep under the monotonous sound of the engine.

Far away, ahead of us, we see a glimmer of light, announcing the start of a new day. We steer to the riverbank. There is a small settlement where the men fill our jerrycans. We appear to be running low on diesel and are still a long way from our destination. A few bends of the Sepik later, the silhouette of the jungle in front of us fades away and the world opens up. We see a distant horizon at the end of Bismarck Bay. In front of us, the sun is rising just as the helmsman steers our boat, which has already been detached from the other one, through the surf. As we go round a cape, we see the Manam rising out of the sea a little further to the southeast. A plume emerges from the huge pyramid-shaped volcano, which rises ominously from the flat sea. What timing to see this spectacle just after sunrise. And this wasn't even one of the wishes I was mumbling into the black sky a few hours earlier.

We have reached the sea and are now sailing parallel to the coast, straight towards the volcano. The golden beaches have a green crown of tropical rainforest. A few times, our engine stops and we float around, drifting towards the open sea. On the river, that wasn't a problem as we went with the current anyway and were tied to each other. Fortunately, there is always the other boat to give us some diesel when we need it, so we sail towards the coast again.

It takes another two hours before the helmsman makes a right turn. We sail into a small bay, right over the reefs, coral and green, yellow, red, blue fish with jolly stripes that I can see very clearly through the water, which looks like it's made of glass. We jump onto a beach with fine white sand. I take photos while the men unload the cargo from the boats and lay it down under the first row of palm trees. I realize that I haven't exercised in a while and help them carry the bags of betel nuts to the pile, which keeps getting bigger. The Papuans obviously think this is very strange: a white man carrying such a heavy load? When my sloop is empty, I see a fish lying on the bottom. So, this is the sad creature that flew from the Sepik into the darkness, towards me, to its death. One of the men carelessly throws it on the sand, where the greedy sea pulls it outwards, bit by bit. Now that the boats are empty, the three boatmen sail away again, across the sea and up the Sepik against the current, back to Angoram. In search of a new load of betel nuts.

After a while, a truck arrives, which will be our PMV for the rest of the day. A green, rolled-up tarpaulin hangs over a scaffold on the back of the truck. The bags have to be lifted again and stacked in the back. A little later, I'm again sitting on the same bags of betel nut, together with the traders with whom I spent the whole night on the boat. We set off on a sandy road towards the southeast. I hadn't expected to leave here so soon. If what they say is true, that it's a three-hour drive to Madang, I can still explore the city this afternoon.

I enjoy the landscape gliding past me, the fresh air blowing through my hair, the pidgin chatter of the traders. I wonder where they are going with all those bags: they don't even know themselves yet. The further away they get, the more the betel nut is worth, but the longer it will take them to get back to Angoram to pick up a new load.

Then, a minivan comes our way. There are shouts, hands are waved; our driver slows down and turns around when we reach an intersection because the road is too narrow to reverse. We drive back to the last small village we passed. The minibus we just saw is parked on a grassy field: the village square. The passengers are waiting for us. They turn out to be traders from the highlands of PNG. Somehow, they knew that a load of betel nut was on its way. My fellow travelers of the night also get out and the negotiating begins.

I jump out of the vehicle and explore the village. Soon, a girl starts following me. After exchanging a few words, she calls a friend over. By the time I reach the sea, I'm surrounded by a crowd of children smiling at me, wanting to touch me, happy to pose for a photo with this unexpected stranger. The children pull me along, show me their huts, introduce me to their parents, show me their school and the field where they play. They take me to the beach where traditional outrigger canoes are moored. From time to time, I glance from afar at the betel nut traders: the negotiations are still going on. I pick a few frangipani flowers and give each girl one. They are beaming, run away and come back with necklaces made of shells which they hang around my neck.

The negotiations are over. Most of the bags are reloaded into the small van so that there is barely enough room for the men themselves. There are sufficient bags of betel nut left in our lorry to sit on. The traders have big smiles on their faces: they made a good deal. When I hear that they got three times the cost of the nuts, I realize that I should also have taken a bale with me.

While the traders are happy with their quick success, the driver isn't. His truck is now half-empty, which is a shame. His lorry is pointing in the direction of our starting point and he decides to drive all the way back to where we started. When we drive away, I wave once more at my Papuan friends in the village.

We drive past the beach where we landed in our sloops and continue, looking for a new load for our PMV. In a field a few villages further on, we find a batch of brown bags with copra. We load this dried coconut pulp so that the truck is even fuller than when we started. We jolt back down the same road, past the point where we left off a few hours earlier and past the village where my fellow travelers did such good business and I got my shell necklaces.

A late afternoon stroll in Madang should still be possible, I calculate. I'm on the left-hand side of the truck so that I can see the coast. Beaches, bays, fishing boats and the enormous Karkar volcano island – several times, I want to get off and explore this region further. Ah, the tragedy of traveling. There is too much to see, time is always limited, there are always alternatives, and you constantly have to make choices. For every place you visit, you skip something else. I will mark this region of PNG in my head for a future visit. This country has already fascinated me so much that I will definitely come back. And I have only been here for a few days – there's much more to come.

We pick up more and more people along the way until the truck gets crowded. In addition to the men who were in the sloop with me last night, sitting on the remaining bags of betel nut, there are now women with children, older men and farmers. People talk, doze off, sing, stare outside, stare at me. I'm the alien here, the curiosity, the stranger from a faraway land that they don't know, can't imagine and will never visit. And I – I stare back, smile, try to understand their *Tok Pisin* and talk to them, enjoying the views that surprise me at every turn.

A deep sense of adventure and excitement races through my body. Sheer happiness. All this while, after lying on the betel nuts during the night, I'm now sitting on those same sacks for a day, having to hold on to a bar so as not to slip, trying to stretch my legs every once in a while because they are starting to feel numb. But sharing this PMV with the Papuans is an important part of the adventure. I can't imagine driving this road in an air-conditioned four-wheel drive, even though I would have arrived at my destination long ago, even though there are a hundred spots where I would like to stop to take a picture, go hiking or scuba dive in the sea.

I have stopped trying to calculate when we will arrive in Madang. The journey is the adventure, the experience, the highlight that I have come for and the destination is becoming increasingly unimportant. I can do that city walk tomorrow. When we stop for the umpteenth time for people to buy something or do their thing behind a tree, I take the opportunity to walk to the rocks on the side of the road for a view of the sea. Then, the driver of the PMV comes to me. 'Sorry for any inconvenience, sorry it's taking so long, I hope you're not disappointed. Here, have a coconut.'

As I drink the delicious water and then crack the nut open on a sharp stone to fish out the flesh, the question keeps going round in my head: how does he see me? How can I explain to him that I'm enjoying an incredible day? Does he honestly think that all foreigners are only satisfied with luxury chauf-

feur-driven, air-conditioned cars and five-star hotels and the
fastest possible transfer to the next destination? That they look
at their watches every five minutes on which time is ticking
away relentlessly and that they are always in a hurry? Then, I
think about the fact that many visitors of PNG go on exclusive
and very expensive organized trips because they are afraid of
the country and its supposed dangers. At most, they might see
the Papuans when they perform in a directed dance show or,
on departure, in the souvenir shop at the airport. Yes, they do
travel up and down that same Sepik River, but in luxury cruise
boats with suites instead of on a sloop with bags of betel nut.

It has been dark for hours when we see lampposts, cars
parked along the road and shops with neon lights. We have
reached the outskirts of Madang and I have to get used to being
in a city again with all the people, noise and stench that go with
it. The PMV driver drops me off at a hotel with simple rooms.
The traders and other Papuans in the back of the truck wave
goodbye to me. When I turn around, I already miss them.

The young lady at the reception desk examines me with an odd
look when I ask for a room for one night. Didn't I come for the
sing-sing? It will be on throughout the next day. I planned to
travel to the highlands the next morning, but to experience a
sing-sing, a traditional festival in Papua New Guinea, is a
stroke of luck. I had no idea that there would be a festival here.
I feel lucky and realize this is a chance I should not miss. I
immediately add a night to my stay.

The next morning, it's already oppressively hot and the streets
are full of people when I walk to the office to buy a ticket.
There is a long queue. When I finally walk onto the grounds,

the large lawn in the middle of town turns out to be filled with Papuan spectators and dozens of groups of Papuans from villages along the coast and the mainland. They have come from far and wide in a colorful and endless display of the cultural wealth of this country. PNG not only has 850 languages; all those languages are spoken by different tribes, all of whom have their own customs, their own clothes, their own way of making themselves beautiful.

I see men with an impressive bow and arrow who point their weapon at me for fun, there are topless women with thatched skirts, with necklaces made of bones and shells, men with enormous crowns of feathers, with fearsome stripes and dots painted on their faces, with bones and feathers pierced through their noses. Without my asking, a guard holds down the ribbon that has been stretched around the grounds and invites me to walk across the section only accessible to the artists.

I can now talk to the different tribes, take pictures, try to wear one of the huge hats (how do they manage to dance with such high, heavy headgear?), pose for pictures the Papuans want to take with me, and shake hands. One of the many men I speak to is completely covered in red oil. In an unguarded moment, he gives me a close hug and I'm now blanketed by the oil myself. The bystanders burst out laughing. For a moment, I feel part of a Papuan tribe. In most countries, this would be a tourist trap. Here, the audience consists almost entirely of locals who come to enjoy the wealth of their own culture. I spot four other foreigners amongst the multitude of people.

After the *sing-sing*, I realize that, within a week, PNG has won a special place in my heart. Their nature and culture, certainly. The surprises and the adventure, of course. But mainly because of the wonderful people. As pure and authentic as I have rarely experienced. I now understand exactly what Jake said in Colombia. This country and its people are intense and compelling and absorb you before you realize it.

There are many more adventures ahead of me. I climb Mount Wilhelm, the highest mountain in the country, towering high and icy above the tropical land. I explore the highlands, where the completely different climate and vegetation make it seem as if I'm in another country, at another latitude. I eat strawberries and oranges instead of mangoes and pineapples. I marvel at the matriarchal culture of Trobriand, also known as Love Island, due to the free sexual morals of its inhabitants. There, I see a festival celebrating the opening of a small church and discover the almost sacred status of the yam. I also witness the devastating effect of a cruise ship that spews out thousands of visitors in a village of probably a hundred inhabitants. The damage they leave behind is appalling. It doesn't earn them any money either because most people pay with Australian dollars or New Caledonian francs. On Rabaul, I climb active volcanoes and marvel at men digging in the volcanic soil for eggs of the megapode. PNG more than lives up to its slogan: *Land of the Unexpected*. The Papuans continue to surprise me, touching me with their humor, their hospitality, their helpfulness, their interest and their respect. And all this, for a country where a UN employee takes a taxi to go across the street because it's too dangerous to do so on foot.

Then, the moment has come for the return journey. I reluctantly check in. My original flight has been canceled, but the attendant has rebooked me onto a flight for which my ticket is not even formally valid. But PNG has one last surprise in store for me. I get into a conversation with the staff at the security checkpoint, who are usually not the friendliest people you meet on a journey.

They ask me all sorts of questions about my experiences in their country, I show them photographs, we laugh and finally, we say goodbye with a tight embrace.

When the plane taxis away a little later, I press my nose against the window. Tears in my eyes blur the last images of the country. It feels as if I am saying goodbye to a loved one I haven't seen for a long time. That love, PNG, remains in my heart, and I will certainly return to her.

Chapter 15
And Then, it All Went Wrong

South Africa/Botswana – 2017

W here am I? What am I doing here? What on earth has happened? My eyes shoot desperately in all directions. Thoughts flash through my head like a slippery eel that is impossible to catch. I'm frantically searching for clues that will help me answer my questions. It's as if I have been completely out of this world and have been catapulted back to a place unknown to me. Or is this a weird dream I soon won't even remember? Let me concentrate.

I discern the musty taste of earth on my lips. Then, one by one, images begin to form. I see that I'm standing on the verge of a road. From the softness of the light, I deduce that it must be late afternoon. In the distance, I notice silhouettes. When I look more closely, I see people looking at me with worried eyes. Strangers.

Little by little, sounds seep into my ears. I hear some of them talking, with excitement in their voices, although I can't understand what they are saying. They point behind me. I automatically follow the direction of their fingers, turn around and see an enormous hunk of white crumpled metal lying in the grass.

It vaguely reminds me of a car. The chassis is dented on all sides, as if a giant had smashed it with all his might against the walls of his giant room. The windows are gone. There is grass between the axles. A refrigerator hangs ludicrously upside down on a wire, its door dangling helplessly in the air. Red lines glint whimsically alongside one of the doors. That car is in a strange position. Upside down. It looks somewhat familiar.

About ten meters behind it, I see a metal frame sticking out of the grass at an angle, with a flat dark green package and a wheel on top. Is that part of the wreckage? Between the frame and the remains of the car, there are all sorts of things hurled haphazardly onto the grass. Pans. Wine glasses. Cutlery. A shoe. Plastic bags with groceries. Or what's left of it.

The longer I walk around, the more it dawns on me that this is no dream. Fragments of memories seep in. They provide me with mnemonic devices through which, step by step, I try to crawl out of a dark tunnel, back to reality. Didn't I put those groceries in the car myself and isn't that my shoe? Wasn't I behind the wheel of that car? And those red stripes on the door: could that be blood? To verify, I walk over to the twisted steel and see a camera bag lying inside. It's mine.

So, it's all true.

The door doesn't open. The windows are shattered into thousands of fragments lying on the floor and I can reach my hand inside, grab the bag and, with some effort, pry it out from under the back seat. I switch on my camera and without giving it any thought, I start taking pictures. The rattling sound of the shutter has a calming effect. It sounds and feels familiar. Now that I'm taking a closer look at the havoc, the situation begins to sink in. But questions remain. Take those openings in the wreckage: they are too small to crawl through. Even if I was in that wreck, how would I have ever been able to wriggle myself out of it?

Then, in the corner of my eye, I see Anneke being placed on a stretcher. Huh, is she here too? I carefully walk up to her, scared of what I'm about to see. She lies still on her back, her arms tight alongside her body, looking straight up. At least she can look. I see her familiar, serene gaze and she nods at me reassuringly as I hover above her face. She blinks her eyes for a moment when a ray of sunlight hits them. Her head lies between two supports. This sight of her frightens me to death. This is not a dream. This is not a nightmare. This is real.

Back at the wreck, I try to gather our belongings. I walk around haphazardly with things in my hands. All sorts of thoughts whirl through my head that don't want to fall into place, like in one of those glass globes where the snow keeps floating around after you shake it hard. After a while, the snowflakes start to fall. Memories become sharper, thoughts clearer.

We're in South Africa. We were on our way to Botswana, where we were supposed to arrive around sunset. All kinds of questions are now running through my head. Is Anneke seriously injured? How soon can we get a new car here? Will we make it to the Botswana border today? In a few hours, night will fall. What about tomorrow? Can we still have that party in Ireland in a few months? I just sent out the invitations a week before. Do I have to cancel those? How weird – only now do I see that my right arm is covered in blood, but I don't feel anything. So those red marks on the door are indeed blood. My blood. I walk on, dazed.

Before leaving, a friend said: 'Oh, Botswana, that's a piece of cake!' That's what it seemed like, beforehand. I had deliberately saved the 'easier' countries – Botswana, Madagascar and Ireland – for last: I had traveled through the 'difficult' countries years before, thinking I should 'save the best for last.' I had put together a trip with a small organization and at the last minute, it seemed possible for my girlfriend and long-time travel partner Anneke to join me. We were looking forward to traveling in a very different way for once. Three weeks with a car and a place to sleep on the roof, with the possibility of cooking for ourselves along the way: it seemed like the ultimate freedom. After all the endless journeys in bulging vans and cars across Africa, which would always fit far more people than you would ever think possible and where there was always the question of whether you would arrive safely, this was a luxury that we wanted to experience.

That morning, Sam, a Zimbabwean from the rental company, had given us instructions. Dressed in a black jacket and with a beautiful slit hat on his shiny head, he explained in a calm voice where we could find everything in this almost new white Toyota pickup. We had tried the use of the jack, both the small and the large one. We had opened all the drawers of the little kitchen in the back and checked off every item on the checklist that came with it. We had checked the fridge, the operation of the gas, the *bush shower* and the satellite phone provided. We had practiced putting up and taking down the tent via an ingenious mechanism on the roof. To our surprise, the mattresses and bedding were in the tent, waiting for us to tuck ourselves in. We were ready for an adventure like we had never experienced before. Off to Botswana. Just a few hundred kilometers away: country 191 was up for grabs. The only thing we didn't know was that we would never use those kitchen utensils and that we would never sleep in those beds.

That was a few hours earlier. Now, all our plans are in doubt. After decades of traveling in almost two hundred countries, is it seriously going awry just before I reach the finish line? After an infinite number of near misses, traveling in countries where I wasn't supposed to, after all the challenges of every kind from which I had somehow managed to escape, often with a fair share of luck? Have all those guardian angels on my shoulder, who have saved me countless times from perilous situations, let me down just now, with only three countries to go?

The stretcher on which Anneke lies, belongs to an old-fashioned, gray van standing on the verge: the ambulance. The South Africans at the side of the road warn us: it belongs to a state hospital. They explain that their health care is slow and unreliable and not of the quality we're used to. They urge us to wait for the ambulance from a private clinic that they have already called. In the meantime, a tow truck turns the car around and is about to haul the wreckage away. Within an hour, only those who pay close attention to the tracks on the verge would be able to see anything at all.

Meanwhile, the police have arrived. They want to interrogate me. After all, I was the driver of the car that is now hanging on a steel cable and will be crushed on the scrap heap before the day is out. Questions from the friendly lady in uniform force me to think back to what happened exactly. My head finally finds some peace. In it, I now see images of the steering wheel that I can no longer hold. Of an enormous blow. A spinning world of blue sky, of grass and trees, oncoming traffic, the blue sky again, grass and trees, then shattering glass, darkness, grit between my teeth, followed by silence. Terrifying silence.

As if I were watching a slow-motion film, I now see what

happened after that blow, frame after frame. I see myself hanging upside down. I ask Anneke if she's all right, loosen my seat belt and wriggle out through the twisted bars of the window. Then, I walk around the wreckage to help Anneke out as well.

The lady in her uniform asks what preceded the blow. I dig into my memory, gathering the fragments. We had arrived in Johannesburg the previous evening and had a short night because we had to show up early at the rental company. After receiving the instructions and saying goodbye to Sam, we had driven west. We had done our shopping at a mall in Rustenburg and then continued towards the border on a road that wasn't too busy. Anneke was stretched out sleeping while I drove along the N4 to Botswana, towards the sun. After that: a black hole in my memory. It's as if I'm standing in front of a collapsed tunnel and the answers are on the other side. Impossible to reach. I can't manage to dig myself out. The officer says she knows enough.

Anneke is still lying patiently on her stretcher when a modern van arrives. The ambulance from the private clinic. Anneke is transferred to their stretcher and placed in the ambulance. As always, we travel light: all our stuff easily fits next to the stretcher in the ambulance. The groceries we had done an hour earlier can be thrown away: they are twisted, crushed, cracked open or have disappeared in the grass. Anneke lies in the middle of the car, the brothers and I sit at the side. Wide-eyed, the men look at the wreckage, then at us, and back. They can't believe that we crawled out of that debris alive.

We drive back. We pass Swartruggens towards the east. Away from Botswana: the wrong way. Away from country 191. Once we arrive at the Netcare Ferncrest hospital in Rustenburg, Anneke is lying on a bed. The doctor is inspecting her arm and hand. They are full of wounds and from each wound, he extracts small shards of glass with tweezers. It seemed this was the extent of her injuries, but Anneke would suffer from this blow for years to come.

Then, it's my turn. The first-aid doctor examines my head and removes pieces of glass. He examines my right arm. At my elbow and halfway down my forearm, there are wounds so deep that I can see his fingers disappearing halfway into it. Still, I feel nothing. He promptly sends me to the X-ray department, but only after I have paid. On examining the photos, it turns out that there are lumps of glass deep inside my muscles. These can't be removed easily. The doctor stitches up the wounds at my elbow. He forgets to check whether the nurse has sedated me and does without it.

By now, it has long become dark outside and it's finally clear to us that we won't be traveling any further today. It turns out that here, too, taxi drivers know when they can make a profit from something. They ask an absurd amount for a ride of a few kilometers to a hotel. We decide to stay in the hospital, with the advantage of care being at hand if we need it. And by doing so, we slam the door in the face of the greedy taxi drivers.

I want to send a few emails so I take out my laptop, which was well protected by clothing deep inside my backpack. However, the sturdy aluminum frame is bent and split. When I pry it open, I see that the screen is completely shattered. A silent witness to the devastating blow we have received. How did our bodies survive that same blow?

That night, we lie on a hard bench in a deserted room. I can hardly sleep because of the pain in my back. Images of rolling cars flash through my head. Desperately, I look for a moment where I can intervene, where I can steer the car further, across the road, towards Botswana. But they all end in a heavy blow and immense destruction.

I wake up in the middle of the night. All kinds of alternative scenarios go through my head. Anneke could have died! I imagine how I would have to go to her mother to break the news, how I would explain it, how I would try to comfort her. I could have been killed myself. We could have perished together. Perhaps even worse: we could have been maimed for life. There could have been children playing on the verge, there could have been a woman walking with a load of firewood on her head and a baby wrapped in a colorful cloth on her back as you see everywhere in Africa. No chance against a car that shoots off the road at 120 kilometers an hour, flipping over twice.

I crawl over to Anneke, hug her and hold her tight. And then, they finally come. Emotions. Tears. Tears of shock, of sorrow, of relief, of happiness, all flowing together. The realization that we have had a serious car accident and that we got away relatively well, is now imposing itself on us. We look back at the photos of the wreck. Only now do we understand the stare of the paramedics in the ambulance. Now, we realize that the first blow to the Toyota was absorbed by the bodywork with the roof tent and the spare wheel, which were immediately torn off at the impact. Then, the seat belts saved us on the second impact. Without that tent and without those seat belts we would have been dead. How could it be that I was worried about traveling to my last three countries, Botswana, Madagascar and Ireland?

Ireland? Less than an hour and a half's flight from home and I had never been? I need to shed some light here. A few years earlier, I was sitting in a cramped van in Uganda that was struggling through one deep pothole after another. The passengers were nodding and I thought about the countries that still laid ahead of me. For the first time, I tried to imagine what it would be like to visit my last country. I envisioned being all by myself, giving my passport to an unknown official in a faraway country and having him complete it with my very last stamp.

Although that moment was still far in the future, it seemed to be the ultimate anticlimax. After all those years of traveling, it would suddenly be over – without anyone to share the milestone experience with. I decided I had to do things differently. I wanted to celebrate the achievement of my life's goal with loved ones. There, among all those sleepy Africans in a rickety van on a dirt road in Africa, I decided to save Ireland for last. Easy to reach – and it seemed an excellent country for a party.

But a party is the last thing on my mind. I only want one thing now: to go home. The next day, it finally dawns on me that I should call the insurance company. An efficient help desk employee explains that I must be operated on as soon as possible. The glass in my arm could cut the artery, so they judge the situation to be life-threatening. Surgery must be done locally; traveling to the Netherlands would pose too great a risk. They advise me to go to a bigger hospital in Pretoria. But I don't feel like sitting in a car for hours and so I decide to stay, in part because it's not at all certain that I will be helped there any sooner. The insurance company provides a payment guarantee so that the hospital can take appropriate action.

The next morning, Dr Van der Merwe comes to introduce himself, just before the operation. A little later, I'm sedated and wheeled into an operating theater for the first time in my life. Next thing I know, I'm recovering, hooked up to an IV for a couple of days. I'm alert because some nurses are more precise than others, some making big mistakes when inserting the needle. Fortunately, Anneke is allowed to lie on a chair in the corner of the room, so at least we're together. We need each other now more than ever before. She also makes sure that everything goes smoothly and calls for help when necessary.

The surgeon sympathizes with us and invites us to his house to rest for a few days. He explains that as long as we take good care of the wounds, we can travel – in case we want to. Now that I have recovered from the operation and the shock, I'm starting to get the travel itch again. If we go back home, we will probably regret it. Botswana is still within reach.

We decide to decline Dr Van der Merwe's offer and try to travel on. Going home is always an option if it turns out to be too hard to travel. Grace, a sympathetic nurse with a name perfectly fitting her profession, gives us a big bag with all the necessities: special gauze, bandages, ointment, scissors, plasters, painkillers and antibiotics. My eyes flicker as I leave the hospital under the bright sun. We get a lift to the border and that same evening I stretch out my thickly bandaged right arm to give my passport to the official. I get a stamp from Botswana. My 191st country. Only two more countries to go.

For the rest of our trip, Sister Anneke would clean my deep wounds twice a day with the supplies Grace gave us and rub them with a special ointment. The journey would bring more perilous situations. The four-wheel drive we hired in Maun almost capsizes, an hour before sunset, in a deep mud pool in Savuti. It's an area that is known for its lions and cheetahs; precisely the reason we wanted to go there. Then there was a lion that roamed around our car at night near the Chobe River while we were sleeping on the roof, at a campsite where we were all alone and where the receptionist simply said that she would go home if it became too scary. Several irritated elephants come very close to our car with their flapping ears. At the same time, we enjoy the abundance of wildlife, the land-scapes, a canoe trip in a mokoro and a walking safari in the Okavango Delta and the captivating sunsets. Still, a vague feeling of disaster looms over our journey.

Even after our return home, the enormous blow of a few weeks earlier is still reverberating. We have already crawled through the eye of the needle so many times – this time it went wrong. To put it more precisely: it almost went wrong. Considering the incredible blow we received, we can only be glad that we came out relatively unscathed. We're confronted with our vulnera-bility and mortality and realize that even guardian angels have an expiry date that can lapse any day. Fortunately, we can continue to live and we can continue to travel. To new adven-tures. On to Madagascar. On to Ireland!

Chapter 16
Boom Boom Buddha/Epilogue

Afghanistan – 2017

We in the West think of unpredictability as a menace, something to be avoided at all costs. We want our careers, our family lives, our roads, our weather to be utterly predictable. We love nothing more than a sure thing. Shuffling the songs on our iPod is about as much randomness as we can handle.
—Eric Weiner, The Geography of Bliss, 2008

Doubt is the precursor of fear.
—Alex Honnold, climber

June 3, 2017, 11:19 AM. Corrasmoor Road, a few hundred meters south of Cullaville, Northern Ireland. In the bend ahead of me is Kingham's nineteenth-century bridge over the River Fane. Under normal circumstances, you would walk or drive over it without giving it a second thought. Yet, this bridge is special because the Fane defines the border. Across the river, on the other side of the bridge, is Ireland. My final country.

Family and friends put an Irish flag and a cloud of balloons into my hands. When I go round the bend, I see that they have marked the border on the road with duct tape. I have looked forward to this moment for months. No: years. I have tried to imagine what this moment would be like. Now that the time has come, a jumble of emotions rises inside me. I feel joy and pride, but also hesitation and regret. Visiting unknown countries has fascinated me all my life. When I cross this bridge, I will never again experience the excitement of visiting a new country, until a new one is born. All my life, I have yearned to cross a border. This time, I hesitate to take the final step.

As always, my curiosity wins in the end. A little later, we all walk into the last country on earth that I have never been to before. What follows is a ceremony that is hilarious and moving at the same time. A strict customs officer who looks very much like Anneke inspects my luggage. She asks awkward questions that remind me of previous challenging border crossings. My passport is embellished with a specially made stamp, by an official who is the spitting image of my brother-in-law Matthieu.

Irish passers-by, who cross this border every day without even blinking an eye, stop and ask what we're doing here. They are flabbergasted when they hear what we're celebrating and ask me about countries they are curious about and dream of seeing one day. I have joined a select club of travelers who have achieved the same feat. Around one hundred and fifty worldwide – that is less than those who have been to space.

That night, we celebrate in a pub in Dublin where more friends and also colleagues join us. We hug, chat, laugh, there are speeches, we eat, watch videos sent by friends who couldn't be with us and cut a world map cake. I look at all the people who have come from Canada, Romania, Switzerland and the

Netherlands to Ireland. I think of all the others who, for whatever reason, couldn't come, but who are thinking of us, and I feel fortunate. I remember the ride in that van in Uganda where I decided to save Ireland for last. It's even more wonderful than I imagined. Much more wonderful.

Ten days later. A sun-drenched day in New York. I walk to the United Nations headquarters. After a tour of the building's striking halls, bursting with international allure, I walk to the flags of all the member states planted in the pavement on the west side of the complex, along First Avenue. At 48th Street, I come to the first flag. Afghanistan. I realize that this is the only country I visited as a mere toddler. My parents took my sister and me to Kabul on the way back home, after we had lived in India for a year. My memories consist only of the glorious tales my parents told me about it. In my mind, I put the country on my travel wish list.

I take my time walking south, along the long row of alphabetically ordered flags. An emotional walk. At each flag, I stop to recall memories of the country. For some countries this is easy because I have been there recently (Botswana! Madagascar! Ireland!); for others, I have to dig a bit deeper into my memory to recall my trips. By the time I arrive at the corner of 42nd Street, at the Zimbabwean flag, my head is spinning with adventures from all over the world. Much more than at that little bridge over the river Fane, it begins to sink in – how much I have traveled, seen and experienced in all corners of the world.

I may have visited all the countries now, but there are many places I still want to see and things I want to do. The curiosity that made me want to travel on and on is still as strong as it was before my party in Ireland. It's time for new travel goals. What will change is that my travels will no longer be dictated by the list of countries I haven't been to yet. Now, I have complete freedom to choose my next destination. The question is: where do I want to go, what do I want to see, what do I want to do? The choice is overwhelming – as is shown by this long row of flags.

There are a few countries of which I only have lousy pictures, or no pictures at all, for my website. I was too young when I visited, my camera was stolen, or I had taken few, bad or even no pictures for other reasons. I definitely want to visit those to make my website complete.

The last years before I reached Ireland, I had attached magnets to a big world map on the countries that were still left on my list. After every trip, I removed one magnet, until the map was completely empty. I now put magnets on the countries I want to revisit. There are magnets on Russia, Pakistan, Sri Lanka, the Philippines, Greenland, Nicaragua, Tanzania and fourteen other countries – because I only have twenty magnets. As soon as I have visited one of them, I put the magnet on another spot I want to visit. The number of magnets on the map will never diminish.

A month after Ireland, I go to Liechtenstein for a few days. It turns out to be a great destination for spectacular mountain hikes. I had only been to Vaduz on one of my youthful Interrail journeys. Even the tiny Alpine country has more to offer than I saw on my first visit. Likewise, every country always has a new region, an unknown city, a World Heritage Site, an unclimbed mountain or what have you, as a reason to go back. Thank goodness for that.

That autumn, I have more time off. I just need to decide where to go. For years, I thought my first trip after 'Ireland' would be to an 'easy' country. Italy was the obvious choice. No long journey, no time difference, no money issues, no visa needed, I speak the language and it boasts probably the best cuisine in the world. Although I had been there many times before, there was still plenty to see and do. Despite all these arguments in its favor, I wasn't convinced. I was missing something, although I couldn't put my finger on what it was exactly.

Then, I come across a report on the Internet by a young couple who have traveled through Afghanistan on their own. I know immediately: that is what I really want. Afghanistan! I only know a little about its recent history. The Soviets invaded the country when I was in high school and occupied it for a long time, the Taliban seized power in the nineties and the US bombed it after 9/11 in their *War on Terror*. Since then, it has only been in the news after yet another attack, bombing and other disasters. It's also known for the gripping books by Khaled Hosseini about how the Taliban's reign of terror has taken a heavy toll on the lives of the Afghans.

It's a country that I have flown over so many times. A country that I looked into from Tajikistan with awe and an irresistible longing, as I traveled along the northern border with its rugged mountains in the Pamir Mountains. Alphabetically, it's the first UN country on the List of 193, as I saw in New York. What could possibly be better than just starting at A again? The longer I think about it, the more I look forward to making Afghanistan the first country to which I should return. Once again, the thirst for adventure and the craving for an extraordinary experience wins out over a trip to a 'safe' destination like Italy.

It turns out to be very easy to get a visa, on the Laan van Meerdervoort in The Hague, a stone's throw away from the Peace Palace and the remarkable building of my secondary school. Kabul turns out to be easy to reach, there are several flights a day and you can choose whether you want to fly through Istanbul or Dubai. A few days before departure, my worried mother suddenly appears at the door. She begs me to change my plans. She has never done this before and it somehow adds some more tension to the trip.

Anneke is coming along. Together we have experienced so many special adventures and visited so many countries after our first trip to Turkmenistan. We survived the accident in South Africa, traveled to Madagascar and celebrated 'Ireland' together. She has her doubts about our destination and we agree to keep an eye on things. If we don't feel safe, we will fly back immediately. After all, there is no point traveling to a place where you aren't at ease – and you simply can't know in advance how it will feel to be there. On our way to Dubai, we meet a Dutch couple transferring to Bali for a beach holiday. When they hear where we're going, the woman says: 'Oh, Afghanistan. That's different!'

Once on the plane to Kabul, I feel that same tension again that I remember from my trips to Somalia, Iraq and other 'red' countries. I'm on my way to a country at war, a country that I mainly know from violent images. A country where you have to trust that everything will go well, but where a distant voice says that it can all go wrong if you're unlucky. You can try all sorts of ways to steer fate and trust in your luck, but there will always be a part you can't influence. And that part is quite large in Afghanistan.

Slowly, the Boeing 777 descends towards our destination, giving us a good view of the Hindu Kush below. We see rugged, desolate mountains, with jagged ridges, a valley in between, winding unpaved roads, rivers with spare green fringes. When we are lower, we see patches of green ground that are being tilled. Seeing it from the sky, it all looks perfectly normal.

Then, the suburbs of Kabul come into view. The expanding city lies spread out between the barren mountains, and sometimes on their lower slopes. Kabul has grown to seven million inhabitants. This means a more than fourfold increase since 2001, making it the fifth fastest-growing city in the world.

A little later, we're outside and don't know where to go. We're supposed to go couch surfing with Sayed, a young Afghan, but he is nowhere to be seen. At least, that's what we think. It could be that man with the turban, or is it the other one? Nobody seems to be waiting for us, nobody is standing there with a sign. Nobody cares about us or looks at us with surprise.

We ask around and are soon offered a phone to call Sayed, who tells us we have to walk to Parking Lot C. For safety reasons, no cars are allowed inside the airport. There, we find a group of taxi drivers who immediately pounce on us like predators stalking welcome prey. So here they are! Taxi drivers are the same everywhere in the world. I feel more at ease already. There aren't that many foreigners here and if they do come, they are picked up by armored four-wheel drives or army vehicles. The drivers look at us covetously. We politely tell them we don't need a taxi.

Sayed enthusiastically shows up a few minutes later. We leave the disappointed taxi drivers. We follow him past high, free-standing walls of concrete and past another checkpoint complete with baggage scanning and another search, after which we leave the airport behind us and arrive at a busy roundabout. Heavily armed soldiers stand next to their armored vehicles around the square. Two days earlier, there had been an attack here during the visit of James Mattis, the US Secretary of Defense. The Taliban fired six rockets, but no one was injured. Sayed hails a taxi and we're on our way through a city that has captured my imagination for so long and is now unfolding before my eyes.

On the way, I ask him what that enormous zeppelin is doing a few hundred meters above the city. He tells me that it belongs to the Americans, that it keeps an eye on the whole city and tries to intercept communications to prevent attacks. With a sneer, he adds that since the airship's arrival there haven't been fewer attacks than before. He soon turns out to be a fierce opponent of the American presence, like almost all Afghans we will meet. They see the Americans as occupiers that they rather get rid of. Sayed will later say that the Soviets have done more for Afghanistan than the Americans: they at least have improved the infrastructure.

Apart from the zeppelin, helicopters fly low over the city almost continuously. The dull chuff-chuff-chuff of the rotors can be heard in the background almost all the time, until the helicopters come closer and their noise drowns out everything. Combined with the countless military patrols, checkpoints and six-meter-high concrete walls, Kabul feels like a military fortress. With half the streets blocked off and the city bursting at the seams between the surrounding mountains, the traffic jams are almost permanent.

Sayed overwhelms us with Afghan hospitality. He buys us drinks and prepares a full meal in his simple flat. That evening, he takes me on a walking tour of the city. I don't protest, even though all the advice I had read said to stay inside after sunset. We end up in a dark bar where I suffer a big defeat playing pool against his friends.

The next day, we criss-cross through Kabul. We play shuffleboard in a park, look out over the city from Wazir Akbar Khan Hill, from which the largest Afghan flag in the country flies, and walk through a huge market. I can't imagine it looked any different when my parents visited it on their honeymoon in the early 1960s. In between hundreds of market stalls with fruits, bread, dead animals, vegetables, toys, clothes and much more, we see the colorful blend of people who can all call themselves Afghans. The country has dozens of ethnic groups and is a true melting pot of Central Asian people. We see those who look like Iranians, we see people who would blend in perfectly in Tajikistan, we see Uzbeks, Hazaras with their unmistakable mongoloid features, and Pathans, who are the largest group of the country. This diversity makes Afghanistan both rich and very hard to control.

We navigate through the filth on the streets, pass slums draped over the hills and see a small monument to a young woman. She was stoned to death here a few years ago because someone had expressed a vague suspicion that she wasn't pious enough. It tells us that many here are still under the spell of very conservative ideas fueled by religion. It shows that Afghanistan continues to be a patriarchy where a woman has an inferior position. At the same time, the purpose of the monument is to widen people's perspective and stimulate emancipation. While Sayed tells the story, I see tears well up in his eyes.

The taxis that we take to get around struggle through endless traffic jams. That, too, was something to be avoided at all costs according to the advice, but all driving here ends up in a traffic jam now that all roads are one-way and the city is so jam-packed. We eat deliciously spicy meals, wander through markets and see shopping malls around Chicken Street. In the 1970s, when Kabul was still high on travelers' wish lists – if only because drugs were easily available – this was a popular destination amongst backpackers. Then, there is the policeman at a checkpoint who stops Anneke and clearly enjoys unabashedly looking at a woman-with-blonde-hair-and-no-burqa.

That same evening, an undercover policeman drops by who has been informed by neighbors that foreigners are staying with Sayed. They have a lively conversation, during which the agent regularly looks at us and points at us. In the end, it seems to be OK. It reminds us that we're in a country at war, where people are alert and it raises questions when an Afghan has contact with strangers.

Still, we feel more and more at ease in Kabul. As I saw in those other countries that are considered 'dangerous', life goes on. People walk the streets to go to work and school, they go to the market to buy food, they run their shops, they sit on terraces to chat about the latest developments in their lives. Often, when they see us, their faces fold into a smile. Then, they wave at us or put their hand on their heart and try to start a conversation. People touch us with their genuine warmth. The country is beginning to take hold of us and there is no question of us returning home any time soon.

We want to see more of the country. Flights to the north turn out to be full and Sayed advises us to take the bus. He tells us that a Polish guy traveled the opposite way a few weeks earlier. Early in the morning, Sayed takes us to an intersection that serves as a bus station. On a piece of paper, he jots down what we have to say in case we're spoken to along the way. He doesn't want to speak English to us in front of other passengers because that would only make it clear that we are foreigners. Although we're both wearing inconspicuous clothes, I feel it would be obvious that we're foreign anyway. When the driver gets in, Sayed salutes us in Dari and we're alone for the first time since he picked us up from Parking Lot C a few days before.

We traverse the foothills of the desolate Hindu-Kush mountains on a Soviet-made road that regularly leads through tunnels crudely carved into the rock. We try to be invisible, especially when we get off for a break. At the end of the day, we arrive in Mazar-e Sharif.

A passenger from the bus helps us find a hotel. The gentlemen at the reception desk don't understand how we arrived this late from Kabul. The only flight had already landed that morning. They call us crazy when they hear that we took the bus: 'even we don't do that!' We decide to fly to the other destinations we still want to see and buy all the tickets we need that same evening. We find out that the manager of the hotel wants to follow his wife to Germany; he is happy to practice his German with us. The hotel is fine. It's centrally located, there is security at the entrance, it's quiet and it even has wifi. Within walking distance, we have the market and the jewel we came for: the Blue Mosque, also known as the shrine of Hazrat Ali.

The next morning, we walk straight there. A haze hangs over Mazar: the wind blows street dust meters high into the air. After a security check, we arrive at a huge square in the city center. We can already see the outline of the mosque in the hazy air, but first, we have to pass through a decorative gate to reach the southern entrance. The building may be small, but the sight of it overwhelms us when it reveals itself in all its splendor. The richly tiled outer walls overwhelm us. The domes and the towers and turrets rising above the structure on all sides overwhelm us. The light blue-green glow of the tiling overwhelms us and seems to lift the building from the shiny white marble floor on which it stands and in which all that splendor is reflected. It's reminiscent of the dazzling mosques and madrasas we saw on our journey through Central Asia. The border with Uzbekistan is less than a two hours' drive away.

We walk with our bare feet on the cool marble around this mosque and its tombs. Ali ibn Abu Talib, or Hazrat Ali, Mohammed's son-in-law, is said to be buried here. This makes it an important pilgrimage site for Shiites, although most believe he is buried in Najaf, Iraq. Over time, political and religious leaders have been interred in this shrine. No matter who lies here, a cloud of serenity hangs around the magnificent temple, in a region where war shows the ugliest side of man.

It soon becomes clear that being non-Muslims, we can't enter the building. Nevertheless, we relish the outside. We find a place in the shade to watch the spectacle in peace. Not just the Blue Mosque itself, but also its visitors. We see a never-ending stream of families walking on the grounds, around the building, or disappearing into it to pray. The dark blue-purple burkas of the women contrast sharply with the white of the floor and the turquoise of the mosque. The women often have to struggle to prevent their wide dress from blowing off. Some visitors approach us, sometimes for a short conversation, a selfie, or just to stare at us. The few foreigners who come here almost always travel in groups – they are accompanied by guides and stay at a distance. We will return here, again and again, to feast our eyes on the different kinds of daylight that make the gem glow in the Northern Afghan dust. The mosque may be called blue, but when the sun shines on it, it looks more like light green.

We wander around the endless market. The people of Mazar are less diverse than those of Kabul: the majority here is Tajik. Men wear Islamic prayer hats or turbans. Almost all have beards. It seems more conservative: even though the Taliban doesn't control this area, almost all women wear blue burqas. We see shops which only sell the dress: all in the same hue of blue. Just like in Yemen, traditions are still strong here, the country is a patriarchate, and it is hard to imagine that this will change any time soon. Once more, we come across the paradox of the traveler, because the very fact that traditions rule the streets here, makes that we stare out our eyes.

We take pictures of vendors posing with their geometrically dotted loaves of bread and observing goat carcasses hanging from their metal hooks, with swarms of flies around them. A beggar woman wearing a burqa keeps chasing us and pulling our arms until Anneke gets into an argument with her. I have a *kameez shalwar* made for me and I buy a *pakol*, an Afghan cap, to go with it. With this Afghan outfit, I'm immediately taken for an Afghan. It's now even easier to make contact with the curious people in the street, even though they are disappointed when they discover that I don't speak Dari and that I'm not Anneke's Afghan guide.

We visit Balkh, the capital of the Bactrian Empire long before our time and now a sleepy town with monumental buildings and ruins from its glory days. In the evening, while we're eating in the corner of a restaurant in a space that is closed off by curtains, a young man comes and joins us, uninvited. He asks us everything he wants to know, without any inhibitions. He pretends to be open-minded and tells us about the lockable rooms that can be found on the top floors of restaurants and where he takes his girlfriends. He is particularly interested in our love life, wants to hear how it works in the West and is shocked when we tell him that we both had other partners before we met. Shaking his head, he finally disappears through the curtains hanging around our table. He had wanted to appear progressive, but this man, too, has such strong traditional ideas of men and women that he cannot understand ours.

We fly back to Kabul. We use the transfer time to walk around for a couple of hours in the Gardens of Babur, the fifteenth-century founder of the Mogul Empire, who is buried here in this same garden. We're almost constantly surrounded by young Afghan girls and boys who want to have their picture taken with us. These youngsters are clearly more modern than those we saw in Mazar. Both the young women and men wear fashionable clothes, address us with a soft voice and smile shyly when we take their picture. I have never made so many online friends in such a short time. Here, too, that ubiquitous curiosity regarding the stranger. Again, the feeling that people long for a safer life, for contact with the rest of the world, for a future without the threat of attacks or a return to medieval practices.

At the end of the afternoon, we fly on to Herat in the west of the country. There, we see the restored citadel, the ornate Friday Mosque and again a colorful market that seems to go on forever. We see the shrine of Sufi Ansari. On the vast grounds near the mausoleum of Gowhar Shad, we see boys launching cheerful kites, trying to bring each other's down.

Here and there, we sit down at a stall, order a glass of freshly squeezed pomegranate juice and watch everyday life pass by. One of the many photos I take is of an old man wearing a turban. I guess he must have been around when my parents passed through this city on their long honeymoon. What must his dark eyes have seen since then? Who knows, maybe the lingering wars have carved those deep furrows in his face, or perhaps those fissures have put me on the wrong track and he is actually much younger than I think.

After another short stop in Kabul, we continue to Bamiyan. Looking through the plane window during the landing, we see huge holes in the rock face that marks the north side of town. Until March 2001, they were filled with gigantic Buddha statues that were many centuries old. Even though we knew we were going to see this, even though the striking statues were destroyed sixteen years earlier and I have seen the videos of their destruction on the Internet, the sight of the empty crevices is still shocking. It's yet another raw reminder of the cruel war that still holds the country and its people in its suffocating and relentless grip.

We sleep in an old caravanserai at the foot of the cliffs. Right under the gap in the rock where the Great Buddha stood, until madness struck. The madness that ripped the statues from their old place in a foolish iconoclasm, in which symbols of a different kind of faith had to pay the price. At the time, the world was filled with indignation at these crimes born of religious fanaticism.

Now, we hear the story that got much less coverage at the time. The Taliban first tried to destroy the statues with tanks and anti-aircraft missiles, but days of shelling only managed to punch holes in the colossal works of art. The statues were simply too big. So, they ordered captured Hazaras from the neighborhood to descend from the enormous heads on ropes with sticks of dynamite, which they had to place at regular intervals in cracks within the statues. Those who refused got a bullet through the head on the spot. The Taliban kept their weapons pointed at the poor guys until all the explosives were in place. A little later, they blew the statues out of the rock face from where they had peacefully looked down on many generations of Bamiyan residents for fifteen centuries. These same inhabitants had been forcibly made accomplices of their destruction.

We start the next day with a visit to the historic rock wall and its missing works of art. To start with, we walk to the Small or Eastern Buddha, get an explanation from the guide who rattles off the dimensions of the statue for us and we climb the steps at the side of the crevice. Here and there, we can still see remnants of colorful wall paintings, heavily tarnished by aging and vandalism. Once we reach the upper gallery, we look out over the surprisingly green landscape in which poplars draw straight lines around the edges of the town and in the surrounding fields at the foot of rugged mountains.

When we look down, we see the thirty-eight-meter emptiness directly below us. Anger bubbles up inside us at the narrow-mindedness that has robbed the town's inhabitants and humanity of its famous statues. Back at the foot of the crevice, we find pieces of rubble patiently waiting for reconstruction. When asked about it, the curator of the museum sighs, saying that Afghanistan has bigger and more urgent problems than rebuilding the statues.

We walk back along the enormous rock face, observing the dozens of rectangular carved openings where monks once meditated, where people lived for centuries long after Buddhism had disappeared. We're approaching the much larger alcove of the Great Buddha. The guide that accompanies us tells the history of this statue that, at fifty-five meters, was a lot higher than its eastern counterpart. This made it the tallest standing Buddha in the world. The statues were carved out of the cliffs in the sixth and seventh century. In their heyday, the statues were painted from head to toe and covered in gold. For many centuries, they were praised in accounts by travelers and traders who passed through here on their journey along the Silk Road.

When we arrive at the spot where the statue's enormous feet once stood, I look up. There is a tangle of gray tubes: scaffolding, although no work is in progress. On the left side, I see an opening in the sandstone wall. That must have been the beginning of the staircase. Only fragments remain: after a few steps, it comes to an abrupt halt. Blown away. The dynamite has done its work ruthlessly well.

My thoughts wander off to my parents. For years, my sister and I heard the stories of their honeymoon, which quickly assumed mythical proportions for us. How, in their early twenties, they told their parents they were going to India for their honeymoon, how they hitchhiked through the Middle East, had the craziest adventures and saw the most beautiful things along the way, how they were welcomed everywhere and finally flew back home via Moscow after half a year of traveling. There, nobody understood exactly what they had seen and experienced.

They must have stood here as a young couple in love more than half a century earlier, at the giant feet of the Buddha. At that time, they saw an immense statue towering above them, where now I only see metal tubes filling the void. I try to imagine how they walked up the stairs here, hand in hand. How they kissed each other halfway up. What they said to each other about that gigantic statue, probably the most impressive thing they had seen on their journey.

How could they have imagined at that time that their son, who would be born a few years later, would travel to every country in the world? That, more than half a century later, he would be standing here, staring helplessly at the ruins of an ancient staircase which they climbed without even giving it a thought? How could they have imagined that one day that staircase and those statues would be destroyed? One of the stories of their amazing journey that impressed me the most was how they had had lunch on top of the Buddha by cracking walnuts on the huge, sandstone head. The shards of that head now lie swept together at the foot of the rock wall.

My parents, young and happy back then, their future ahead of them, would see their stormy marriage end in devastation twenty years later, just as these Buddha statues now lie in ruins. In the meantime, they had taken me to Greece as a baby and passed the travel bug on to my sister and me with trips through Europe, the Middle East and Africa. We regularly went off the beaten track and always sought adventure. That same bug had led me to embark on endless journeys and live adventures, a few of which I describe in this book.

What if they had had a 'normal' honeymoon and taken us on all-inclusive beach holidays or to a nearby campsite? Would I be standing here now, in this alcove of destruction? Would I have traveled all over the world, with an unstoppable curiosity and drive to experience new adventures and discover new places? Would I have embarked on this fantastic quest to visit all the countries in the world? Would I have got the idea to travel to countries you weren't supposed to go to? Would this book have ever seen the light of day?

In an earlier chapter, I mentioned the all-important influence of fate on travel and love. Of course, its impact reaches much further. To begin with, it determines where you're born and who your parents are. Whether they give you a taste of all sorts of adventures and thus shape you for the rest of your life. How many times have I tried to imagine what my life would have been like if I had been born in a slum somewhere in a poor country's metropolis? A street brat with rags on his body, trying to beg for food or money, or sell homemade stuff for a pittance. A rascal who looks in confusion at those rich foreigners who come to photograph the slums of his neighborhood and then vanish into a world of luxury that he will never see for himself. What would I have become in his place? What would I have seen of the world? Would I ever have crossed a border?

Fate decided that my path crossed with Nana's in Yemen, that I ran into a military base in Iran, that I bumped into a bear in Kyrgyzstan, that I wanted to go to Nauru just when Australia had opened a refugee camp there, that the attack on Brussels airport took place on the day I was to fly there, that al-Shabaab didn't attack my hotel in Mogadishu during my stay, and that Anneke and I survived a ghastly accident in South Africa. I could extend this list endlessly with so many other incidents that were spine-tingling and somehow ended well, but over which I had little or no influence. By traveling to the unknown and by taking risks, I gave fate every chance to let me live all kinds of adventures.

Of course, it's wise to try and give fate a push in the right direction. Pay attention and think before you throw yourself into harm's way. You can do a lot to influence or even avoid the whims and caprices of fate. Take a later bus, walk down a different street, don't climb that lava-spewing volcano, stay inside and just do nothing at all. But when it comes right down to it, Lady Luck has the last say. The essence of travel is precisely its unknown and unpredictable nature.

Once you accept the uncertainties and risks involved, adventure is guaranteed. Then, you experience the stories that you can later tell when you get home. Those are the stories of which I have narrated a few in this book. And that is why there is always a moment when you have to accept whatever fate throws at you. A moment when you must embrace it, believe in a happy ending and trust in your guardian angels.

Wasn't it dangerous? To visit all the countries in the world? That was the question I posed at the beginning of this book. I was looking for adventure and that came naturally by traveling to countries unknown to me. If my destination had a red-letter travel warning, it made the journey even more thrilling. Excitement, unexpected events, meeting unfamiliar people who become friends, discovering that countries are often very different from what you think beforehand: adventure by nature is a positive concept and makes your travels memorable. Danger, on the other hand, has negative connotations; a bad outcome is a definite possibility. While I was aware that things could go wrong, I always threw myself into adventures, believing that they would end well. The lure of adventure was always stronger than the worry of possible danger.

Looking back at all the risks I took, a few occasions come to mind where I narrowly escaped. It wasn't in countries often considered dangerous, such as Somalia, Yemen or Afghanistan, the country I'm traveling in now. The real danger came from a completely different direction, in places and at times I didn't expect.

There was that sunny Sunday morning when I walked home from Leiden Central Station after a flight from Toronto. There was nobody on the street. I was listening to music through my earphones and longing for my bed after a night of work. On the Blauwpoortsbrug, barely a five-minute walk from my front door, I was startled by the shrill sound of screeching brakes behind me. In a reflex, I turned around and saw a glimpse of a car breaking through the bridge's metal fence. It disappeared into the Morsgracht, leaving a trail of bubbles in the brown water.

I realized immediately that if my train had arrived a few seconds later, if I had walked just a little slower, or if I had stopped to select another song on my iPod (it's been that long), the car would have crushed me to a pulp against the fence. Then it would have thrown me, suitcase and all, into the canal and left me, badly injured, to drown under its weight. With goosebumps on my arms, I called 112. In no time at all, the police, an ambulance and the fire brigade were on the scene and divers were busy rescuing the occupants and hauling the car out of the water.

Or that time in Lomé, where the doctors told me that they wouldn't have been able to save me from a severe case of malaria if I had come in a few hours later. The guy who jumped on my back in Mauritius, threw me to the ground and put a knife to my throat while his accomplice cut my backpack from my shoulders. The police couldn't believe that this had happened, because crime, they said, didn't exist in their paradisiacal country. Then there was the mugger in a good neighborhood of Buenos Aires who, in broad daylight, repeatedly slammed his pistol on my head, began to yank at my camera and continued pummeling my skull when I refused to hand over the camera and my lens bag. Why didn't he shoot? Was the gun real? I will never know. I got away with six stitches in my head. And with a camera, because the brute finally ran away, just before the police arrived, having been alerted by bystanders.

But by far the greatest risk was the transportation. The thousands, tens of thousands of kilometers in cars and vans that would never pass any kind of test, with drivers who acted as if they were immortal, with total contempt for death. Drivers who had an unshakeable faith that a higher power would always protect them, who overtook where they couldn't, who competed with other drivers and who took pleasure in testing the speed limit of their vehicle. Drivers who made it a sport to keep as little distance as possible from other cars and who carried far more passengers than they were supposed to. I remember a small Japanese car in Africa where the driver shared his seat with someone else and there were three people in the front passenger seat, which seriously impaired his driving skills, if only because the gear stick was virtually inaccessible.

There were the crammed boats and dinghies that plunged deep into the waves of lakes and seas and were mercilessly lashed by a raging storm. Lifebuoys were rarely present and if they were, there were always far fewer than there were people on board. There were the helmet-less rides on the back of motorbikes over unpaved roads in Africa, driven by boys who had learned to ride from their brother or a friend. And of course, there was that terrible crash in South Africa, when I was driving a car myself, flipped it twice and crawled out of the wreckage alive, together with Anneke. We were saved by the tent on the roof which absorbed the initial impact, and then by the seatbelts which held us down and kept our heads from being smashed.

Some would say that I was brave to travel to all those countries, even though I didn't know beforehand what I would find, even though there was war, even though it wasn't always possible to know how I could escape if things went wrong, even though loved ones asked me not to go. Others will say that I was crazy to keep looking for 'danger'. And indeed, if it had gone wrong once, I wouldn't have seemed brave anymore, but stupid, naive, irresponsible or reckless. The dividing line is wafer-thin.

Not going was never an option. I have an ingrained urge to always take the unbeaten track, the hidden path, go to the not-so-obvious destination. This almost always results in the most remarkable experiences. Take this trip to Afghanistan. After all those years of adventure, of all places, I decided to come here. I didn't have to, I could have chosen Italy, Thailand or Australia. Yet, I fell for the excitement of a 'red' country.

Destiny rubbed its randomness and cruelty under my nose long ago. Within a few years, four loved ones were snatched from my life out of the blue. Mark and Marilyn, who took all kinds of inspiring trips and long ago opened my eyes to travel in countries I had never heard of, died in an unfortunate canoeing accident in the ice-cold waters off Baffin Island in their native Canada. They were forty and forty-three. A year later, my cousin Sander, a journalist, had interviewed people in Dili about the upcoming referendum on independence for East Timor. On the way back to his hotel, he ran into an Indonesian army patrol who killed him with a bullet through his heart. He was thirty years old. My Argentinian travel friend Walter left his office in Buenos Aires just after the 2001 crisis and was attacked by two armed robbers. Even though he handed over all the money he had on him, one of the men shot and killed him on the spot. He lived to be fifty-five years old.

Four people whom I had said goodbye to when we last met, without ever thinking that I might never see them again. Four people who dared to do things and to live from the bottom of their hearts. Four people who had the terrible misfortune of being in the wrong place at the wrong time. Four people who regularly came to my mind when I found myself in dire straits. Their accidents made me realize how incredibly fragile we are. That you have to take life as it comes, that you have to get out of it what your heart tells you and that destiny can strike ruthlessly and unexpectedly. You just never know when that will be. However sad their deaths made me feel, I found comfort in the conviction that they had made the most of their lives and I could only try to follow their example.

Some of my trips over the last ten years I wouldn't have dared to make fifteen or twenty years ago. Risks come in degrees. Gradually, my confidence grew and I dared to always do more. At the same time, I realized that there are no guarantees for a good outcome. Just as life involves risks, safe travel is an illusion. Things can go wrong in the most unexpected ways, moments and places. My fallen friends are the ultimate proof. Wrong time, wrong place.

This book is by no means an appeal to throw all fear overboard and travel blindly to countries that are known as 'dangerous.' Rather, it's a plea to face the fact that risks are a part of life and therefore also of travel. That you can have the most beautiful adventures if you're prepared to embrace the potential risks involved. And that the best way to do that is to always stick to your wits and your senses, to collect trustworthy information beforehand and once on the ground, to believe in your luck and to establish a good relationship with your guardian angels.

After the great empty crevices of the Buddhas, it's time to explore the surroundings of Bamiyan. We drive to the deep blue lakes and green-white waterfalls of Band-e Amir, which lie spectacularly in the barren, wild, light brown landscape. We walk through the Qazan Valley and see the ruins of the medieval Shahr-e Golghola, the City of Lamentations or City of Screams, which lies near Bamiyan itself.

When Mutukan, the favorite grandson of Genghis Khan, was killed by an arrow shot from the city, the legendary Mongol conqueror swore revenge. It's well known that for him, revenge was never gentle. Watched by the Buddhas, he destroyed the city; all its inhabitants were exterminated. The name of the ruins refers to the wailing of the population on the wretched day they were massacred. To maintain control over the area, he left behind a battalion of soldiers. Legend has it that this is where the Hazaras originated. The name is said to derive from the Persian *Yak Hazar*, meaning thousand, a unit of the Mongolian army. Indeed, it's easy to see how the population here has Mongolian traits and differs from the other Afghan tribes. A little to the east of Bamiyan is Shahr-e Zohak, the Red City, destroyed by the same Genghis Khan when he took his merciless revenge for the loss of his grandson. How different would it all have been if that archer had missed Mutukan?

After Bamiyan, we fly back to Kabul. Travel over land is strongly discouraged, even though there is a new road and the distance is less than two hundred kilometers. A few hours' drive. But there are too many cases where buses are stopped by the Taliban and that often ends in a bloodbath or, if you're lucky, a kidnapping that can last years.

Not wanting to embarrass Sayed, we decide to look for a hotel. Instead of one of the five-star hotels, which are the main targets of suicide missions due to their high-security status, we choose to stay in a backstreet hotel. The entrance is at the back of a shop. A watchman guards the entrance with a machine gun and a walkie-talkie. The reception desk is located on the first floor behind thick bars and an armored door that is only opened when everything has been confirmed to be in order by cameras and when the guard has given his permission. We're convinced that this isn't a place where attackers can make headlines around the world. This is one of the many ways to give fate a helping hand.

In the capital, we see the National Museum, restored after having been demolished by the Taliban. A large part of the collection has unfortunately been lost – destroyed or traded on the black market to buy new weapons, cause more destruction and wage more war.

After other walks in the city, past the inevitable checkpoints, a stroll over the bird market and spontaneous conversations with Afghans, we visit the landmine museum on the last day. After decades of war, the country is full of them and they still claim fatalities every day. The museum shows how many different weapons can be found in Afghan soil and who the probable victims are. Mostly children, whose natural curiosity is brutally punished when they playfully touch or unsuspectingly step on a mine. The thought that, even if the war ever ends here, the mines will continue to take their toll for a long time is disgusting.

This journey has confronted me with the tragedy of Afghanistan and I can only sympathize with its people. They have the incredible misfortune of living in a country of great strategic value. In the middle of Asia, it acts as a buffer zone to keep large neighboring countries apart. All the powers from inside and outside the region want to exert their influence here: Pakistan, Russia (as successor to the Soviet Union), China, India, Iran and the United States, to name just a few. On top of that, the Afghans have paid the highest price for the al-Qaeda attacks on US soil. According to the latest reports, the Russians are secretly backing the Taliban to fight the American troops, just as the Americans once armed the Taliban to fight the Soviets.

When will this country ever be able to live in peace? The people have become hardened by the enormous losses they have suffered. Tired and numb from all the wars that took place in their country over their heads and the violence that followed. With hardly any prospect of improvement. Despite everything, they bravely continue with their lives. They can still manage to warmly welcome the foreign visitor even though, given their history, they have every reason to treat foreigners with deep suspicion.

It's time to go home. We struggle to get through all seven checkpoints at the airport and then, once more, we experience that strange sensation that flying brings. In half a day, we are catapulted back to another reality. That same evening, we're safely home.

The next day, we read that a few hours before our departure, a lorry had been intercepted in Kabul. Under crates of tomatoes, the police found a load of three thousand kilos of explosives. The same old questions pose themselves. Was it dangerous to go to Afghanistan after all? Obviously, I knew there were risks involved in our journey, but I embarked for the adventure, just like I did on all my previous travels. Where possible, we have tried to minimize the risks.

But then again, suppose that truck hadn't been intercepted and that the driver would have carried out his gruesome mission. What would have been the chances of us being exactly on the spot he had executed his crime, in the megalopolis of Kabul? Exactly at the moment he detonated his cargo? You can hardly protect yourself against a truck full of explosives. The only thing you can do is avoid crowds, sleep in backstreet hotels and pay attention to your surroundings all the time.

Fortunately, my guardian angels have taken care of me again this time. My destiny hasn't turned into my doom. More than for ourselves, I feel relieved for the Afghans who didn't perish in yet another senseless attack. For them, the only question is when the next one will take place and if they, or their loved ones, will be able to survive.

Would I embark on this kind of journey again? Definitely! Rather today than tomorrow. Always following my heart, always in search for the next adventure!

Did You Like Reading
The Long Road to Cullaville?

Now, it's your turn to write! Please consider leaving a review at Amazon.com, Goodreads, or Bookbub to help others find *The long road to Cullaville*.

You can find more on this book, the author, his passion for travel, and the upcoming sequel at BorisKester.com. This is also where you can sign up for the newsletter.

You can contact me, follow me, and get inspired to travel or to write about travel, at: boriskester.com/contact

Instagram: @boris_traveladventures
Facebook: facebook.com/Boris.Kester
TikTok: @borisbooks

Goodreads:
goodreads.com/author/show/21974345.Boris_Kester

Excerpt from the Next Book

In a few kilometers, I should be there. Then, the most exciting of all my adventures will start. Unbridled curiosity and vague fear run through my body like a swirling cocktail. At the same time, deep inside of me I feel a reassuring certainty. Conviction that I cannot do anything else than what I am about to do, simply because it comes straight from my heart.

I am on the way to bring Nana a copy of *The Long Road to Cullaville*. She plays a deciding role in the first chapter, and the book would not have seen the light without her. We have never seen or heard from each other since the terrible end of our frenzied relationship more than thirteen years ago.

Nana doesn't know that I am on my way. I don't know if she's home, I certainly don't know how she will react when she sees me - if I will even find her, because I also don't know exactly where she lives.

Be the first to know when the new book arrives...

Signup for Boris's Email List at BorisKester.com/mailing-list

www.ingramcontent.com/pod-product-compliance
Lightning Source LLC
Chambersburg PA
CBHW061137120626
46546CB00005B/1820